P9-DNZ-065

Black's Law

A Criminal Lawyer

Reveals His Defense Strategies

in Four Cliffhanger Cases

Roy Black

Simon & Schuster

SIMON & SCHUSTER
Rockefeller Center
1230 Avenue of the Americas
New York, NY 10020

Copyright © 1999 by Roy Black

All rights reserved, including the right
of reproduction in whole or in part in any form.
SIMON & SCHUSTER and colophon are registered
trademarks of Simon & Schuster Inc.

Designed by Sam Potts

Manufactured in the United States of America

10 9 8 7 6 5 4 3 2 1

Library of Congress Cataloging-in-Publication Data

Black, Roy, [date]
   Black's law : a criminal lawyer reveals his defense strategies in four
cliffhanger cases / Roy Black.
      p.   cm.
   Includes index.
   1. Black, Roy, [date]. 2. Lawyers—United States—Biography. 3. Defense
(Criminal procedure)—United States. 4. Criminal justice, Administration
of—United States. I. Title.
   KF373.B537 A3   1999
   345.73'05044'092—dc21

                                                          98-31544
                                                          CIP
                                                          Rev

ISBN 0-684-81022-0

To the criminal defense lawyers of this nation: who fearlessly tread into hostile courtrooms, armed only with their briefcases and their native wit; who turn the Bill of Rights from an abstraction into a reality; who protect the rights and privileges that keep us a free people; who fearlessly fight against a federal government that has become the enemy of individual liberty; and who valiantly attempt to stem the steady erosion of our civil rights by a growing number of uncaring judges.

Contents

Introduction

In January 1971, on my first day as a real lawyer, I was a little cowed as I walked up a flight of marble steps into the Metropolitan Justice Building. The concrete-and-steel structure seemed overwhelming. Its cavernous lobby was a stream of bodies: uniformed cops swaggering like gunfighters, rumpled detectives with loosened ties, teenagers in harsh gang colors, sequined drag queens, blue-suited yuppie lawyers, ponytailed surf bums in shorts. The walls reverberated with a din of voices in English, Spanish and Creole.

I was stepping into the terrible and unpredictable branch of the law labeled "criminal." More than any other place in the city, this building is a scene of great drama, where some are raised to great heights, while others fall to their ruin. On that bright Miami day I was unaware of the many years of study and struggle that lay ahead to master this discipline.

On the fifth floor I searched for my boss, Phil Hubbart, who had just been elected Dade County public defender. On election day I had spotted Hubbart, one of my law school professors, at a busy corner of U.S. 1. He was holding an election poster and waving at motorists. I stopped to talk and ended up with a job.

His waiting room was full of dirty, wounded people who looked like refugees from the county jail, which they probably were. Hubbart was in a small, cluttered office. He apologized that he had no time to orient me. There were only ten of us to defend all the indigents in a county of more than a million people. "Your first trial is tomorrow," he said, handing me a thin file. "A woman charged with second-degree murder of her boyfriend."

"What do I do?"

"You can start by talking to her." He pointed out the window to a looming ten-floor dungeon behind the courthouse. "She's right over there."

My on-the-job training began the next day. Another rookie lawyer and I fumbled through the murder trial and somehow, probably from pure luck, we won. Then I was given a case of my own. The defendant was a drifter who had broken into a house and put a gun to a child's head. He threatened to shoot unless the mother cashed a check and came back with enough money to buy a couple of dime bags. The woman ran to the police. SWAT teams surrounded the house. After several hours of intense negotiation, the guy surrendered.

The textbooks don't have a lot of defenses for hopeless causes like that, but I tried some kind of insanity angle. At about ten o'clock in the evening the jury came back with the inevitable guilty verdict. Only a handful of people were in the courtroom. They included the mother and child who were the victims and the defendant's girlfriend.

Suddenly the girlfriend jumped on the mother and wrapped a chain-link belt around her neck. As they rolled around on the floor, the woman's face turned purple.

I stood there exhausted, numbed from losing my first case, shocked at what I was seeing. I couldn't move a step.

Fortunately, a burly bailiff separated them, but I went home that night thinking, "I took seven years of higher education to do this?"

My three years at the University of Miami Law School had provided excellent instruction in contracts, torts and securities—but little about criminal law and nothing about trials. I had chosen the Public Defender's Office because I didn't want to spend my life worrying whether clients may or may not have breached subsection C of paragraph 2, and I knew that virtually all civil suits ended in out-of-court settlements. Still, as I dragged myself to work the next morning, I wondered if I could face every day the raw, bizarre life of the criminal courts.

My doubts vanished after the first case on the docket. A young black man, just off a bus from the state mental hospital, had arrived with psychiatric papers stating that he was now mentally competent to stand trial. The judge asked him if he had a lawyer. The defendant bent over the court reporter and peered at the machine on which she was typing.

"Are you looking for your lawyer down there?" the judge asked. Everyone in the courtroom laughed, except for the young man, who replied: "The lady is picking on that piano but there ain't no music."

This pathetic soul had not a friend in the world, except for his young and inexperienced public defender. I realized in an instant that he needed my help, and if I didn't help him, no one else would. For the next several days I searched for a livable refuge outside the psycho ward for this disposable youngster. When I found one, I also found my calling. I learned that one committed lawyer can change the future for at least a few who couldn't save themselves.

The more I worked at the Public Defender's Office, the more I realized the value of the defense attorney. I loved the work-hard, play-for-broke attitude. I loved the image of being a single crusader representing the despised riffraff of society against the State with its well-funded, popular prosecutors. The Miami justice system blended law and economics to create a monster conveyor belt capable of speeding each defendant to the state penitentiary at the lowest possible cost per unit, and it was a pleasure to derail that factory machinery by throwing a constitutional monkey wrench into its gears.

Miami was a great place to learn about the law, precisely because there were so many chances to gain experience in the courtroom. As I once told a law journal, Miami is "a criminal lawyer's dream come true." In two years, I defended more cases than many defense attorneys do in a decade. During one frantic stretch, I tried three jury trials in a single week. I did close to fifty in my first two-year stretch. What more could a young lawyer dream for?

I had stepped into a real life that seemed right from the pages of Kafka or Stephen King. There was the crazed man who stabbed his girlfriend fifty-six times with a butcher knife. A lunatic threw a bloody severed head at a rookie cop. A punk from Las Vegas cut off women's fingers for their diamond rings.

By the time I left the Public Defender's Office to go into private practice, I had a mature appreciation for the inner workings of the justice machine. I had found that prosecutors and police officials are often motivated by their own agendas. They figure the bigger the fish, the greater the glory. Most judges aren't any better. They too are concerned mostly about their image. Few in the black robes have enough steel in their spines to risk ruling in favor of an unpopular defendant. I appreciate Theodore Roosevelt's complaint about one judge: "I could carve out of a banana a Justice with more backbone than that." With everyone pursuing personal interests, defendants find their slim chance of survival in the hands of a citizen jury.

That's where I come in. When most people see me on the nightly news, I am striding into a courtroom beside a person who has been charged with an awful crime: murder, money laundering, rape at a historic mansion. Time and again I hear friends ask me, "How could you defend him?" Or: "Certainly he must have done something or he wouldn't have gotten in trouble, right?"

The answer is one that comes out of hard experience in the courts. Ours is an adversary system of justice. This means we determine truth through testing both sides of the story at a trial, not by means of a sixty-second news clip or a talk-radio rant or the latest CNN poll. We have *inalienable* rights, meaning ones our government can't take away.

Rights are not self-executing. They don't exist unless you have a lawyer to enforce them. Article 125 of the Constitution of the U.S.S.R. issued by Stalin in 1936 provided that "the citizens . . . are guaranteed by law (a) freedom of speech, (b) freedom of the press, (c) freedom of assembly including the holding of mass meetings and (d) freedom of street processions and demonstrations." But these were just so many words, because Stalin did not provide for attorneys independent of state control to speak for those rights vigorously. He did not offer his people our crucial Sixth Amendment, which allows the accused to "enjoy . . . the assistance of counsel for his defense." Lawyers are the ones who transform abstract rights into reality.

That reality comes only when people have a concrete understanding of why we need rights. Too many times in America we have our work cut out for us because the public looks at the man in the defendant's chair as a bad guy without any human qualities. In this book, I want you to see the defendant as a flesh-and-blood human being, not a hunk of meat. I want you to feel how he is scared, humiliated, confused and desperate. The only experiences that come close to being a defendant in a criminal trial are awaiting the confirmation of a diagnosis of terminal cancer or suffering the death of a child in an accident.

When you learn what it's like to walk into a packed courtroom, with all the power of the State arrayed against you, fearing for the end of your life as you know it, I believe you will have a completely different appreciation of our criminal justice system and the rights of the individual. You will see for the first time why a defense attorney must do everything in his power to protect his client.

As I once told a reporter when I was defending a police officer who had started a riot, "I'm going to do whatever I can to see justice is done in the courtroom. If the town burns down because of it, so be it."

Those were tough words, but true. My job is to represent people as best I can, nothing else. That's what makes criminal law the most demanding branch of the legal profession. It's the one area of the law in which the individual matches his wits against the State. The government has far more resources: police officers, investigators, crime labs, plus federal and state law-enforcement agencies, all of them tied together by computer networks that can pluck out obscure information half a continent away at the flick of a button.

I often say, "A lot of people don't understand the need for defendants to have rights until they themselves are accused of a crime." Certainly, in three of the four cases I write about in this book, the defendants never envisioned hiring a criminal defense attorney, and they were shocked to see how powerful and unfair prosecutors can be. The only reason the fourth man wasn't shocked was that he was deranged and frequently didn't understand what was happening in the courtroom.

The first case, that of Luis Alvarez, shows how intense pressure from politicians and the media can threaten justice. Luis was a young cop assigned to patrol Miami's toughest ghetto. His split-second decision to shoot a black man ignited one of Miami's worst race riots.

The media frenzy began when the mayor, the city manager and the police chief held a televised press conference demanding that Luis be punished. They were quickly abetted by self-proclaimed activists who exploited Miami's ethnic politics. Janet Reno, then our local state attorney, mobilized her top prosecutors and investigators, with no expense spared, to throw all they had against one street cop. Thanks to their pronouncements and the spin the media gave the story, everyone assumed that Alvarez would be quickly convicted.

The trial was conducted in a racial tinderbox poised to explode in the unlikely event of an acquittal.

This was my first experience in a massive case, and it was one of the toughest I ever had—not only because of what happened in the courtroom, but also because of the outside pressures that I knew the judge and the jurors couldn't ignore.

In the second case, that of Thomas Knight, there was a massive outcry not just for his conviction, but also for his execution. He was a vicious, insane killer who grew up in one of the poorest, most oppressed black neighborhoods I've ever seen. His childhood was a brutal nightmare that would have warped any young mind. That information did not come out at his trial, where he was represented by four attorneys who did virtually nothing to defend him.

In the other cases in this book, you will see how solid defense work can make a difference. In Knight's case, I delved not only into the mind of a multiple killer but also into the minds of his multiple defense lawyers. His capital trial is a cautionary tale of how bad lawyering causes a mockery of justice. The rules of American law are carefully structured so that two opposing forces battle it out in the courtroom. When one side abdicates its responsibilities, the result is a miscarriage of justice. The actions of our judges in covering over the inadequacies of lawyers shakes our faith in the fairness of the system.

In the third case, you'll meet Stephen Hicks, a young bartender with no criminal past who faced a death sentence when he was charged with murdering his girlfriend. This was a classic murder case based on circumstantial evidence, and everything depended on the way that the police detectives had conducted the investigation. They made up their minds before looking for the evidence. This timesaving attitude freed them from searching for evidence they didn't want to find. The botched investigation made our task extremely difficult, because there was no way we could retrieve evidence once it had been lost. This case shows how powerful the police are and how they can tip the scales of justice.

And finally, you'll meet Fred De La Mata, a Cuban immigrant who worked his way up to president of a major bank only to see his career shattered by federal prosecutors who apparently decided it was easier to go after a respectable banker than elusive drug dealers. Prosecutors acted like schoolyard bullies, making deals with admitted drug dealers, so that they could, in my opinion, reap publicity for nailing a big-time corporate executive. This case shows how relentless prosecutors can be when they believe the ends justify any means.

I regard each trial as a war of eighteen- or twenty-hour days in which I use every bit of energy and experience and knowledge that I possess to help my client. In all my trials, the stakes are high, because people do not come to my kind of practice with small problems. Thomas Knight and Stephen Hicks were confronting death. Fred De La Mata was facing a twenty-five-year prison sentence, but he felt his life was in the balance because the respectability that he had spent decades to achieve was threatened with destruction. Luis Alvarez was charged with manslaughter, but we feared he too might face a death sentence if convicted—plenty of his fellow prisoners might be eager to kill an ex-officer linked to a racially explosive killing.

Come with me now into the courtroom. Pull up a chair at the defense table. The judge just walked in and the clerk is calling our case for trial. I feel a rush of anxiety as I think of how much is at stake. Who will be the State's first witness? Do we have all the files to cross him? How much do we disclose in our opening? Should the client testify?

Alvarez

DECEMBER 28, 1982. THE TRIGGER ENGAGED THE HAMMER, PUSHING THE FIR-
ing pin into the base of the cartridge. The ensuing explosion blew the 158-
grain, pure-lead hollow-point bullet out of the barrel at 950 feet per second,
mushrooming as it punched into the bony forehead. I was fifteen miles away
enjoying a plate of jumbo stone crabs dipped in mustard, with a side of hash
browns, at Joe's in South Beach. The riot broke out as I was digging into one
of Joe's celebrated key lime pies.

Fifteen minutes later I drove my elderly Mercedes 190 north on Alton
Road, past the Miami Beach marina, and on to MacArthur Causeway. The
concrete parkway rises over Biscayne Bay, then slices into the heart of downtown Miami. To my left was the vast port of Miami, a steel-and-glass island
city, with sleek white cruise ships docked end to end along a two-mile-long
wharf. To my right were the celebrity mansions of Star Island and, next door
on Palm Island, the fortified mansion Al Capone lounged in during the St.
Valentine's Day massacre.[1]

---

[1]. On February 14, 1929, Capone's henchmen in Chicago, posing as police officers,
gunned down seven members of the Bugs Moran mob. The murders gave Capone control of the Chicago underworld. After serving a prison sentence for tax evasion, Capone
returned to Florida. Suffering from syphilis, he could be seen wandering around Palm Island in his bathrobe.

I rode past Watson Island and on to the labyrinth of expressways, raised on tall concrete columns, that bridges drivers safely over crime-infested streets and the crumbling housing projects of Miami's oldest black ghetto, Overtown. The transportation system was an expensive conspiracy to shield our eyes from unsightly poverty and disease in one of the world's richest playgrounds.

I was reminded of what lay below when I saw the Twelfth Avenue exit ramp blocked by police cars, blue-and-red lights flashing. I turned on the radio to WIOD 610, an all-night news station. "A cop just shot a black youth in a video arcade on Third Avenue," a street reporter yelled. "Police cars are rushing to the scene." A mob was bombing passing cars with rocks and bottles. Police cars and garbage dumpsters had been set on fire. Snipers were reported to be shooting at cars on the expressway. The frantic reporter warned drivers to stay out of the central city. I had just passed within a few yards of the arcade. Too close for comfort.

The rioting lasted three days. Two persons died. Another twenty-five, including two police officers, were injured. Property damage was in the millions. The networks showed helmeted riot police with plastic shields and batons battling rock-throwing black youths and looters toting television sets and cases of beer and groceries out of broken storefront windows against a backdrop of bright yellow fires and columns of black smoke.

Civic leaders were particularly disturbed because the shooting occurred three days before the Orange Bowl festival, Miami's premier tourist attraction. Extra security had to be brought in for the Orange Bowl parade and the football game, both sited near the edge of Overtown. Commentators gave breathless, detailed descriptions of the riots before a national television audience. The "Magic City," as the tourism people like to call it, was back in the news.

Most of the city's leaders thought there was only one way to get rid of the problem: Blame Luis Alvarez, the young police officer who had shot the youth. Carrie Meek, then a state legislator, now a congresswoman, insisted that "justice be served" by convicting Alvarez and threatened that if it were not the city would burn. Five official agencies—the Miami Police Department, the Federal Bureau of Investigation, the Dade County State Attorney's Office, the Miami city manager's office and something called the Community Relations Board—held press conferences to announce that they were starting investigations. The elected officials of the Miami City Commission promised there would be "no whitewash" of its own investigation. An associate U.S. attorney general in Washington said that the federal government wanted to see if there had been "a deprivation of civil rights" of Nevell Johnson Jr., the twenty-year-old who had died twenty-four hours after being shot.

If anyone had doubts about who was victim and who was villain, they could turn to *The Miami Herald*, which featured side-by-side stories of the two main participants. The one about Nevell Johnson was topped by this headline: "Victim had good job record, respect of his co-workers, love of his family." Alvarez was portrayed less sympathetically: "Record of Officer who shot Johnson includes five departmental probes."

Johnson's story described a model citizen who worked as a courier at a county agency. His co-workers adored him. The story claimed he had no police record and was never a bother to anyone. "All our boys," Nevell Johnson Sr. said, "we raised them right. They're not bad boys."

Alvarez was portrayed by the *Herald* as a hot-tempered officer with an internal affairs file packed with citizen complaints. In this and subsequent stories, he was described as a macho cowboy. On the night of the shooting, police officials claimed, he had left his patrol zone without permission to roust the arcade. Eyewitnesses insisted he had stormed into the arcade cocking his gun. TV news shows starred Overtown residents describing Alvarez as throwing down a Saturday night special near Johnson's hand after the shooting, to make it look as if the youth had lost a shoot-out.

These stories and the opinion pieces that followed made out Alvarez as guilty. I remember thinking that if this cop thought the shoot-out was bad, just wait for the backlash from an establishment desperate to keep racial peace. Several days later Ron Cohen, a former student of mine who had become counsel to the Fraternal Order of Police, called and told me it was only a matter of time before Alvarez was indicted. Did I have the balls to take on his defense?

Without a second thought I said send him over. But as soon as I hung up, I felt a frisson of doubt. The local press smelled blood, and wouldn't turn its nose up at mine. One miscalculation, gleefully emblazoned on every TV show and in the *Herald*, and my fledgling career was history. Clients didn't stand in line to hire the lawyer who blew the biggest case of the year. Still, I had agreed to see him, so I did, late the next morning.

He was a handsome guy, with a sharply clipped Latino-style moustache. He had pale skin, curiously untanned for a cop, framed by black hair. He had sharp, suspicious eyes that perhaps had seen too many nights in a police cruiser. He was slim, too—not one of those macho bodybuilder cops on steroids. He stood still as he scanned my office, which, as usual, was cluttered with shelves stuffed with books, a desk piled with unopened mail and old newspapers. It looked more like a used-book store than the cool minimalist office suites of the grand corporate law firms.

The way his eyes moved I could see he was tightly wound. But there was a dignity in his erect bearing, and I sensed a certain solidity in his demeanor that indicated, even as tense as he was, that he had an inner confidence that might carry him through the even more intense pressure that lay ahead.

I also sensed a wariness. Why should he open up and trust me? I wondered. I had just left the Public Defender's Office, where the street cops saw us as their sworn enemies, the hated opposition who put the scum back on the street.

To break the ice, I asked him how he was holding up. Sinking into a chair, he expressed shock that the police department had succumbed to political pressure. His bosses had yanked him from street patrol and put him behind a desk, doing nothing, making him look more guilty. "How can they abandon me? That man tried to kill me. When a young punk goes for his gun, the last thing I'm thinking about is his color."

Luis thought the media, particularly *The Miami Herald*, was generating all the hatred against him. "These stories are all garbage," he complained. "There isn't anything in them that's true." The newspaper was treating him like a mobster. For several days Al Messerschmidt, a *Herald* reporter, had sat in a car in front of the duplex where Luis lived with his mother. She was terrified. The guy kept insisting that he wouldn't leave until he got an interview.

"Everyone thinks I'm guilty. Only the street cops, the guys on my shift, support me. They keep coming to my house, all night long. You'd think it was a wake. I don't care what reporters say—I don't see any of them walking down Third Avenue at 3 a.m."

Luis thought the whole experience was a bad dream. He expected to wake up one morning and see the problem had vanished. Once the police and State Attorney's Office finished their investigations, he would be vindicated and that would be the end of it. He thought it would speed up the process if he went to the investigators and explained what happened.

"Listen, you don't quite get it," I said. "They don't want to hear the truth. Everyone else gets off the hook by blaming it all on you."

Luis blinked, then stared down at the floor.

For a long moment he didn't say anything. Then he stood and paced around the room, hands clasped behind his back. "I can't believe it," he said in a low voice, talking to himself. "What do you think they'll charge me with?"

"Manslaughter, I bet."

"But he was trying to kill me!"

He was looking so distraught that I calmed him down by asking him about his background. He told me that he had been born in Cuba and came to the United States with his mother when he was eight. She had worked as a waitress six days a week, twelve hours a day, to keep them going. Luis found a part-time job when he was fifteen as he went through high school and then junior college. He had been a police officer for eighteen months. He was twenty-three years old, earning $450 a week.

"I've always wanted to be a cop," he said. "But a real cop. Somebody who arrests bad guys. I'm not a paper cop. I'm not one of those guys who just fills out the forms at the donut shop."

Abruptly, he changed the subject. "So you want me to tell you what happened that night?" He said he had been showing a rookie cop, Luis Cruz, the worst spots of Overtown. That's what brought him to the arcade, where he encountered Nevell Johnson. "I shot him in self-defense. What should I have done, let him shoot me? It happened so quickly, so fast, I didn't have time to think."

"Let's slow it down," I suggested. We replayed the shooting many times, first in slow motion, then at full speed. Years of listening to stories in jail cells and courtrooms force you to become a fairly accurate judge of character. I was sure his fear of death that night wasn't faked, but I also knew that wasn't enough to prove self-defense.

"Look," he said, "I know my whole life is on the line. How long would I last in Raiford [the notorious state penitentiary]? Fifteen minutes? I always defended myself, but I can't do it here. I need someone who believes in me, who's not just going through the motions."

He had seen his life transformed in an instant from respected cop to

pariah. He desperately needed help. How could I say no? Like one of my partners said: Good thing you're not a girl, you'd always be pregnant.

William Perry, president of the Miami chapter of Jesse Jackson's group Operation PUSH, and others organized a massive six-mile march from the Overtown game arcade to Miami's City Hall, chanting slogans, singing "We shall
overcome" and carrying signs demanding Alvarez's arrest. When the marchers
arrived, the mayor and two elected commissioners were waiting to listen to
their demands that Alvarez be brought to "justice." Howard Gary, Miami's first
black city manager, calmed the crowd by assuring them that Dade State Attorney Janet Reno had all the evidence and Alvarez would soon be brought to
"justice." The crowd cheered.

Only Reno stood between Alvarez and an indictment. She was just launch-
ing her meteoric rise through the legal firmament and was no stranger to
strong-arm politics. At the knee of her father, Henry, who for decades had
served as a police reporter for *The Miami Herald*, Reno had learned all about
the subtle ways in which prosecutors can manipulate the media. She had
learned her lessons well because the media had begun canonizing her into
Saint Janet of Miami. Ironically it was her country girl appearance—tall,
lanky, ungainly-looking with mousy brown hair shaped like a helmet, thick
square glasses, given to frumpy fashions—that made her popular with the average citizen, precisely because she looked so different than the carefully manufactured elegance of most politicians.

Faced with riots and blaring newspaper headlines, Saint Janet did what any
savvy politician would do—cut Alvarez up into little pieces and throw him to
the mob. What did we expect? *Profiles in Courage?*

She could be so charming that people tended to overlook the little incon-
sistencies in her ethics, like claiming personally to loathe the death penalty
but not hesitating to ask for it in headline-hunting cases. While campaigning,
Reno liked to style herself as the policeman's best friend, but with the heat on,
she decided that prosecuting cops was more politically advantageous than defending them, and in our case, she forged ahead.

Reno assigned three top prosecutors and two investigators to work full-time
on the case. She presented the case to a grand jury that included Fred Graves,

an attorney who was one of her former prosecutors. The grand jurors listened to a parade of alleged eyewitnesses, each of whom gave shocking testimony about how Luis had abused Johnson.

Neither Luis nor I was allowed to be present at the grand jury proceedings.[2] We couldn't ask questions or put on our own witnesses. The outcome was predictable. Grand jury proceedings are supposed to be secret—in fact, in Florida it's a crime to disclose grand jury testimony—but after the indictment Graves appeared on a half-hour television show and proclaimed Alvarez was guilty beyond any doubt.[3]

When the indictment came in I was told Luis had to surrender at the Northside Shopping Center police station, right in the heart of Liberty City, a black area a few miles from Overtown. What better way to show the black community that the State Attorney's Office was "solving" blacks' problems? Someone made sure that this backwater police substation was swarming with dozens of journalists.

We had to elbow our way through the crowd to get in the building. For the next half hour I stood beside Luis as he went through the grim ritual of booking—filling out the arrest form, being fingerprinted, being photographed. Luis kept grumbling that he was being treated "like any asshole on the street."

After he was released on a personal recognizance bond, we tried to avoid the journalists by leaving by the rear door, but reporters and cameramen were waiting. They trailed us to my car, shouting questions.

The next day the newspaper headline showed that black leaders weren't going to be satisfied with a mere booking: " 'We Must Have Conviction' of Alvarez, Activists Say." Ray Fauntroy, leader of the black coalition, demanded:

---

2. Grand juries are decidedly one-sided affairs dominated by prosecutors. By law the defense is prohibited from addressing the grand jurors or presenting witnesses. Thus the grand jury hears from only one side and usually does what the prosecutor wishes, hence the expression "A good prosecutor can indict a ham sandwich."

3. Mr. Graves appeared on a local half-hour television news show and discussed the Alvarez indictment with a panel of local reporters. He commented that the grand jurors were "shocked" by police shootings and opined that the State Attorney's Office would obtain a conviction because "the evidence will show at trial his guilt beyond a reasonable doubt." Another grand juror was quoted in *The Miami Herald* describing grand jury deliberations and concluding that Alvarez was criminally negligent.

"We want him convicted and sent to jail with the maximum penalty." Another activist, Georgia Jones Ayers, warned what would happen if he wasn't convicted: "Take it from me, baby, this city is going to burn."[4]

Perceptions of the Alvarez riot depended more on race than fact. Either it was a mob of drunks using the shooting as an excuse to rob and loot or a legitimate rebellion against decades of racism and poverty. None of this overheated ideology was news to me. I have the dubious distinction of having firsthand experience in each of Miami's race riots in the past quarter century as a legal mercenary for one side or the other. But for Miami's leaders this riot was one too many. They had a dread of black gangs burning down the city. This paranoia even had a name—McDuffie.

This was the name given to the biggest riot, which occurred just two years before Alvarez, in May 1980, sparked by the trial of four police officers charged with beating to death a black insurance man named Arthur McDuffie. The trial was moved to Tampa because of prejudicial pre-trial publicity in Miami. When the cops were acquitted, Miami's black neighborhoods erupted in violence, producing the worst riot in the city's history. Eighteen people were killed and 270 were injured. Property damage approached $100 million.

The McDuffie riot produced the concept of the "Miami Riot Syndrome": White cop killing black suspect leads to riot. White cop getting acquitted of killing black suspect leads to another riot. After a while, as the people of Los Angeles were later to learn, when someone in a poor black neighborhood was shot by a cop, neighbors felt almost compelled to riot, as if it were a civic duty, and they felt the same way when the cop was acquitted. After verdicts, TV camera crews roamed the areas looking for "action," and, of course, the residents provided it. Authorities could figure out only one way to break the cycle: Convict the cop.

The McDuffie destruction was a constant theme in the media, and our prospective jurors kept hearing about it nightly. "We'll never forget McDuffie

---

4. Once again, Janet Reno's political instincts proved deadly accurate. Ayers was so appreciative that she later renamed her school the Janet Reno New Chance Alternative School. At present there are no plans to open a branch in Waco, Texas.

here," legislator Carrie Meek told Channel 7. "We want justice, and we want it right now. If we don't get it, there will be a repeat of McDuffie."

My first task was to assemble the right team of lawyers and investigators to fight this war. Reno's office had the full-time help of several police detectives and I was certain it was searching for the best experts on police procedures that money could buy. Reno's team was led by two of her toughest prosecutors, Benton Becker, who was the U.S. Justice Department official who drafted the Nixon pardon for Gerald Ford's signature, and Robert Beatty, the highest-ranking black in Reno's office.

I needed an expert in firearms and police procedure on the trial team. There was only one name on my list—Mark Seiden. Mark was a stubborn, disciplined loner and a dedicated scholar. After eleven years as a cop and years of self-study, he was an encyclopedia on guns. We met when he was a Metro-Dade police arson detective, orchestrating the prosecution of a client whose failing clothing store burned to the ground. I was surprised one day to find him sitting in my law school evidence class and even more impressed when he turned out to be the top student. But a devastating personal tragedy had recently befallen Mark and I hesitated to even approach him. While he was in the middle of the two-day bar exam in Tampa, his wife, Cheryl, a Metro-Dade detective, was ambushed and shot by two thugs in the parking lot of their condo. Her spine severed, she clung to life for two weeks before she died. Mark dropped from sight and I wondered if their dream of his becoming a lawyer died with her.

I had no other way of contacting him, so during a break in the trial of the man accused of killing his wife I approached Mark in the courthouse corridor. "Mark," I said, "I know this is a difficult time, but I'm working on this Alvarez case, and I need some help. Would you give me a call when this is over?"

Several days later he dropped by. He told me he had already been offered a plum job. I shamelessly went for the jugular: "This is a chance to make a statement about the dangers of police work that won't come again. If we lose, think of the consequences to street cops in Miami." He agreed. We shared the sense of mission, but I sensed he needed the challenge to put his life back on track.

•   •   •

Next we needed a writer, someone who thrived on spending long hours in the law library reading cases and drafting motions. We found the perfect candidate, also a former student of mine, Ralph Barreira, who had just graduated fifth in his class. He dressed like a '60s radical and had long hair, but his politics were to the right of Ronald Reagan. Ralph could have had his pick of jobs with the biggest, best-paying law firms in town, but he preferred to join us in defending Alvarez.

Our team's first meeting was in temporary office space in a run-down building grandly named for the defunct Northeast Airlines. The war room was uncomfortably hot due to a malfunctioning air-conditioning system, but we loosened our ties and started to work. I took a yellow legal pad and sketched out a checklist of jobs. I assigned Mark to brief investigators, collect police and lab reports, and start calling possible defense witnesses. Ralph was to do a rough draft on our change-of-venue motion, pick up the discovery documents and assemble our files. My first job was finding friendly cops for intelligence gathering. We were a small team compared to Reno's specialists. We might be outmanned, but we would not be outworked.

For our own investigation, I wanted bodies to walk every block of Northwest Third Avenue, both sides of the street, to knock on every door, go into every tenement, have a drink in every bar, to talk to every single person in the area to find witnesses who saw what happened in the arcade. I knew white faces wouldn't get any useful information, so we hired black investigators, mostly ex-cops. I went through four before giving up. They all came back with the same story: It wasn't healthy asking questions about Nevell Johnson, and no case was worth getting killed over. Any investigation we wanted done, we would have to do ourselves.

My downtown office was less than two miles away from Overtown. The only greenery were tufts of weeds in vacant lots. Youths lounged against lampposts on street corners. Elderly men sat on the sidewalk in lawn chairs, watching the world go by.

Decades before, Overtown had been a thriving neighborhood filled with shops and tailors and supermarkets and restaurants. Then the government built a huge expressway system that slashed through the area, destroying many of the area's landmarks and casting huge shadows on what remained, precipitating a downward spiral from which it never recovered. By the time of the shooting, the population of Overtown had shrunk from 40,000 to 11,000. It had become a vicious battlefield, where razor wire and random gunshots were ordinary. On every block derelict buildings served as drug houses. Gangs of belligerent youths roamed the streets carrying semi-automatic weapons. The mantra of no jobs, no money, no future made a convenient excuse to become a predator. Crime beat the minimum wage at McDonald's. Overtown was a place of burglaries, robberies, rapes. Tourists got mugged in Overtown. They got shot. So did blacks and so did cops.

From my days at the Public Defender's Office I had firsthand experience of Overtown's streets. Without investigators, we had to do our own street work, hunt up witnesses, track down shaky alibis. One spring morning in the early 1970s, I was walking up Northwest Second Avenue, one block east of the arcade, right across from the marquee of the abandoned Lyric Theater, when a black youth jumped out of a doorway behind me, snaked his forearm around my neck, put a knife to my throat and demanded, "Give it all up, motherfucker." I foolishly twisted around and stood face-to-face with Willie Williams, one of my PD clients who was charged with a string of armed robberies. We looked at each other in shock for a moment, before Willie apologized, saying he hadn't known it was I. Then, not wanting to waste our time together he inquired how his case was going. Back at the office I dumped Willie's file on my trial partner, Jack Denaro. I had lost some faith in Willie's presumption of innocence.

Now that I was the attorney of record for Public Enemy No. 1 in Overtown, the place was not exactly at the top of my list of fun spots to visit, but in every case the first job is to carefully examine the crime scene. Pictures are no substitute because they never reveal everything. I needed to know where every game was in the arcade, what the windows looked like, how the place *felt*.

For security reasons, Mark, Ralph and I usually went to the arcade early in the morning, shortly after it opened, when few people were around. It was in a stark concrete building, painted tan and orange. Bullet holes pockmarked the facade. Its glass doors were heavily tinted. Next to it was the Third Avenue Pool Hall. Across the street was a bar. A few yards away was Interstate 395. The roar of the elevated traffic made the street feel as if it were part of a noisy factory. Underneath the roadway, in perpetual shadow, was a colony of cardboard shacks — homes for the homeless. In the distance, I could see the shining glass and steel bank towers of downtown.

Walking into the arcade was like stepping into an electronic fantasy land:

Space Invaders, Robotron, Galaxy, Pac-Man, Frogger, Asteroids, Ms. Pac-Man. Each was a man-sized box with a large electronic eye staring out. The machines lined the walls and surrounded the columns. The walls were orange-yellow, the floor a brown-yellow linoleum. Nevell Johnson had been playing a spaceship game called Eagle, which was against the east wall, near a column. It was a tight spot, at the edge of a corridor only two and a half feet wide. Luis would have been dealing with an armed suspect in cramped conditions—a fact that we had to make clear to the jury.

I spent so much time studying the layout of the arcade that after a while I could close my eyes and tell you where each machine was. When we learned that four teenage girls had been playing Pac-Man, I knew that meant they were close to Johnson. When a witness said he was playing El Dorado or Captain Fantastic, I knew his view would have been blocked by a column, so he couldn't possibly have seen Luis and Nevell Johnson at the Eagle machine.

Outside, as I walked down the cracked concrete of Third Avenue past broken neon signs, I affected a casual air I didn't feel. My stomach tightened as we entered the three-story, U-shaped tenements, climbing on concrete steps that smelled of stale urine so rank I breathed through my mouth. No one wanted to talk. Each time I went, a crowd gathered. Curses, threats and, occasionally, pieces of stale fruit filled the air. Mark, as an ex-cop, could carry a gun. For our trips to Overtown, he packed three. Thankfully, he never had to use them.

Weeks before the trial, I engaged in further research by seeking out Dr. Joe Davis, the Dade County medical examiner. I thought after thirty years of studying bullet wounds, Doc Davis could supply an answer I needed.

I found him behind a large, flat desk loaded with scientific journals, jars with body parts floating in clear solution and some medieval-looking surgical instruments. He cleared a chair piled high with medical books and case folders so that I could sit. I questioned him about the bullet's path through the brain, getting him to sketch out the trajectory on my legal pad.

Davis theorized that Johnson immediately lost all conscious control of his body when he was shot. If so, I asked, how did Johnson's autonomic nervous system react to the blow of the shot? Did Davis have an opinion on how Alvarez and Johnson were positioned? Left unsaid was my question that perhaps physics could prove that Johnson was going for his gun. Davis swiveled around and pulled a thick, well-fingered book off a shelf. He laid it on the desk, opened to the unforgettable photo of Jack Ruby thrusting the gun into Lee Harvey Oswald's stomach as he squeezes the trigger. Oswald, his face open-mouthed in pain, jerks back. "Perhaps this is how Johnson reacted," Davis said, "but can we ever really know?"

From the beginning, I thought it was important we get the trial moved out of Miami. Disc jockeys at WMBM, a black radio station, were making fiery calls for "justice." Several times, black demonstrators rallied at the Criminal Justice Building, where our trial was to be held. A survey by Metro-Dade police showed that 60 percent of county residents—our potential jurors—agreed with the statement: "Police officers' use of deadly force has been on the increase and cannot be justified." Fifty-eight percent agreed with the statement: "Miami is a potential powder keg, and the threat of violence is imminent."

Every time Luis Alvarez was mentioned on the local television news, video-tapes of the post-shooting riot were shown: buildings and cars burning, angry youths throwing rocks and bottles, the injured arriving at the emergency room.

At the hearing about moving the trial, I proved that the case dominated the news by submitting over five hundred newspaper articles, several hundred videotapes of newscasts, numerous affidavits of residents and finally our own public opinion poll. It revealed the undercurrent flowing through Miami: Two-thirds of all those questioned didn't want to sit on the jury. Half were convinced that an acquittal would cause another riot. Another third were unsure. That meant that four out of every five prospective jurors would weigh Luis's guilt or innocence while thinking about a riot. Would some think it worth the price to send one individual to jail for a few years to spare a county of a million and a half residents the turmoil of another riot?

I argued that the constant threats of more riots made the jurors afraid to return a not-guilty verdict. "Judge, it's not the poisonous publicity alone, it's the fear caused by it. The type of fear that pumps through the arteries of this city. Fear of racial violence. Fear of more burning cars and buildings. Fear of more people beaten to death. Fear of finding Alvarez not guilty."

Our judge was David Gersten, a thirty-one-year-old who had served on the bench less than two years. With a thick beard and wire-rimmed glasses, he had the look of a graduate student. Gersten was not predisposed to the prosecution. He was not swayed by the politics surrounding the trial, and he was not impressed with the intense emotionalism of both sides. In many of his rulings in our case, he would prove astute and impartial, but on this point he was implacable. Judges are human beings and $50 black robes don't insulate them from outside pressures. The accepted wisdom in Miami was that the hyperviolence of the McDuffie riot was due to moving the trial to Tampa. No judge wanted to be held responsible for eighteen deaths and $100 million in damages. The trial was staying in Miami.

One last job before the trial began was to design the appearance of our client. Psychological research proves that we have five minutes to be accepted or rejected when we first meet someone. We also gather 87 percent of our information by sight and only 7 percent by hearing. So what the jury sees in the first few minutes is vitally important. No detail is too small if it will provide an edge—including appearance.[5] Urban-cop fashion has a dark, hard-edged, almost threatening look. It's a survival mechanism. The clothes send out a message—don't fuck with me. Alvarez's moustache added to the rough image. We selected classic tailoring to soften him—single-breasted suits, in muted hues, with non-designer ties—to reflect our serious purpose. We wanted the image of a professional—a man you could trust, a man who wouldn't panic, a man who would do his job in a solid, competent way.

When Luis hesitated, I told him an anecdote related by Edward Bennett Williams, the famed Washington attorney, in his book *One Man's Freedom*, about representing Frank Costello, reputed head of the Mafia during the 1950s. Early in the morning of the first day of his trial, Costello came to Williams's hotel room. The lawyer was astounded to see a mafioso wearing an exceptionally expensive suit. "You can't wear that suit," Williams told him. "Go get a cheap

---

5. The Menendez brothers' fuzzy-sweater look was a brilliant haberdashery gambit, but it won't fly again because prosecutors are tuned in to it and will expose the now transparent ploy to the jury.

suit." Five minutes later the lawyer heard a knock on his door. It was Costello—
still wearing the expensive suit. "I'd rather be convicted," he said.

Not Luis Alvarez. He shaved off his moustache and bought several conservative suits.

It took thirteen months for Luis to get his day in court, but finally in January
1984, the State was ready. Just before the trial began, Judge Gersten called us
into chambers and handed over a police intelligence report. A black extremist
group called the Yahwehs planned to disrupt the trial by an assassination. I was
the target. "This isn't a trial," I moaned. "It's hand-to-hand combat." I was jok-
ing because none of us had then heard of the Yahweh group, but a few years
later I stopped laughing when Yahweh Ben Yahweh and other cult leaders
were convicted of killing fourteen whites.

Meanwhile, community leaders were preparing for more riots. The Miami
Police Department canceled all vacations until after the trial. Patrol cars were
outfitted with bulletproof vests, face shields, riot batons and gas masks. Even
plainclothes detectives were given riot gear. A county-wide emergency operations headquarters was put on standby.

The first bomb threat came on the first day of jury selection. The National
Liberation Front called at 8:30 a.m., warning that a bomb would go off in the
Criminal Justice Building an hour later. All the courts and offices in the nine-
floor building were evacuated. Our prospective jurors stood outside on the
street, where they heard prisoners chant from the Dade County Jail next door:
"Kill Alvarez! Kill Alvarez!" Nearby marched pickets from black organizations
carrying placards demanding a conviction. Quite an auspicious start to a trial
guaranteed by the Bill of Rights to be calm and dispassionate.

Two hours after the threat, the bomb squad reported the building was
clean, and we were allowed into the Criminal Justice Building, which even
under usual circumstances is something to behold. A repulsive stench hit us
as we passed the southwest corner of the building, nicknamed "chicken central," which doubled as a concrete altar for Santeria, an Afro-Cuban religion.
Small chickens with their throats slit and a disemboweled goat, its bloody vis-
cera exposed, cooked in the white-hot Miami sun. The animals were somehow linked to the deities who guided judges and jurors. Some people, more

considerate of our olfactory response, tastefully hid their ritual sacrifices in plastic bags. Others simply deposited the stinking carcasses on the ground.

Inside, as usual, the corridors were a noisy sea—uniformed cops and detectives and lawyers and witnesses mingling with corrections officers and reporters. Dazed grandmothers came to see what their kids were accused of. Wives and lovers of defendants sat on hard wooden benches next to victims waiting to testify. Elderly gents in checked sports coats hopped from courtroom to courtroom, looking for hot testimony to spice up their retirements. It's the kind of place where a Nebraska-born accountant in a business suit, accused of drunk driving, can be found waiting next to an impoverished Puerto Rican woman who's a rape victim.

On this morning you could add to the list one young Cuban-born suspended police officer. With a clean upper lip, wearing one of his new single-breasted dark suits, Alvarez walked with us through the special security precautions that had been set up for the trial, including a metal detector right outside Courtroom 4-1, which was to be our home for the next two months. Inside the courtroom were security officers in plainclothes, carefully watching the spectators for signs of trouble. I knew Judge Gersten himself was so concerned he carried a Smith & Wesson .38 bodyguard revolver under his robe.

At the table to our left, in the choice spot right next to the jury box reserved for them in every courtroom in the land, sat the prosecution team. By this time, Reno had brought in an even tougher group, led by Abe Laeser, her chief assistant prosecutor. He had a chalky complexion, heavy, hooded eyes and a dour, almost funereal expression that masked a subtle and ingenious mind. What Laeser lacked in social skills he more than made up for in legal talent. The lawyers of a score of death row inmates had underestimated Abe. It was my understanding that he had never lost a case. He was flanked by Ed Cowart, a former chief judge of the Miami courts who began his career as a Miami motorcycle cop, and Ira Loewy, the sharp-tongued chief of the law division, to handle legal arguments.

When the judge took the bench, I renewed my plea to move the trial out of Miami. Gersten again said no. He believed that sequestering the jurors for the two or three weeks he thought the trial would take would be sufficient protection against outside influences. The judge then ordered the bailiff to bring in forty-eight prospective jurors. As they entered, they looked furtively around the large room. They didn't talk to each other, but sat nervously, as if they were in a dentist's waiting room.

As we began jury selection that morning, many of the spectators seemed bored. They probably thought the lawyers and jurors were engaged in polite conversations that had no particular point. But what could be more important than picking those who would decide the case? Both sides had invested serious time in thinking out the beginning moves of this subtle, multi-level chess game called voir dire. My team was working on meager donations from Luis's fellow officers, and we didn't have money for jury selection specialists or intricate polling procedures. What funds we did have had been spent on the poll to support our futile change-of-venue motion.

Our poll results showed that 20 percent of all respondents were convinced of Luis's guilt before the first witness had testified. Only 9 percent thought he was innocent. The rest weren't sure. The data revealed what we suspected: Dade County was polarized along racial-ethnic lines. The poll showed that 48 percent of all blacks were firmly convinced of Alvarez's guilt. Only 3 percent thought he was innocent.

It also revealed that I had to be cautious of Hispanics, too. One in five Hispanics thought Luis was innocent, but another one in five assumed he was guilty. I wasn't sure why this was: Perhaps some Hispanics, usually heavily pro-prosecution, assumed that because he was indicted, he *must* be guilty. Many of Miami's Hispanics, especially those from Cuba, come from the upper classes of Latin America and are far more conservative than Hispanics in other parts of the country.

Judging from our poll, our best strategy was to select non-Hispanic whites. Only 9 percent had already decided that Luis was guilty. That was a number I was willing to live with.

Journalists were guessing publicly that we would seek Hispanic jurors, under the intuitive assumption Hispanics, particularly Cubans, would be sympathetic to Luis. I did nothing to disabuse them of that notion. Let the State knock Hispanics off the panel, while we would challenge any other juror black, white, or Hispanic—prejudiced against Alvarez. The result would be a white non Hispanic jury, which the poll projected as our best bet.

Jury voir dire requires an improbable intellectual feat mastered by few lawyers. Imagine the task: Put at ease nervous, anxious recruits; probe through their personal histories; expose their biases and prejudices, while forcing them to sit on uncomfortable chairs in a warehouse-sized room studded with legal symbols designed to intimidate. On top of that most judges frustrate any attempt to ask revealing questions, preferring instead the tried and worthless legal boilerplate which sounds magisterial but accomplishes little. In an effort to overcome these factors I followed a strategy of probing their fears of riots but with a hidden agenda. While seeming to seek riot-related stories I was rating their fear indexes. How would they relate to Alvarez's fear in the shooting?

I asked anyone who had faced his own death to raise his hand. Several did so. I had each describe what had happened to him in detail. What made you feel afraid? Did your heart pound? Did your body feel flushed? Did you start sweating? How did your stomach feel? Did you think of anything other than survival? Did you have time to think, or did you just react?

Each time someone shared an experience, I threw it out as bait, like Phil Donahue, to get the others talking. One juror described how he had narrowly avoided a fatal car crash, then caught everyone's attention by dramatically describing how his heart kept pounding for several minutes afterwards. This man's story—and that of others with similar experiences—educated the rest of the panel. These jury candidates were becoming our witnesses. In my summation I planned to play back to them their same descriptions of emotions and sensations to show how Luis had felt.

What's more, my conversation with each one allowed me to forge a personal bond. I was able slowly to draw most of them out of their shells and turn nervous strangers into something approaching friends. Without their being aware, I studied each one, running him through my own personality tests, with a view to creating the right chemistry in the jury box.

The first black juror I questioned was an elderly widow who had known the dead man, Nevell Johnson, since he was a boy and had been friends with his father for forty years. Several times I asked her if she had already made up her mind about Alvarez's guilt. She insisted she hadn't, but obviously, she was too close to the Johnsons. The judge agreed: She was removed for cause.

Another problem was a black unemployed janitor. "If the officer did it," he said to me, "he's a jive turkey."

"What does that mean, 'jive turkey'?" I asked.

"It mean he is no good," the fellow answered. Then, turning to Luis, he added: "If you're offended by that, I'm sorry, sir."

The janitor said that I must prove that Luis acted in self-defense. "If you don't do it," he warned, "you lost your case."

After considerable argument I persuaded the judge that this juror, too, should be dropped for cause, for requiring us to prove Luis's innocence.

The last black was also a problem. He was a thirty-seven-year-old painter who lived and worked in Liberty City. He said he had never had any problems with the police and claimed he could reach a verdict based only on the evidence.

"But if your verdict is unpopular with your neighbors, could you return home?"

"It will be tough," he admitted.

As I questioned him, Luis stared at him intently. When court was adjourned, he whispered to me that he was sure he had seen this painter before. "And if I recognize him, it ain't because I go out with him."

That night Luis found a buddy on the midnight shift who sifted through records and came up with a police report: The painter had been arrested during a shift that Luis had worked. Luis wasn't listed as the arresting officer, but he was certain that he had been at the scene as backup.

Luis came to court the next morning carrying the guy's arrest record. Always a man of action, he was happy that he was able to do something other than sit passively at the defense table. He felt great until Judge Gersten studied the arrest record and declared it was insufficient evidence to drop the painter for cause. A man's being arrested, the judge declared, didn't automatically mean he was prejudiced against police officers. We used one of our preemptory challenges to excuse him from the panel.

Our one other tough decision concerned a Hispanic male, Guillermo Marrero, who owned two Burger Kings in Liberty City. One of the restaurants had burned down during the McDuffie riots four years before and then been rebuilt. As soon as the questioning began, he made it clear that he didn't want to be on the jury.

"I can be fair," he told us, "but I have reservations, like what would happen to the sixty people I employ." He worried that if he voted for acquittal, his places might be destroyed and his employees would lose their livelihoods. Still, he said no threats could alter the facts: "The truth is always the truth."

One detail persuaded me not to strike Marrero: He carried a gun to work. Obviously he knew how dangerous life could be in Miami's ghettos. We decided to keep him. So did Laeser, who apparently assumed that Marrero would be terrorized into supporting the prosecution.

We ended up with Marrero and five non-Hispanic whites. I ordered each member of the defense team to memorize the jurors' faces, their seat locations and their biographies. The individual jurors would now fade to the background as more dramatic events in the trial took center stage, but we could not afford to forget them. They were:

—Donald Moore, sixty-two, a marine chemist at the University of Miami. We felt he was the perfect juror for this case, a researcher able to penetrate the technical nonsense that the State was going to present about Luis's gun.

—Robert Mendelson, sixty-five, a retired dock foreman. He remembered the Johnson shooting because he was working a part-time job that required him to drive through Liberty City, and his colleagues warned him to be careful. He said people weren't entitled to riot. He knew some people would be unhappy with the verdict, no matter which way it went, and that wouldn't bother him.

—Janice Winn, a forty-three-year-old real estate agent with two children. She didn't believe what she read in the newspapers and thought the shooting was an "absolute tragedy" for both the Johnson and Alvarez families. Like many people, she said the prospect of riots terrified her, but "whatever the verdict, it will be unpopular."

—Mary Ellen Hoodwin, a retired medical secretary who had lived in Miami for thirty-seven years. She said she never read *The Miami Herald*. She didn't socialize much and didn't care what others thought.

—Victor King, fifty-three, the father of eleven children and an Eastern Airlines mechanic for almost three decades. He had read or seen little about the case.

Each side had used only four of its six challenges—a low number in such a high-pressure, high-publicity case. I think the reason was that we and the prosecution were looking for the same kind of jurors—non-Hispanic whites who were strong on law enforcement.

After eight days we had a jury—almost. The court clerk raised her right hand, ready to swear in the panel. Guillermo Marrero, the Burger King man, announced: "I can't do it."

At the defense table we stared at each other. This kind of twist is generally found only in bad trial movies. Judge Gersten quickly ordered the five other jurors and two alternates sent to the jury room. Marrero was left alone in the jury box.

"I have already received threatening phone calls," he stated. "A caller told me that if I was going to be on the jury and the guy was found innocent, I'd be in trouble." The manager of one of his restaurants had received similar calls. Marrero feared his Burger Kings would be burned.

Both Laeser and I wanted Marrero replaced, but we differed in our suggested solutions. Laeser wanted the whole panel dismissed because there were no blacks. I told the judge that the incident was another example of how impossible it was to get a fair trial in Miami, but if he didn't agree to a change of venue it would be best to replace the Burger King man with an alternate and get on with the trial.

At 11 p.m., after hours of reading legal cases, the weary judge emerged from his chambers. "I'll tell you," he said, "you'll never find anything in the law books about this. Clearly we don't have a jury yet." He said he would contemplate the matter overnight and have a solution by morning.

As we drove back to the office, Mark, Ralph and I talked about how crucial this moment was. The young judge must be feeling immense community pressure to impanel black jurors, and I wasn't about to let anyone on the jury who had a preconceived notion of Luis's guilt.

After eight tough days, I had the jury that gave us our best shot and I intended to fight for it. Anticipating that Gersten might throw out the entire panel, we rushed back to the office to prepare a petition for a writ of prohibition. I pulled law books off the shelves and spent the next several hours reading jury selection opinions until my eyes burned. Our plan was to have the petition waiting in the clerk's office of the Third District Court of Appeal. If Gersten dismissed the panel, we would file our pleading within moments and demand that the jury be retained at the courthouse while the appellate judges considered whether Gersten had the power to throw out the panel. The plan was that a messenger would hold the motion at the appellate court until we instructed him to file it.

The next morning, however, we showed up in court to see the judge looking uneasy. "Mr. Black," he said, "I've just been called by the appellate court. They say you've already filed this motion."

Chagrined, I explained my plan. I hadn't meant to file yet; the messenger made a mistake. I could see Gersten mulling the effect of this petition. Judges deny ever being influenced by the threat of an appeal, but this time I swear it worked. He announced he was appointing the first alternate, Lourdes Mangas, a twenty-two-year-old travel agent, to take Marrero's place. Our lone Hispanic had been replaced by a Hispanic.

For opening arguments, all 120 spectator seats were filled. Directly behind the defense table sat a row of young off-duty police officers. The hierarchy of the Miami Police Department had decreed that they couldn't wear their uniforms in the courtroom, but the brass couldn't stop them from attending. They were all street cops, and they knew what had happened to Luis Alvarez could happen to any of them. The group had vowed that, no matter how long the trial lasted, officers would be sitting behind Luis each day.

Laeser began with a surprise, setting up an eye-catching, brightly colored schematic on an easel. Drawn to scale by an architect, it displayed in detail the interior of the video-game arcade. Each machine—Omega, Robotron, Harlem Globetrotters, Sinbad—was clearly marked. Round one to Laeser, once again proving that money is the mother milk of law as well as politics.

Pointing to the floor plan, Laeser, in the soft voice of a professional mortician, ran through a list of Luis's alleged errors that night: He deliberately left his assigned patrol zone without his supervisors' permission and without radio clearance. He left his patrol car and entered the game room without notifying the dispatcher. He had no right to confront Johnson, who was peacefully playing a game. He violated accepted police procedure by getting too close to Johnson and by cocking the hammer on his service revolver—a dangerous procedure in which the revolver could go off with just a quarter of the pressure usually required on the trigger. His gun had been illegally modified into a deadly and dangerous weapon unauthorized by the Miami Police Department. The rebound spring had been clipped, creating a hair trigger.

The prosecutor claimed Luis told Johnson, "We are going to walk out of here nice and easy." Johnson simply was obeying that instruction, turning slowly, with hands up, in a gesture of surrender. As Johnson turned, Laeser claimed, Alvarez flinched and the gun accidentally went off. The prosecutor kept repeating the word "flinch," and I scribbled it down. The courtroom is a war of words, and this was a word I needed to deal with.

Before the grand jury, witnesses had claimed Luis planted a throw-down gun on Johnson as a cover-up for killing him. This accusation fell apart when witnesses surfaced who had seen Johnson toting the gun before the night of the shooting. So the prosecution had shifted its focus to manslaughter through culpable negligence, a kind of malpractice case, like a surgeon amputating the wrong leg, except you go to jail for thirty years. Laeser's theory was aimed at proving that Luis had accidentally shot Nevell Johnson through a series of unprofessional mistakes. Since cops are supposed to be knowledgeable about weapons and their use, a cop's carelessness with a gun is tantamount to criminal activity. So words like "flinched" spun the argument toward the accidental.

Laeser said he had proof of what happened. A blood spatter expert had studied photographs and noticed "five droplets of blood near the Eagle machine" that substantiated the State's theory. He promised we would hear more about these "droplets." Then he hammered at Luis, claiming he was a cop out of control, compounding one mistake with another, which ultimately resulted in the unnecessary and tragic death of Nevell Johnson.

As Laeser strode back to his seat, I glanced at the jurors and gathered from their deepening frowns that Laeser had struck a chord with his detailed list of Luis's alleged sins. I decided I had to take them out of the comfortable courtroom and drop them onto the dirty, grim and dangerous streets of Overtown.

Without preamble, I painted a portrait of Overtown, where violence is a daily reality. Fear makes the decent people prisoners in their dingy apartments. The cracks of gunfire and the risk of stray bullets force their children to sleep below window level. Police officers walk down hostile streets, watching their backs like enemy soldiers.

"Overtown has overwhelming problems for police officers," I told the jury. "Most of the street signs have been stolen or vandalized. Ninety percent of the streetlights don't work. Overtown is only ten blocks wide and twenty-five blocks long, but it gets 50,000 police calls a year." That's more than a hundred a day.

The jurors sat on the edges of their seats. It was time to set the scene in the arcade. Again, I painted a vivid picture. Alvarez warily walks into the room, leading rookie Luis Cruz. "The jukebox is going full blast. Thirty to fifty people are playing video games so noisy they would drive you crazy." Alvarez focuses on details significant only to a street cop. His eyes quickly scan everyone there, searching for anything out of place. "Out of the corner of his eye he sees Nevell Johnson playing the Eagle video game. Over his left kidney, there is a bulge." The cop has no choice but to confront him. The situation quickly falls apart. Johnson's eyes lock on his. This isn't going right. Johnson's hand reaches for his gun. Luis fires his gun. "The key event in this case took one second.

"Ladies and gentlemen," I said, looking straight at the jurors, "this is the first time that we've had an opportunity to make known our side of what happened that night. After enduring thirteen months of biased newspaper articles and inflammatory television shows, we for the first time are given an opportunity to refute these charges."

To examine Laeser's claims of violations of police procedure, I walked over to a corner of the courtroom and pulled out a blackboard. This was a spur-of-the-moment idea. To contrast with the expensive, high-tech visual the State was putting on, I wanted to show that we were a low-budget, low-tech defense, the only kind a street cop could afford. Never underestimate the power of a piece of chalk.

Apologizing for "my very poor penmanship," I roughed out a diagram that showed Luis's path through the arcade, and then I asked about Nevell Johnson. "Crime is a risky business, and the riskiest of all is to carry an illegally concealed firearm and to go out and threaten the people." I told the jurors Johnson was not the benevolent bystander that Laeser described, but rather a more sinister character nicknamed Mr. Snake. "Mr. Snake is dead, but he has to be part of this trial. His actions cannot be ignored or forgotten. We grieve for his family and friends. We, too, wish that he was alive today. We, too, wish that he had not taken the actions that he took on that night and put himself in that position so that he got killed. If it was up to us, ladies and gentlemen, we would spare Nevell Johnson. We would spare Luis Alvarez. We would spare this community the trauma of reliving that night some thirteen months ago, a night in which there were no winners, only losers.

"The State has spent a fortune to second-guess everything Officer Luis Alvarez did. They've hired experts from all over the country, armchair quarterbacks, who will second-guess everything that this police officer did. But did they spend one thin dime to determine what Nevell Johnson was up to that night? Through the testimony you are going to know that Nevell Johnson of his own free will illegally concealed a stolen firearm on his body the night of December 28.

"In the safety of this courtroom, we'll debate for weeks what happened in that one second, but that was a luxury that Officer Alvarez did not have."

My opening stretched to an hour and a half. After I sat down, I had the sinking feeling I had tried to stuff in too many details, events and people. I had skated perilously close to committing the cardinal sin of overtrying my case.

Laeser's first witness was John Buhrmaster, a young homicide detective who had led the police investigation. A chiseled, clean-cut marine type, with a hard face and sandy brown hair, he had been on the force for a decade, the past five years in homicide. He was a formidable witness who had garnered thirty commendations and was a six-time officer of the month, a runner-up for officer of the year, and officer of the year. He had received two silver medals for valor. It was easy to see why Laeser wanted to lead with him.

Buhrmaster testified that he was at his desk at police headquarters at 6:05 p.m., December 28, when he heard an excited officer shouting over the radio: "238 emergency, 238 emergency. Get me the squad, get me the squad, please. I'm on, ah, Fifteenth Street and Northwest Third Avenue. Somebody just pushed me and a shot went off and there's a, a, um, a black male down."

Luis was 238. The "squad" meant an ambulance. I knew Laeser wanted to get this transcript into evidence immediately because it smelled of an accidental shooting. This was one of his strongest pieces of evidence.

Buhrmaster said that he and Sergeant Bobby Cheatham jumped in a car and drove to the arcade, which was less than two miles from police headquarters. They arrived at 6:15—about ten minutes after the shooting. A crowd of 150 to 300 was blocking the street, and the detectives had to push their way through to get to the game room.

Laeser handed the detective a photo of the game room taken through the front door and asked him to identify it. He did. The prosecutor asked that the photo be introduced into evidence. I scanned the photo and saw the Eagle machine had been moved out from behind the column, making a larger space for the confrontation than there had been. The Robotron machine which blocked the view of some witnesses had also been conveniently moved. I objected and the judge granted me a voir dire, in which I was allowed to do a mini–cross-examination of the witness on this point. It turned out the photo was taken eight days after the shooting and Buhrmaster sheepishly admitted the machines may have "inadvertently" been moved.

Despite my objections the judge allowed the photo into evidence. First witness, first exhibit and the gamesmanship had begun. When I walked back to the defense table, Luis grabbed my arm and asked in a hoarse whisper, "How can they get away with that?"

"This is just beginning," I replied.

I had lost a round but scored a point against Laeser, who was a methodical man, accustomed to following a time-testing formula for presenting a case. I had upset his rhythm and it showed.

Steaming from my interruption, Laeser returned to Buhrmaster's narrative. The detective said that when he arrived paramedics were lifting Johnson onto a stretcher. There was a large pool of blood "back by the Moon Patrol." Luis was nervously pacing back and forth, speaking under his breath. He told Buhrmaster that he had picked up Johnson's gun—a .22-caliber RG Model 14, blue steel with a three-inch barrel—and put it in his belt so that some kid didn't run away with it. The detective took that gun, then asked for Luis's service revolver. He inspected it and made a note: "stainless steel service revolver, Smith & Wesson model with brown wooden grips." *Wooden* grips. I made a note of that. Another technical violation.

Buhrmaster said that at 6:35 p.m. he talked with Luis, who told him how he and his partner, Luis Cruz, had walked through the arcade and were about to leave when Luis spotted the bulge under Nevell Johnson's sweater. He felt the bulge. It was a hard object. He asked Johnson what it was. Johnson told him it was a gun.

Buhrmaster: "He said he told the guy that they were going to leave the game room and he wanted no problems from him. At that time he withdrew his service revolver and lifted the sweater to show his partner the gun, and he took his hand off the gun and put it on the left shoulder of Nevell Johnson. He said at that time while he had his hand on the shoulder and his partner was in the process of reaching for the gun, the individual turned toward him suddenly and he jerked back away from the individual. And his gun discharged." Buhrmaster testified that Luis had not told him that he had shot in self-defense.

The detective claimed that Luis had given him a demonstration of how Johnson had turned toward him. He showed the jury a motion of swiveling slowly, with his hands raised up by his head. By this time our defense table was roiling with anger. This was not in Buhrmaster's police report. Someone had gotten him to add this detail. I was trying to take notes while pushing Luis back in his seat.

Now it was my turn. I started cautiously. Cross-examining a smart witness with an agenda is like a razor fight. You don't know you've been cut until you are bleeding to death.

I opened by describing the unpleasant atmosphere that night at the arcade. Supervising officers, crime scene technicians and other detectives had to push their way through screaming crowds to get into the arcade. Soon, the angry mob was pushing against the doors, trying to get inside. Buhrmaster and the other officers felt trapped. I was sure they were more worried about firebombing and snipers than carefully collecting evidence.

The jurors were watching me. I think most jurors understand intuitively that direct examination is always carefully rehearsed; it's on cross-examination that they lean forward in their seats, waiting for the clash that is about to come. As John Wigmore, dean of the Northwestern University School of Law, wrote in his famous multi-volume treatise on evidence: "Cross-examination is the greatest engine for determining the truth. A lawyer can do anything with cross-examination." It's such a powerful tool that more clients end up in prison cells from inept cross than from any other blunder.

The formula for successful cross-examination is simply stated: Use plain declarative sentences, add only one new fact per question, and lock in an answer before administering the coup de grâce. Think of cross-examination as a series of statements by the lawyer, only occasionally interrupted by a yes from the witness.

And your interview with Officer Alvarez took place at 6:35?"

"Yes sir."

"By then the crowd was even larger?"

"Yes."

"Still a steady stream of rocks and bottles?"

"Yes."

"Did people begin pounding on the windows of the arcade?"

"Yes."

"Were the officers handling the crowd outside forced back inside the arcade?"

"Yes sir."

"Things were too hot for them standing outside the front doors?"

"Yes sir."

"You could hear gunshots ricocheting off the walls of the building?"

"Yes."

"It was like the last stand at the Alamo?"

"Very close."

"You know, Davy Crockett," the judge interjected, getting in the mood. Things were going well.

Through a series of questions Buhrmaster described how the crime scene technician, Rafael García, ordinarily a meticulous collector of evidence, was allowed only thirty minutes to work in the arcade. Usually he needed at least six hours to inspect even a simple homicide scene. Under my questioning, the detective acknowledged that the rush caused García to make ten errors in his diagram.

García was still working when a police major ordered everyone out of the arcade. Luis and Cruz were rushed to waiting patrol cars. García and other officers managed to escape. But then the crowd surged, trapping Buhrmaster and Sergeant Cheatham. They hid in a back room for forty minutes, until a SWAT team rushed up in a phalanx of squad cars. Officers in body armor jumped out, threatened the crowd with rifles and fired tear gas. The homicide investigators slid into a squad car and got away.

When the detective was finished describing his harrowing escape, I pulled out a videocassette, shot by TV news crews, showing the street scene outside the arcade immediately after the shooting. Laeser hurriedly objected, and the judge sent the jurors out. I popped the cassette into the VCR. The judge watched as angry young men shouted obscenities and threw rocks at the arcade. Squad cars were on fire. Police officers dashed about in riot gear—bulletproof vests and helmets with plastic visors protecting their faces—as they formed a defensive line against the rioters.

"Focus on the police officers," I told the judge. "They're all watching their backs. It's a bad case of nerves. What better proof why mistakes were made?"

Laeser objected to the tape. It was an ugly display. Gersten decided the jurors would be overwhelmed by the impact of the video. They would not see it.

When the sidebar was over it was 6 p.m., time for adjournment. We went back to our office and huddled in the library around the conference table, trying to figure out what to do. Not being allowed to show the video was a blow to our defense. The antiseptic atmosphere of the courtroom diminishes the reality of chaotic events, and I was certain the visual impact of the flames and rocks would have been more powerful than the detective's dry description. I wanted *something* because the next day I had to cross-examine Buhrmaster on the statement he had allegedly taken from Luis. If we could show jurors how chaotic the situation was at that moment, we'd go a long way to explaining why the detective might have gotten his facts wrong.

As we talked, I noticed a box in the corner. It contained hundreds of hours of audiotapes of all the police radio channels from the night of the shooting. We had listened carefully to Luis's transmissions, but there were many other channels, used by other police groups, that we had never bothered to listen to. Could an audiotape give the same mood as a videotape? Maybe if the sounds were real enough.

Deep into the night, we listened to the tapes. Much of the stuff was indecipherable codes, with officers shouting at each other. But on some tapes we found unnerving sounds in the background: breaking glass, occasional pops of sniper fire, rioters shouting obscenities at the police. Suddenly, we heard the number 1941. Someone checked a code list we had. The number belonged to Detective Buhrmaster.

We played the rest of the tape. Buhrmaster had forgotten one small detail.

For day two of Detective John Buhrmaster's testimony, I focused on the toughest subject he had raised on direct: Luis's statement to him in the arcade. In the detective's version, Luis had made several incriminating statements, and I needed to get across two points. First, Luis was under extreme stress at that moment. Second, Buhrmaster's recollection was flawed because of the chaotic conditions in the arcade and perhaps because of political pressure later.

I elicited from him that Alvarez seemed dazed and was entering post-traumatic shock, not uncommon in police shootings. Yet Buhrmaster sought no help or comfort for him. He didn't take him back to the station for questioning, but left him unarmed in the midst of a riot while attempting to interrogate him.

I asked about the alleged interview at 6:35 p.m. Buhrmaster said he and Luis were both standing up. The detective took notes with his pad on top of a video machine. The whole interview lasted less than five minutes.

I pointed out that he had made numerous mistakes in his notes. He had noted that Luis's revolver had wooden grips, when in fact they were plastic— a minor point that we knew the State was going to make into a big deal.

"You said Officer Alvarez told you he *jerked* back."

"Yes."

I wheeled over our blackboard so that the jury and Buhrmaster could see it. "And you used the word 'jerked,' did you not?"

"Yes."

I spelled out the word on the blackboard in huge letters, enunciating each letter as I printed it: "J-E-R-K-E-D. Is that accurate?"

"I don't understand your question."

"Well, let me see if I can perhaps make it a little more understandable. You know that you can change the meaning of a sentence by a small change in the words of the sentence, don't you?"

"Yes."

I showed him his fifty-page, single-spaced police report and pointed out he used the word "pulled" the trigger without any mention of "jerked." "Now, one of the things that might happen—I am not saying this *did* happen, but one of the things that might happen is that people might try to influence you to change words. It's possible that could happen?"

"I don't understand what you mean," Buhrmaster replied cautiously.

"For example, perhaps an unscrupulous person might want you to perhaps change one or two words in what was said to you. Could that be possible?"

"I can't answer that," he said with a defensive tone I was sure the jurors caught.

"How many times since December 28 have you had conferences in the State Attorney's Office?"

"I couldn't tell you."

"A large number?"

"I really don't know."

"And you know what their theory in this case is, don't you? I mean, they certainly discussed that with you, didn't they?"

"Somewhat, yes."

If this were *Perry Mason*, I would have asked him if the prosecutors had told him to use the word 'jerked' and he would have admitted I was right. But in real life it would have been an example of the lawyer committing the error of one question too many. Buhrmaster would deny that Laeser suggested he use the word. He'd claim the change had been unintentional. I left it to the jury to decide why the word was changed.

He had testified that Luis said Johnson's hands were up in the air in an obvious surrender position, and he had demonstrated with Laeser by raising his own hands up by his head. Now, I showed him, and the jury, a transcript in which he had clearly stated that Johnson's hands were at chest level.

"Has anything happened since that perhaps caused you to lift up your hands?"

"No."

"Has the intense political pressure caused your hands to go higher?"

"No."

His denial was spoken in a low, hesitant voice, and I saw disbelief in the eyes of a couple of jurors.

Buhrmaster's recounting of Luis's statement right after the shooting had crumbled a bit, but not enough. Now it was time for the sound show. We brought Ralph's stereo into the courtroom. When Laeser realized we were about to play a police tape, he knew we were going to upstage him. He sensed that the tape wasn't going to be good for him, so he complained to the judge. He said our cassettes of the radio broadcasts were "a copy of a copy." He planned to play the originals later in the trial.

Gersten overruled the objection. Audio, without the powerful images of the video, was more acceptable to the judge. Laeser was annoyed at this further disruption of his plans.

Mark punched the play button. After a moment of static Luis's panicked call at 6:05 blasted out of the speakers. "238 emergency, 238 emergency. Get me the squad, get me the squad." The words rushed out, frantically. Hearing Luis shout, hearing the tremor and horror in his tone was far more powerful than Buhrmaster's dispassionate reading of the transcript of the day before.

Next we played the tape of a secondary channel. This one was new to Buhrmaster, as it had been new to us the night before. I led the detective along slowly, not telegraphing what was coming. He was smiling, thinking he was simply our expert, guiding us through the confusing jumble of numbers and letters.

I knew I was taking a risk. Cross-examining a hostile witness is a zero-sum game. For one side to win the other must lose. If Buhrmaster survived unscathed, we wouldn't.

First, I firmly established that Buhrmaster had taken notes of his interview with Alvarez, and at the top of the page he had carefully noted the time the interview began as 18:35, using military notation, meaning 6:35 p.m. After making certain that he was locked into 18:35, I led him through the chronology of the tape.

Every few seconds, I noted, the dispatcher announced the time. "This is so you professionals in the police department have a record of the time things happen?"

"Correct."

We heard squad cars from 30 sector and 40 sector reporting they were on the way to the scene. An officer requested a lieutenant and an internal affairs investigator. The dispatcher announced it was 18:14.

"That's 6:14 p.m.?"

"Correct."

Next we listened to a report that the internal affairs sergeant and a lieutenant were racing to the scene. Officer 447 was setting up a roadblock south of the arcade, to keep cars away from the mob. Then a report came that 27 Alpha, a major, was going to the arcade.

I led Buhrmaster through an explanation of how police use codes to communicate a lot of information quickly without tying up the frequency. "You don't simply say, 'This is Detective Buhrmaster of the homicide unit.' You give a code number."

"We have a call number."

"What's your call number?"

"1941."

I signaled Mark, and he played more tape. We listened as the harried dispatcher ordered squad cars from the northern zone of Miami—the Liberty City area—to go to the arcade. A lieutenant asked for canine units. All downtown units were ordered to the arcade. Then all south-end units. The riot accelerated with astounding speed. Within twenty minutes of the shooting, every squad car in the city had been ordered to the scene.

At 18:30 the SWAT team was ordered. In the background we could hear the noise of the riots—obscenities and broken glass and gunshots. Then 1941 yelled that the crime scene technician still wasn't there.

"Your number is 1941?" I asked.

"Yes."

Mark played more. In the hushed courtroom everyone could hear the clamor in the background as Buhrmaster frantically called for support. The tension in his voice showed how chaotic the situation was. The dispatcher announced the time: 18:35. The precise time Buhrmaster claimed he was interviewing Luis.

"That's 6:35 p.m.?" I asked.

"Yes sir." Buhrmaster swallowed hard.

"You testified that your conversation with Officer Alvarez began at 6:35 and lasted three to five minutes?"

"Yes." Suspicion dawned in his eyes.

"It is now 6:35 p.m.?"

"Yes."

"Play the tape."

Again, we heard 1941—Buhrmaster—screaming for support. The dispatcher announced the time: 18:36.

"We just heard 18:36," I said to the detective.

He shook his head. "I didn't hear 18:36."

"Well, let's play it again."

We played it again, and he acknowledged that he was on the radio at 18:36, or 6:36 p.m. That was supposedly a minute into his interview with Luis. The blood suddenly drained from his face.

"It said 1941?"

"Right."

"That's you?"

"Yes."

"You were talking to the dispatcher?"

"Correct."

"The operator reports back 1941?"

"Correct."

"So you had to be listening on your radio?"

"Correct."

"That's between 18:35 and 18:36?"

"Right."

"You're talking to Officer Alvarez at the same time?"

"Correct."

"But you have one ear on the radio?"

"I'm sorry?"

"One ear on the radio?"

"I don't know if I can answer that."

"But you're talking on the radio."

"Yes."

"Things are getting hot. The crowd is getting boisterous?"

"I tell you, you could hear the crowd the whole time."

"Things are chaotic?"

"I would say yes."

"You are rushing García to collect evidence before it gets worse?"

"Yes."

"The major is telling you that you must leave before it gets any worse?"

"Yes, he did."

Buhrmaster was on the air, intermittently, for the next three to four minutes. Left unsaid was the one question too many: How could you take an accurate statement of Alvarez while you're talking on the radio? I turned to the judge and announced, "Your Honor, we're finished with all this equipment. Perhaps if you want to take a very short recess, we can move all this and disconnect it." I wanted to give the jurors a few minutes to let the significance of the tape sink in.

• • •

I had already spent far more time with the prosecution's lead witness than Laeser had, and I was just getting started. Laeser's methodical approach was right out of Homicide Prosecution 101 and easy to read. I banked on unpredictability to force Laeser on the defensive.

When the afternoon session began, I introduced into evidence the bullets that had been taken from Johnson's gun. They were CCI stingers, high-velocity bullets intended to bounce around inside a human body until they slammed into vital organs. Then I picked up Johnson's gun, the RG-14, which had a nasty little two-inch muzzle. "This is what's commonly called a Saturday night special?"

Buhrmaster admitted it was the gun of choice in muggings and 7-Eleven robberies, and had no legitimate sporting use. He also conceded Alvarez had no choice but to make an arrest on a charge that carried a five-year prison sentence. Next, I used him to introduce Johnson's sweater into evidence.

In order to establish Alvarez's state of mind, I spent time establishing Miami's place as number one in the FBI national crime statistics for the past few years. Then we moved on to an interesting footnote to the riots. The first night of the riot, a team of prosecutors appeared at Miami police headquarters, which towers like a fortress on the edge of Overtown, to launch the Alvarez prosecution.

"At eight-thirty in the evening, assistant state attorneys came to the police station?"

"That's correct."

"Now, did they come to begin the prosecution of the people who were burning the cars?"

"No sir."

"Did they come to the police department to begin making cases against the people who were throwing rocks and bottles at the arcade building?"

"I don't believe so, no sir."

"Did they come to begin the prosecution of the people who were shooting at the police officers?"

"No sir."

"Burning police cars is still a crime?"

"I would say, yes."

"Is shooting guns a crime?"

"Yes sir."

"A serious crime, to shoot at police officers?"

"Yes sir."

"Who was appointed to track down these people who were shooting at the police officers?"

"To my knowledge, nobody was instructed to do that."

I had started Buhrmaster's cross-examination with the limited goal of disputing the detective's version of what Luis had told him in the arcade, but as I went along I kept finding other lodes to mine. As the prosecutor gritted his teeth, I asked a series of questions about a witness at the arcade who was beaten and threatened by Overtown thugs after saying that he had seen Johnson with a gun. Then I probed the detective about how one of Laeser's alleged eyewitnesses hadn't even been able to identify Luis in a photo lineup.

Under direct examination Laeser had asked Buhrmaster if he had been subjected to any political pressure from Dade State Attorney Janet Reno or anyone else. The detective had responded no. Laeser had opened that can of worms, and I wanted them to crawl all over the courtroom. "Let me explore that," I said. "Have you in the last year seen Janet Reno on television regarding this case?"

"Objection," Laeser shouted. "It would call for hearsay." Laeser was in a trap, trying to keep out the statements of his own boss, the lead prosecutor of the county. But he had invited this line of questioning, and the judge let me proceed. It was easy to prove Reno's personal involvement since she eschewed PR flacks, spin doctors and anonymous leaks in favor of doing it all herself.

On day three of my cross-examination of Buhrmaster, I explored the personal background of Nevell Johnson Jr. and his Mr. Snake street name. Judge Gersten had never ruled whether Johnson's criminal past could be admitted or whether we could mention that he was carrying a stolen gun. Both these issues bore on Johnson's behavior. Jurors were going to wonder why Johnson would go for his gun when he had an armed officer standing behind him. To answer that, we had to get into Johnson's past.

I started by asking the detective about the business cards, gold necklaces and bracelets all with the Mr. Snake logo. This was a prologue to where I wanted to go—the checkered history of Johnson's German-made, RG-14 blue steel revolver. The Bureau of Alcohol, Tobacco and Firearms had traced its pedigree from manufacturer to distributor, through all its owners, right up to its theft on a Miami Beach street.

Laeser raised an objection that I was asking for hearsay. The judge overruled him. Buhrmaster said he had indeed called ATF, but before he said what ATF told him, Laeser again complained of hearsay. The judge sustained this objection, though Laeser should have known better than to object. Sooner or later the jury was going to hear that Johnson was carrying a stolen gun. We had the weapon's rightful owner scheduled to testify. Laeser knew that, so his objections only served to show the jury that he was trying to keep evidence out.

I tried a new tack: "Did you ever find in your examination of the public records of the city of Miami that Nevell Johnson Jr.—"

"Objection! Counsel knows it's going to call for hearsay."

"Well, before we get to the objection, let's hear the whole question," the judge replied.

Laeser: "Your Honor, the question is as damaging as the response." Laeser's vehement statement caused the jurors to lean forward in their seats.

"Well," the judge said, rocking back and forth in his chair, "I believe that counsel would be entitled to ask a question."

For the next few minutes we battled over this terrain, with Laeser shouting objections. This was intense psychological warfare. Finally, the judge allowed me to establish that Buhrmaster had obtained Johnson's photo from the criminal identification unit. I was pushing the issue as hard as I could to send the jury a message that Johnson was not the model citizen *The Miami Herald* portrayed him. Gersten stopped me at that point. When I sat down, I was said Laeser was so incensed when his last objection was overruled that he gave the judge the finger under the table.

Over the lunch break Laeser made an unexpected decision. When court resumed, he surprised us by venturing back to the subject of Johnson's photo: "What types of photographs are kept in that grouping?"

"Persons who were arrested."

Under Laeser's questioning, the detective testified that Johnson had never been arrested as an adult, but was arrested once as a juvenile. He hadn't been convicted of the charge.

One of my aims in crossing Buhrmaster for three days was to frustrate Laeser and impair his judgment so he would make mistakes. I could not have predicted his response. He had become so concerned over my questions about Johnson's mug shot that he had decided to enter the quicksand of Johnson's criminal past. It was a bad decision. Tactics are the same in trials and chess. You better be sure before you make your move because the rules don't let you take it back.

I pulled out a file with all the papers on Johnson's criminal history.

The 1980 arrest occurred after an officer spotted Johnson and several accomplices wheeling a safe containing $11,000 down the street, away from a broken window at Friendly Finance. The records showed that he had been charged with two counts concerning this crime; he was found guilty on one count.

There was more. The file contained Johnson's juvenile record that we had obtained during discovery from the state attorney's own investigator. It showed two additional arrests. Was it possible Buhrmaster and Laeser were unaware of them? Or were they hoping we wouldn't know about them? Either way, we had caught them. Now was the time for a knockout punch.

On re-cross-examination I brought the document up to the witness stand. "Are you aware," I asked the detective, "that on December 7, 1976, Mr. Johnson was arrested for burglary?"

"Not to my knowledge, no."

"Are you aware that on August 18, 1977, he was arrested for dealing in stolen property?"

"Your Honor," Laeser shouted, "most respectfully, I just—I heard two lies."

"I have the paper right here," I said, waving the documents in my hand.

"There are no papers."

"I'll introduce them into evidence," I offered.

"Was that typed by Mr. Seiden or your secretary?" It was an astonishing accusation.

Judge Gersten tried to calm things down: "Let's not have any arguments in front of the jury," he warned.

By this time, Mark was on his feet: "I would take exception to being accused of falsifying evidence. I mean, by someone with Mr. Laeser's reputation."

When we reached the bench, Laeser hissed at Mark: "My reputation was good enough for the people who killed your wife."

Mark glared back. If there was one subject that might make my colleague lose control, it was his murdered wife.

I stepped between them. "Why don't we take a recess," I whispered to the judge. "If he's going to say something like that, I would prefer that he stop it before it goes any farther."

"Yes, I agree," said the judge, turning to the jury: "Ladies and gentlemen, we're going to take a recess."

We ended up adjourning for the day. On the drive back to the office, Mark turned to me and said, "When Laeser dies I'm going to pour a bottle of my best Scotch over his grave." When I looked shocked, Mark quipped, "Oh, I forgot one detail. I'm going to process it first through my kidneys."

It was clear to me that Laeser's blunders had been caused by the mounting frustrations he had felt over the past several days. In this pressure-packed trial, his meticulous plans had gone out the window during the testimony of his first witness. When his careful preparations were destroyed, his control slipped away. Finally, the anger and pressure had become too much, and he had blown up in a way that seriously hurt his case.

After Buhrmaster, Laeser called Antonio Bell. A high school junior, Bell claimed he was standing on the street corner outside the arcade at the time of the shooting. As the officer approached Nevell Johnson, Bell said, he looked through the arcade's glass doors and saw Luis pull his revolver and cock it. Bell demonstrated with Luis's service revolver, pulling back the hammer with his thumb. He claimed the muzzle had been pointed directly at the head of Johnson, who kept staring at the Eagle video game, his hands on the controls. The way Bell described it, Johnson was executed in cold blood.

I stayed in my seat for a long moment and forced myself to think methodically. Just keep in mind, I told myself, several basic facts that had to be true if

Bell was even there: He was over thirty feet from Johnson, looking through a tinted glass door, and his view must have been blocked by Luis's partner that night, Luis Cruz, and a video machine.

I decided to begin the cross-examination abruptly, exposing Bell's hatred of the Miami Police Department: "You are not exactly friendly with police, are you?"

"What do you mean?" I could not have wished for a better response. Gratefully I took up his invitation by detailing his numerous run-ins with the cops. For all of them he had a response: police harassment. He just hung out with his buddies on the street corner in front of the arcade and the cops would roust them for no reason. I had interviewed the cops on the street narcotics unit who said they made a lot of undercover buys at that corner but, like Louis, the police inspector in the movie *Casablanca*, Bell expressed surprise that any illegal activity was going on there.

"Those doors are tinted, aren't they?"

"No sir, not as I know them."

"Well, let me show you." I handed him a photo showing darkly tinted windows. Still, he insisted the windows weren't tinted.

I handed the photo to a juror, and he passed it down the row to the others. The glass doors were black. Out of the corner of my eye I watched one of the jurors hold it out at arm's length to get a good look, then smile.

Next, I inquired into Bell's experience with guns, hoping to leave the impression he was more than a little dangerous. I struck a richer vein than I anticipated. "Prior to the night of December 28, 1982, had you ever fired a gun?"

"No sir."

"Has anybody ever showed you how a gun worked?"

"Yes sir."

"Who showed you?"

"The sir right there, Mr. Laeser."

"He was showing you how to cock a gun?" I allowed surprise to creep into my voice.

"No. You trying to get me confused. I said he showed me a gun."

"Mr. Laeser was trying to show you how a gun operated?"

"No. He ain't trying to show me. He had the gun and he say, he hold the gun back. He say, 'Is this how the gun work or is this?' "

"You had no idea how to cock a gun, did you?"

"No sir."

"The first time, I take it, according to your testimony, you ever heard about a cocked gun or ever saw a cocked gun was the night of December 28?" Yes. "Despite having no experience with guns, you saw a hammer move back half an inch from a distance of thirty feet?"

"Yes sir."

Not only did we score with that improbability, but Bell then admitted it was Laeser who had taught him how a gun was cocked.

"Mr. Laeser very helpfully pulled the hammer back like that?"

"Yes sir."

"With his own little thumb?"

"Yes sir."

When court resumed the next morning, Laeser called Jeffrey Hoskins, a hulking youth with massive biceps. He had obviously borrowed someone's suit: The sleeves stopped four inches short of his wrists and his pants ended several inches above his ankles. Hoskins's voice surprised me; it was an octave higher than his body mass suggested.

A friend of Nevell Johnson's since childhood, Hoskins told Laeser that he usually went to the game room twice a day. When the police officers approached Johnson, Hoskins said, he was a few feet away, playing Galaxy.

"I had just completed, you know, shooting of a fleet and like there is a ten- to fifteen-second break for the new fleet to appear on the board. And out of the corner of my left eye I saw the police officers' dark uniforms as they walked up."

"At some point did you ever see Nevell turn to or look at the officer?"

"No, I didn't—until the officer turned him. He spinned him, Nevell. And when he turned, his hand was at a low, and he backed up in between two machines. And the officer raised his gun, and that's when the shot went off, when he was close to his head." He said Johnson never moved toward the police officer or reached toward his waist. He didn't know Johnson had a gun.

Once Hoskins was turned over to me, I threw him a couple of hard body blows. In his sworn statement he claimed to have seen a gun beside Johnson's body, accusing Alvarez of planting a throw-down. He quickly denied it now, with the excuse that all the other guys said there was a throw-down so he just picked up on it.

"As I understand it, you gave those lies under oath?"

"Well, whatever," he said diffidently.

I showed him his signed, sworn statement and asked if it helped refresh his recollection. It did.

"You lied under oath."

"Yes," he said, giving up.

I felt sure Hoskins hadn't been anywhere near the arcade, and his testimony was a mixture of neighborhood gossip and media stories. That's where he picked up the now discredited story of a throw-down. Wielding his police statement, I read the answer in which he identified the officer's gun as black, while handing him Alvarez's stainless steel police revolver. Then I asked about his original statement that the gun was in the officer's left hand. This was an obvious problem since Alvarez is right-handed. He proudly answered that he corrected this minor error.

I quickly rejoined it was only after the prosecutors told him it was the wrong hand.

I went over other areas lightly. He said Johnson's hands had been at waist level—another nail in Buhrmaster's version. Then the clincher: Only two days after the shooting, he hadn't been able to identify Luis from a group of photos. Instead, he had identified another officer.

"And you told them that you were positive, didn't you?"

"Yes."

"And then sometime later somebody told you that you picked out the wrong officer?"

"Well," he said, "they should have put on hats." I quickly interjected that Alvarez wasn't wearing a hat that night. Then he came up with excuse no. 2: He was too tired to make an accurate identification. I was tempted to suggest three days of rioting had sapped his strength, but I didn't want to test Judge Gersten's sense of humor.

• • •

Hoskins stepped down on the eighth day of the trial. Combined with the eight days of jury selection, we were now in the midst of our fourth week in Courtroom 4-1. It was tough going. At the end of every trial day we devoted hours to dissecting the day's testimony, calculating gains and losses. We previewed upcoming witnesses, mapping out lines of cross-examination, then drafted legal arguments for the next day. A decent night's sleep was one commodity in short supply.

Each morning the four of us gathered at my law office. Luis usually began by reading out loud the *Herald*'s story of the previous day's testimony. He was constantly astounded by how the articles emphasized the State's points and virtually ignored our own. "Was that reporter really there?" Luis yelled morning after morning. "Are they seeing the same trial?" There were two trials, the one we faced daily in the courtroom and the other, an unrecognizable version we read about in *The Miami Herald*.

The electronic media weren't much better and were far more visible. Each morning, to get to the courthouse, we had to navigate through a forest of TV vans sprouting satellite dishes, and trucks packed with space-age electronic equipment. Thick multi-colored cables snaked across the sidewalks. As we walked up the front steps of the courthouse each morning, we were assaulted by an army of reporters, video camera crews, sound technicians with boom mikes and still photographers with whirling motor drives.

I worried that somehow, through leaks, the sequestered jurors would be infected by these news stories. My fears were confirmed when the jurors' guards reported that the radios in some of the jurors' hotel rooms, disconnected so they wouldn't be influenced by outside news, had been mysteriously reconnected. When that discovery was made, the radios had been removed, but I continued to be concerned about what outside information the jurors might secretly be hearing.

The next witness was Officer Luis Cruz, Alvarez's partner the night of the shooting. I tensed when I heard his name called. This twenty-three-year-old rookie could do us a huge amount of good—or cause us big trouble.

Since he was a rookie, he could be fired without reason, meaning he was susceptible to pressure from the prosecutors and police hierarchy. Ordinarily the dangerous world of patrolling inner-city streets forges a close bond between partners as a survival mechanism, but Cruz had been assigned to Luis only that day. On the other hand, Cruz knew all the street cops supported Luis. That meant he was trapped between warring sides, and as he settled down in the witness chair he was clearly nervous, crossing and uncrossing his legs.

Ed Cowart, Laeser's trial partner, was handling Cruz. As he approached the podium, I was sitting on the edge of my seat, nervously doodling on a legal pad.

Slowly, Cowart worked Cruz through what happened that evening. Cruz described how Luis, his field training officer, showed him the danger spots of Overtown, including the alley where Officer Nathaniel Broom had been killed the year before.

Cowart didn't dwell on Broom, for obvious reasons, but this was a powerful story, and I made a note to ask about it later: Broom had chased a suspect into an alley behind a church. The suspect was waiting for him. He shot Broom before the officer could react. As Broom lay badly wounded on the filthy pavement, the suspect shot him again. This had happened six blocks from the video arcade, and I could imagine how Luis's recounting of the story would have been a powerful reminder to both officers how one mistake could get a cop killed.

Shortly after leaving the alleyway, the two officers drove by the arcade, which Luis wanted to check out. They strolled through the place and were about to leave when Luis suddenly went over to Johnson and patted his waist.

Luis drew his revolver and pointed it upward. "Don't move," he instructed Johnson. "We are going to walk out of here nice and slow, and I don't want any trouble."

At this point, Cruz said, Luis clearly directed his voice to him: "Get the gun."

Cruz crouched a little and reached toward Johnson's gun as Luis raised Johnson's sweater to reveal a revolver in the waistband of his slacks.

From this point on, Cruz testified, he couldn't see what Luis did because he had "tunnel vision" as he concentrated on Johnson's revolver. "As I was reaching for it, I saw Nevell Johnson turn quickly toward Alvarez. I stopped my motion of reaching for the gun. At that time, I heard a bang."

Alvarez looked down at his uniform, Cruz said, as if he thought he might have been shot, then stared at Johnson's body on the floor. "Oh, my God," Luis mumbled. "Oh God."

Cowart asked if Johnson's hand came near the .22 revolver.

"I don't know," replied Cruz, shaking his head. He seemed confused. "It happened so fast, it was all a blur."

"Did it seem the gun went off by accident?"

"I can't say."

Cowart didn't press Cruz much. Neither did I. I handled his cross-examination with kid gloves, restricting myself to bringing out a few details about how cramped that area of the game room was.

"Could you have Mr. Johnson spread-eagled?" I asked, referring to one of the techniques recommended when a suspect is armed.

"There was no room," Cruz responded.

I carefully left one question unasked. The rookie Cruz had frozen in the midst of sudden combat, but in my eyes he had redeemed himself by telling the truth. Even with his career in jeopardy he didn't shade his testimony to help the prosecution or us.

Next came Sergeant Nancy Olon, leader of Luis's patrol group. She testified that she heard his frantic emergency call and arrived at 6:13 p.m., nine minutes after the shooting. She said her conversation with Luis was brief: "All I recall him saying to me at that particular time was 'the gun went off.' He indicated to me there was a jerking type motion by Mr. Johnson." She demonstrated what she said Alvarez had shown her: Johnson spinning counterclockwise, palms outward, hands at waist level—another clear contradiction to Buhrmaster's claim that Luis had shown him Johnson's hands had been raised.

On cross-examination we brought out that she wasn't concerned that Luis had been assigned to 30 sector and the arcade was in 40 sector. Patrolmen crossed sector boundaries all the time, she said, and she had never disciplined anyone for it. Here was Luis's *boss* saying there was nothing wrong with the sector shift—a fact that the State and the media had made into a violation of epic proportions.

Laeser next shifted the trial's focus to Luis's service revolver, a technical maze that was to be a point of contention on and off for days.

In both the pre-trial newspaper stories and in Laeser's opening statement, the alleged "hair-trigger" action of Luis's gun was one of the main points against him. The prosecutors had looked all over the country to find an expert who would say the gun was dangerous. Harry Sefried was a former gun designer with Ruger, Winchester and Colt (but *not* with Smith & Wesson, the manufacturer of Luis's gun) who wore a string tie with a turquoise stone and a gold-gun pin in his coat lapel.

Under Cowart's questioning, Sefried testified that Luis's gun had been modified. Pieces had been buffed to make them smoother, and the rebound slide spring was cut, reducing it from 15 to 13.5 coils. This change meant that it required slightly less pressure to pull the trigger. The modifications increased the gun's "deadliness." He pointed out that the grips were non-standard plastic, which he claimed were "extremely slippery."

Under Mark's cross-examination, Sefried acknowledged that the revolver was within Smith & Wesson specifications.

The gun testimony had gone well, but just as I had feared, events outside the courtroom threatened to interfere with the trial. Judge Gersten gave us the news: The wife of one of our jurors, Robert Mendelson, the retired foreman, had complained she was being harassed.

This was serious. Over our strenuous objections, *The Miami Herald* had published the names of all the jurors. Had Mendelson's wife told her husband about this harassment during one of the weekly visits allowed by the judge? And what if Mendelson had told the other jurors about his wife's worries?

We had to find out what the jury was thinking. For once, Laeser and I agreed. We both thought it best for the judge to interview the jurors in private. However, we were shocked to hear him say that he would leave in the television camera that was taping the entire trial for the local stations and networks. When the judge ordered the courtroom cleared, we lawyers rushed to the hallway, where we huddled around a TV monitor and listened to every word.

With only the judge and a court reporter left in the building's biggest courtroom, the bailiff sent in the jurors one by one. First was the elderly Mr. Mendelson. He said his wife was agitated because she was getting phone calls from an anonymous breather at all hours of the night. Strange cars appeared in front of their house, with men sitting inside staring at their windows for up to an hour.

Judge Gersten asked him: "Do you believe you can still be fair and impartial in this case?"

"I would imagine so." Other jurors knew about his wife's complaints. "They feel concerned because I'm concerned."

"Has anything outside the court proceedings affected your ability to remain fair and impartial in this trial?" he asked.

Mendelson replied, "Outside of that, I have no other reason to feel that I couldn't act as a juror."

Outside of that? One's spouse being threatened was a *powerful* influence. When I heard Mendelson's shaky voice describing this, the comfortable feeling I had about the trial vanished. The other jurors had all sworn to Gersten that they weren't going to be affected by this incident. I disagreed, arguing for a mistrial and a change of venue. Once again, Gersten rebuffed us and ordered the trial to resume.

The next day was my thirty-ninth birthday, but there was no time to celebrate, for the witness was an important one: Pamela Smith, a Florida Department of Law Enforcement expert on the interpretation of human bloodstains.

Mrs. Smith, a very pregnant young woman, asserted she could decipher the patterns and geometry of Johnson's bloodstains on the linoleum floor. From studying photos of the arcade, she had noticed that, by the Asteroid machine next to the Eagle, five droplets were smeared slightly before drying. She testified that these droplets were consistent with Johnson leaning against the Asteroid game when he was shot. The implication was that Johnson had been headed *away* from Luis, turning to go out the door, not to attack the officer.

After Cowart's direct examination, we took a short break. She was Mark's witness, and he had prepared a lengthy, complicated cross-examination. I knew he was going to have a tough time because he was woozy from the flu.

When the judge returned to the bench, Mark wasn't in the courtroom. Someone rushed up and told me that Mark had fainted in a private corridor behind the courtroom. He was being rushed to the hospital.

I told the judge that I wasn't prepared to cross-examine Smith in such a complicated specialty without considerable study. Since it was Friday, I asked that court be adjourned until Monday, to give me time to bone up. The judge agreed.

I raced back to the office and gave myself a cram course on blood spatters. It is a forensic field that has always intrigued me. At its core, it's a matter of basic physics—tiny bits of liquid fly through space, ending up as drops, smears or blobs with tails. An expert can study them and see how fast the blood spurted out; how far the blood went; how it pooled near the body; how it dribbled down a wall. Each detail implies an action by the body and the mechanism of death.

That weekend I pored over everything I had on bloodstains, rereading some passages, looking for explanations that might help decipher these "five droplets." I called up Herbert Leon MacDonell, who has written over one hundred books and articles on the subject, including the classic *Bloodstain Pattern Interpretation*.[6] We couldn't afford to hire him as a witness, but he generously gave me suggestions about how the droplets might not show as much as the State was claiming.

Meanwhile, Mark was recovering in the hospital. When he was feeling a little better, I went to see him with a former student of mine who had become a forensic technician with the FBI. She had agreed to help us off the record.

We used Mark's bed as a desk, spreading the photos of the blood spatters on the covers. In discovery we received over three hundred photos, but no numbered contact sheets denoting their sequence. We kept rearranging them, shuffling them into different spatial relationships. Only then did I see it. Laeser, you clever bastard, I thought. The photos were a jumble until positioned from the right angle. He was using the floor tiles like spaces on a board game. He would link the five blood drops to specific tiles, then work backwards along the floor to the tiles where he would claim Luis and Johnson stood. But his plan was to set the pieces on the board, then wait until summation when he would argue the five drops would prove Johnson had been

---

6. MacDonell at the time was well known to criminal lawyers. He later became a public celebrity by jousting with Marcia Clark as a defense expert in the O. J. Simpson case.

standing still, not twisting his body to draw his pistol. It would be too late for me to debunk it.

When court resumed I was ready to take on the blood spatter expert. I began by emphasizing her lack of experience—she had finished her training less than two years before—and the chaos of the crime scene. Paramedics and detectives had smeared the blood all over the place, spoiling what could have been important clues. She acknowledged she wasn't certain of many details.

"You can't tell us where Johnson was when he was shot?" I asked her.

"No, I can't."

"The only thing you can tell us is your estimation of where Mr. Johnson hit the ground?"

"Yes," she said. The bloodstains were too small, and the chance of contamination too large, to support an opinion on whether the shooting was intentional or accidental.

I got her to admit that "one explanation" for the blood spatters was that Johnson had been spinning and reaching for his revolver when he was shot.

By the time I finished I had destroyed whatever the State had hoped to gain from her testimony. Laeser must have thought so, too, because he complained to the judge that I had obviously lied about my lack of knowledge on blood spatters. I took that as a compliment. Ultimately, we decided the cross-examination had been so conclusive that we had no need to call a blood spatter expert to refute Smith's testimony.

With Dr. Joe Davis, the medical examiner, on the stand, Laeser spent a day going over every gruesome detail of the autopsy. He accompanied the testimony with scores of bloody photos, designed to nauseate, even going so far as to introduce the glass slides mounted with pieces of real human tissue removed during autopsy. On cross I sought to detail the body's history with a catalogue of needle marks and old knife wounds, but the judge ruled them irrelevant.

Davis, a matter-of-fact expert who never shaded his testimony, acknowledged to me that it was equally possible, as far as he could tell, that Johnson had his arms up in a motion of surrender when he was shot or was reaching for his gun.

• • •

The State's next witness was John Campbell, the instructor of the department's officer survival course. A fourteen-year veteran of the force who had the military bearing of a marine drill instructor, Campbell agreed with Laeser that Luis had apparently done some things that were contrary to Campbell's recommendations. "We told 'em, 'Don't let your gun get close enough to someone you're arresting so he can get a hold of it. . . . Don't ever let go of the suspect's gun until you've got control of that person. Hang on to that gun for dear life, because that's what will kill you. . . . ' We told them there is only one time when firing a weapon single action is acceptable." "Single action" was the technical phrase for cocking a gun. "That is at a long distance, preferably when you have something to rest the gun against."

The instructor seemed to be making points for the State, but Mark's cross-examination demolished whatever gains the State had made. Campbell agreed with him that it was proper for an officer to draw his gun when confronting an armed suspect, and an officer is *not* taught that the criminal has the right to shoot first.

That night we sat around the conference table brainstorming ideas for the rest of Campbell's cross. Luis described the officer survival course, held on Virginia Key, an island on the Rickenbacker Causeway which had been Miami's black beach in the not far distant days of segregation. The survival course, set beside a garbage processing plant, was a mock-up of several Miami streets. The world-weary cops who thought they knew it all after a few months on the job typically treated such exercises with disdain, so Campbell would grab their attention with a harsh primer on how the streets killed cops. Why not have him do it in court, shake up the jury just like the cops? The next morning Mark finished his cross by asking Campbell to recite the speech. Laeser made objections. After an hour of legal arguments, Judge Gersten agreed with us: It proved Luis's thinking that night since he had taken the course just prior to the shooting.

Campbell climbed down from the witness stand and stood in front of the jury box. Jamming his hands into his pockets, he launched into his lecture, pacing back and forth in front of the jurors, talking to them as if they were his students.

For the next twenty minutes the jury listened attentively as Campbell described, one by one, the eighteen area police officers who had been killed in the past fourteen years. One officer was killed in Overtown by a fleeing suspect. Another officer was shot walking out of a house. A female officer in Hialeah was shot with her own gun by a suicidal woman. "It can happen to anybody," Campbell said.

Some jurors nodded in agreement. Several had tears in their eyes. In virtually every case, the instructor stated, the officer had died because he was caught off guard. The most dangerous situation was arresting an armed suspect. If an officer got into a gunfight, he usually lost, since the suspect knew what he was going to do while the officer waited to respond. Once the suspect draws his gun, Campbell warned, it is too late. "It can happen on every call. I personally have been to too many funerals."

I could imagine—and so could the jurors—that Luis would have this lecture fresh in his mind as he approached the armed suspect: *Once the suspect draws his gun, it is too late.*

Campbell refused to second-guess what Luis had done at the arcade because each situation was unique and called for a different response.

"The one thing you did teach them," Mark asked, "was to go home alive at the end of their shift?"

"Correct," Campbell replied.

The next morning, just as we were leaving for court, we encountered a graphic confirmation of Campbell's warning. Mark rushed into the office. He had just heard on the radio that a Miami Beach police sergeant named Donald Kramer had just been shot and killed by a psychotic vagrant nicknamed El Loco. The vagrant had been carrying a concealed weapon. Kramer was a conscientious cop who had been patrolling the streets even before his shift started with roll call at 7 a.m. He had arrested this same guy several times before, but this time El Loco turned on him because he was "tired of being hassled."

Luis agonized over whether his indictment had somehow caused Kramer's death. He knew cops all over town had become hesitant, fearing that if they shot to protect themselves they might suffer the same fate.

The prosecution's next witness was Robert Hill, a tall, lithe man with a military haircut. He stared at me with cold eyes behind gray-tinted aviator glasses. Hill was a sergeant in internal security, the unit whose mission is to prosecute other cops.

Cowart attempted to establish Hill as an expert on patrol techniques and procedures. I challenged his credentials, and the judge allowed me to ask him questions to determine if he was an expert. I forced him to admit that very little of his eleven-year police career had been spent on street patrol. His training was in Special Forces, SWAT and hand-to-hand combat. He had never worked in homicide, never done any scientific studies of police shootings or written any articles about them. This was the first time, he confessed, that he had ever been an expert in court.

Through a series of questions I showed that Sergeant Hill was far from an impartial analyst. For the past year he had been the police's liaison with the State Attorney's Office. He had conferred almost daily with Laeser's lead investigator, and he had a desk in Cowart's office. Putting him on the stand was like allowing Laeser himself to become an expert and testify to the jury.

At a sidebar I objected to Hill's being classified as an expert witness. Judge Gersten turned me down, but I figured that my lengthy voir dire had raised questions in jurors' minds as to whether Sergeant Hill was impartial.

With the stage thus set, Cowart was finally allowed to question Hill, who repeated most of Laeser's criticisms of Luis's actions. He claimed Johnson wouldn't have resisted arrest because as a street-wise kid he knew his were minor offenses and that he would be back home before Alvarez finished his report.

Hill said that an officer should not put his gun too close to a suspect, that he should keep his hand on the suspect's gun and not let go, that he should not cock the hammer. "You freeze that subject by saying, 'don't move.' You take the weapon. You don't give conflicting orders. You don't say, 'Don't move,' then say, 'We're going to walk out of here without any trouble,' then say, 'Take the gun.'"

"Officer," Cowart asked, in a question that was about to open doors for us, "do you know in 1982 approximately how many carrying concealed firearm arrests were made by the city of Miami?"

"There were over three hundred carrying concealed firearm arrests made by the city of Miami Police Department."

"And how many of those people were shot?"

"One."

When it was my turn, I asked Hill about another statistic, one that had been on our minds all morning: "In the last twenty-four hours, sir, how many cops have been killed trying to make a concealed firearm arrest?"

Both prosecutors leaped up.

Cowart: "Objection, Your Honor."

Laeser: "It has nothing to do with this case."

The jurors leaned forward. Since they were sequestered, they had not heard the news.

We had a lengthy, heated sidebar that ended with the judge agreeing that Cowart's question had opened the door. I turned back to Sergeant Hill, who told the jury about the officer who had just been shot that morning.

"Isn't it a fact, sir, in the last three months three police officers have been shot and two have been killed with handguns?"

"Yes sir," Hill said.

I decided to try an experiment to show how difficult it is to disarm a suspect. "Stand up for a second," I asked him. "Let's say, for example, you had your gun *here* under your jacket so I couldn't get to it."

Sergeant Hill stood up and carefully removed his glasses. Suddenly, he looked ready for combat, and as soon as I saw that expression I knew I had made a serious mistake. The Special Forces veteran and SWAT team expert was getting ready to make a sedentary lawyer look like a fool. For a moment I stared at the sergeant as he stood poised for a fight. "Oh no," I said, walking away and shaking my head, trying to defuse the situation with humor. "Now you're getting too serious."

The jury laughed, allowing me a dignified retreat. I had almost violated a sacred rule, now known in the legal lexicon as the Darden glove rule: Never, ever, do a demonstration with a hostile witness.[7]

To counter Hill's analysis of what Luis should have done and why Johnson wouldn't have resisted arrest, I asked him hypothetical questions about real

---

7. California prosecutor Christopher Darden made headlines when he demanded defendant O. J. Simpson try on the bloody gloves found at the murder scenes. While the complex DNA evidence was too abstract for many people to understand, the jurors had no problem seeing that the gloves didn't fit. Defense attorney Johnnie Cochran made the bad fit the theme of his summation: "If it doesn't fit, you must acquit."

cases. "Assume," I said, "that a motorist runs through the toll booth and doesn't put the ten cents in and is stopped by a police officer. Now, hypothetically, would you think that person would shoot and kill the police officer over that ten-cent toll?"

"Logically, no sir, but it *has* occurred."

"It's not hypothetical that a police officer is dead?"

"No sir, it is not."

"I ask you hypothetically, would you think that a fourteen-year-old boy driving his father's car would shoot and kill an officer who pulled him over?"

"Logically, no sir."

"Nevertheless, it happened in this county, didn't it?"

"Yes sir, it did."

I ran through other examples, all from Miami. Three officers walked up to a house to ask about a stolen car parked out front; all three were killed. Another officer was shot after stopping a car with a broken taillight. Then I asked about the shooting of Nathaniel Broom, the officer killed in the Overtown alley that Luis had shown his partner shortly before going to the arcade.

"When Officer Broom was shot, he stopped three people in a car driving the wrong way down a one-way street, and he got shot and killed over that, didn't he?"

"Yes sir."

When I was finished, it was 10 a.m. on Friday, February 24, the twenty-seventh day of the trial. As we waited for the next witness, Ira Loewy, the no. 3 prosecutor, suddenly stood up and announced: "May it please the court. Ladies and gentlemen, the State rests."

At the defense table we stared at each other. In his opening statement, Laeser had promised to put on two eyewitnesses who claimed they saw Luis cock his gun. They had produced only one. Also missing were several police officials and expert witnesses, notably a $1,400-a-day expert on criminal procedures. I made a quick note to myself. Before we began our defense we needed a strategy session to decide what Laeser was holding back and why. What surprises did he have in store for us after we showed our hand? A powerful rebuttal could seriously damage us if we didn't anticipate it.

Judge Gersten was as surprised as we were. "Would you say that again, Mr. Loewy?" he asked. "I want to make sure I heard it."

Loewy repeated that the State was resting.

I told the judge that we hadn't been expecting this sudden decision and had no witnesses ready to call. Gersten ordered court adjourned to Monday morning.

The end of the State's case signaled that the trial was nearing its conclusion, and reporters went to Overtown, where they reported threats from angry young men: "If he is not convicted, people will turn Miami upside down."

Almost daily, we had been getting intelligence briefings in the judge's chambers informing us that attacks were being planned against Luis, the judge and the defense team. Black Panthers and Mel Mason, the presidential candidate of the Socialist Workers Party, spent an afternoon in our courtroom and then called a press conference to denounce the racist police. Tensions mounted even more when Jesse Jackson arrived and threatened that the trial was creating a "formula for explosion."

As we entered our seventh week the jurors were exhausted and restless under the strict sequestration that the judge had thought would last only "two or three weeks." I feared the combination of racial tension, intense publicity and bloody photos dumped on them daily would trigger an adverse reaction to us. I worried a juror might cave in to a verdict just to escape the stress. One juror was caught with an unauthorized bottle of wine in his room. Another had to miss her son's eighteenth birthday party. Another missed his sister's wedding. One good sign: The jurors voted to view *48 HRS.*, the Eddie Murphy film depicting the brutal deaths of several cops.

We were running out of resources, physical and financial. Our law firm had to take out a loan to keep going, and we were constantly scrounging for money to pay expert witnesses and other trial expenses. To help us, we put out a flier entitled "Officer Needs Help." Luis went to the police union and spoke on several Spanish-language radio stations, asking the public for donations. We received about $50,000 — which went to pay research expenses, expert witnesses and Ralph's salary. Mark and I didn't take any money. But, as we prepared to begin the defense part of the case, we were flat broke, and we needed to pay several experts whom we were about to put on the witness stand. The Hispanic Officers Association gave us their entire treasury — about $9,000. With that, we kept going.

• • •

The first day of the defense's case, we ran through a half-dozen witnesses. We wanted to get them on and off fast. We knew the jurors were tired, and we wanted to send them a message that we respected their time. This strategy had a side benefit: It left few openings for the prosecutors, as we had culled out any witness who could backfire.

We started with Edward Neal, a black AFL-CIO union representative from Washington, D.C. He testified about visiting Miami in 1980 and going with a friend to some nightspots in Liberty City. In a briefcase he carried a .22-caliber revolver that his nephew had given him. At one of the stops someone broke into his car and stole the gun.

I held up the RG-14 that Nevell Johnson had been carrying that night. "Is this your nephew's gun?" I asked, knowing the serial numbers matched.

"Yes it is."

Next we called a county police officer who testified that Johnson was not licensed to carry a concealed handgun.

"Is it a felony to carry a stolen gun?" Mark asked.

"Yes sir," he replied. The maximum sentence was five years.

We also called José Seiglie, Miami's officer of the year for 1982. He had once patrolled Overtown on the same shift as Luis, and he reported that he had seen stolen cars and "narcotics activity" in the arcade's parking lot. "I've assisted in making arrests there for purse snatches, street brawls, assaults."

Shortly after Seiglie testified, we discovered alarming news that could disrupt our entire defense. Seiglie had been immediately transferred to a beat guarding the garbage midnights on Virginia Key. We were certain, but couldn't prove, that this reassignment was orchestrated by the prosecutors as a deterrent, so other cops would get the message. I knew this would have a chilling effect on all officers' testimony.

Next came Alfred Johnson, the senior firearms examiner for the Bureau of Alcohol, Tobacco and Firearms. This guy was the no. 1 firearms expert in the country. Johnson said he found Luis's revolver to be "functional, safe and mechanically sound." Nothing had been done to the weapon to make it unsafe. He said that the minor modifications made to the revolver were an "action cleanup." It was "common for the knowledgeable police officer to have it done." He said it was acceptable to snip the coil to reduce trigger pressure slightly.

Our next witness was William Rogers, a former FBI agent who designed and sold the $18.95 plastic grips that Luis and other officers had put on their guns. Rogers, a champion target shooter, said that police around the world used his grips and found them superior to the factory grips.

We also called Robert Edmonds, an employee of the Money Tree Enterprises pawnshop near Overtown. He testified that Nevell Johnson had pawned a 12-gauge 500ATP Mosburg shotgun for $25 on November 15, 1982, and redeemed it on December 14, two weeks before the shooting.

What was Nevell Johnson planning to do with such a shotgun? Certainly it wasn't to go hunting; it was the most effective close-in mankiller on the market. It didn't require any thought or skill. You didn't even need to aim. Just swing it around and shoot. Edmonds had brought along another gun of the same model. Mark picked it up and asked several questions while holding the gun. Edmonds said the purpose of the shotgun was solely "anti-personnel."

Mark racked the shotgun. The sound made a nasty, thunderous clap in the courtroom. Everyone jumped—including the jurors.

Fred Doerner, a University of Miami law professor, retired FBI agent and director of security at the University of Miami, offered a legal opinion that Luis's arrest and search of Johnson was within the bounds of stop and frisk under the Supreme Court case of *Terry* v. *Ohio*. When pressed on cross as to whether Luis should have used non-lethal force, he quoted Justice Oliver Wendell Holmes Jr.: "Detached reflection cannot be demanded in the presence of an uplifted knife. Therefore in this court, at least, it is not a condition of immunity that one in that situation should pause to consider whether a reasonable man might not think it possible to fly with safety or to disable his assailant rather than to kill him."

After the first day of the defense, we kept the focus on the basic questions we knew jurors were probably asking themselves: Why hadn't Luis waited? Why hadn't he watched until Johnson drew the gun before firing? Wouldn't it have been prudent to delay a little bit?

We first presented David Churilla, a shooting expert from Orlando, who testified that it could be a fatal mistake to wait too long. Even a novice would be able to draw a gun stuck in his back waistband in a little over half a second. "You are creating a life-threatening situation to yourself and others to let the criminal have a weapon in his hand," he said.

This was good testimony, but I thought we had to personalize it. I tried to call two police officers who had been shot. One had serious brain damage because of his wound and talked with an awful slur. But Laeser objected, and the judge agreed. Fighting back, I called Parke Fitzhugh, a clinical psychologist and board member of the Law Enforcement Stress Foundation, who testified that Luis would have been in severe shock after the shooting and was in a state of denial when he yelled at the dispatcher for help.

Our top cop expert was Robert J. di Grazia, a tall man with glasses who had headed police departments in Boston, St. Louis and suburban Washington. Di Grazia testified that Luis had done nothing wrong in the game room and considered it "definitely" possible that Johnson was reaching for his gun. "In this type of situation," di Grazia testified, "the only thing an officer can do is take aim at a person who is going to come around with a firearm in his hand."

Di Grazia approved of Luis putting his revolver inches from Johnson's head because "it's important for the officer to let the subject know who's in control." It was proper also for Luis to take his hand off Johnson's gun so that Cruz could get it. "If it's a one-on-one situation, hold on to it," he said, but since he had a partner, it was best for Cruz to reach for the gun.

"Would you have shot the man under those circumstances?" I asked him.

"Absolutely," di Grazia replied.

As we started the second week of our defense case, I tried once again to give the jury a graphic presentation of how sudden and deadly a shooting can be. We had failed to get the news video of the riot admitted. We had failed to get the stories of the wounded police officers told. Now, I launched a new bid, with a man named Massad Ayoob.

Ayoob was a onetime holder of three national marksmen records and president of the Lethal Force Institute. He traveled nationwide giving seminars to police, the military and civilians about the use of deadly force and self-defense. In his spare time, he had written seven books and more than two thousand magazine articles.

Ayoob had made a seven-minute videotape for us. In it, he used an RG-14, the type of revolver that Johnson had been carrying that night. He put on a loose, open-front button sweater like the one Johnson had been wearing that night, and then demonstrated how a man could pull out the gun, spin and fire in only a second.

In the final sequence, Ayoob began with his back to two paper targets, shaped like human torsos, to represent Alvarez and Cruz. As Mark held the video camera, Ayoob spun and drew the .22 revolver. He put two shots into the chest of the first target, then two shots into the chest of the second target, finishing with two more shots to the head of the second target.

All six shots took less than two seconds. The tape ended with the camera zooming in on the targets, showing the ragged holes, as Ayoob off camera said, "This is what could have happened."

When I prepared to play the tape to the jury, Laeser objected. The jury was excused, and the judge watched the tape on an eighteen-inch monitor in the courtroom.

Laeser complained that the tape was speculative "It's a what-might-have-happened scenario. . . . An inaccurate representation. . . . Highly prejudicial. Totally irrelevant."

I fought hard on this one. This tape was graphic and powerful. The sound of the shots, the picture of the jagged holes in the target paper had a frightening authenticity that no words from the witness stand could duplicate. I was certain it should have been admissible because it proved Ayoob's conclusion.

Judge Gersten turned us down. He told us Ayoob could demonstrate his draw in the courtroom.

Making what we could of the situation, we called Ayoob to the witness stand. He explained that the winner of the gunfight is the person who draws first: "Action always beats reaction."

Several times Ayoob stepped down from the witness stand to demonstrate what could have happened, showing how quickly Johnson could have fired if Luis had hesitated.

Ayoob said that if Luis had waited, it would have been "suicide." When

Johnson moved suddenly in the arcade, "a homicide becomes justifiable under the rules a police officer is taught."

Laeser tried to get him to admit that he could draw and fire much faster
than Johnson. Not true, Ayoob said. "I'm five ten, 170. He's six two, 140. I'm
thirty-five. He's young, twenty years old. He has the reflexes and the supple-
ness—look he even has the nickname Mr. Snake. That shows you how supple
he is." Ayoob said that if Johnson had wanted to draw very fast, he could have
grabbed the gun and, while it was still behind his back and hidden by the
sweater, pulled the trigger. It was quite possible that Alvarez and Cruz both
would have died without ever seeing Johnson's hand on the gun.

Our last scheduled witness was a slight, five-foot grocery store employee,
Martha Velilla. She walked to the witness stand looking anxiously around the
courtroom. Clutching her handbag, she testified that, after the shooting, she
saw Johnson's photo in the newspaper and recognized him as the mugger who
had attacked her two months before, ripping off her necklace and stealing her
purse. She had waited four months before calling the police. "I was afraid,"
she said, close to tears.

On cross-examination Laeser asked why Velilla had waited so long. "You
called because you wanted to help Officer Alvarez out?"

Velilla: "Yeah, because he killed a crook."

Laeser: "And you are allowed to kill crooks in this country? You can just
walk up to them and shoot them?"

"No," Velilla replied, "but I was glad he killed him."

The hardest question for any criminal lawyer to answer is whether the defendant should testify. We had put on two weeks of defense witnesses who had attacked the credibility of the State's case. Why should we take the risk? On the
other hand, a defendant's failure to testify, especially if he's a police officer,
will weigh heavily with the jury, regardless of the judge's instruction not to
consider it.

Back at the office, we sat around the conference table and debated. Luis was adamant that he wanted to tell the world what had happened. Mark and Ralph disagreed. If something went wrong, if Laeser goaded Luis into losing his temper, the jurors might conclude that Luis was a hotheaded macho gunslinger. Why gamble?

Luis was sure. "Well, I've testified in court before. There's no problem."

"But that *is* the problem," I told him. Most police testimony comes across as detached, devoid of emotion—a technique drummed into them in the academy.

"It's my life, my decision. I'm testifying," Luis said, ending the debate.

"All right," I warned, "one piece of advice. Laeser has been cramming for months, and he's quick and smart, but you have the advantage. Theory is no substitute for experience. Only you have patrolled those streets. He can't outsmart you on this unless you let him. He is going to try like hell to make you mad. He wins if you do. If you lose control here, the jury will figure you lost control in the arcade."

At nine o'clock the next morning, the courtroom was packed. The supporters took separate sides. Miami's street cops sat behind the defense table, while the Johnsons, several well-dressed ministers, and street people with slogan-filled T-shirts occupied the other side. In between were political activists, lawyers, prosecutors and courthouse regulars. A dozen reporters, many of them from national publications, were in the courtroom. Other journalists were squeezed into the nearby media room. All were waiting for Luis Alvarez to describe for the first time what had really happened.

We didn't disappoint them. "At this time," I said, rising, "the defense calls Luis Alvarez."

There was a rustle of paper—reporters flipping open note pads—as Luis marched to the witness stand like a soldier doing his duty. I began with some soft questions about his background so that he could settle down and the jury could get to know him. We talked about his coming to Miami at an early age and starting to work at fifteen.

"Why did you work while going to school?"

"Well, I had to. My mother and I lived alone, you know. We needed the money."

I had suggested to Luis that he keep his answers simple, with little elaboration. The direct examination of a defendant is best kept short and concentrated on the main points. Rambling feeds the prosecution.

"Do you still live with your mother?"

"Yes sir." He was sitting ramrod straight in the witness chair.

To make myself inconspicuous I stood toward the back, behind the jury, so when the jurors looked at Luis, they wouldn't even see me. Luis had to be the center of attention now. Questioning a man with whom you have worked closely for a year becomes a dance of almost balletic timing and grace. I had told him what my opening series of questions would be, and what the closing would be, but I dislike a defendant doing detailed memorization because it makes his testimony seem artificial. I wanted Luis to move naturally through the rest of his testimony.

Under my questioning Luis described the service revolver he had been assigned. It had tiny rust spots and an officer-buddy suggested someone he knew could make the gun "nice and shiny." Luis gave his revolver to the buddy to have it buffed up. He never asked that the trigger be made easier to pull. When he received the gun back, he didn't notice anything about the trigger, but he decided that the wooden grips now looked old and grungy. He replaced them with Rogers grips, which many officers used. He bought them at a police products store that the Miami Police Department had a contract with. That's where all the officers went.

"When you purchased these grips, did you know what they were actually made of?"

"Well, I know now. Then I thought they were wood," he said, taking a sip of water from a white Styrofoam cup. "Nobody knew that those grips were plastic until it was brought out in my case."

We discussed the fact that his superiors respected him so much that, even before the end of his first-year probation, he was selected to be a field training officer and was given a forty-hour course in how to train young officers. December 28 was the first day Cruz was assigned to him.

Following my instructions, Luis looked at me when answering an ordinary question. Only when he reached the crucial parts of his testimony did he swing his head and speak directly to the jurors.

"Why did you take Cruz into Overtown if it was outside your assigned zone that evening?"

"I was assigned to train and test Cruz on December 1, but I was injured from a dog bite, and December 28, the day of the shooting, was my first day back on the street. I had to make up for lost time." A field training officer has to teach the raw recruit the job of being a real cop. "I wanted to show him the quote unquote bad spots, places where we've had problems before, places where we've made arrests." He said they stopped at the arcade because it was on a rough corner. "There is a lot of dope used there. And the owner of the arcade is known to us as a drug trafficker."

On our counsel table was a two-hour video of the instructional ride that Luis had given Cruz through Overtown the afternoon of the shooting. The video had cost us a lot of time and energy, but despite the investment, I abandoned it. I couldn't afford to break up Luis's testimony.

Luis stepped down from the witness stand and showed how he had strolled through the arcade, with Cruz trailing behind, until he spotted the bulge in the sweater at Nevell Johnson's waist. At first, he wasn't certain whether it was a gun. "A lot of people carry those big Afro picks. At the top, they have like a hand and it sticks out. Or it's a brush. So I went up to investigate. I tell Cruz to come on."

Luis picked up his service revolver from the evidence table. He said Johnson was hunched over the Eagle machine. He asked me to play Johnson's part. I turned, facing away from him, my hands on the wooden podium, which became our substitute for the Eagle machine. At one time I had thought of subpoenaing the machines into the courtroom to reenact the shooting, but had decided it would be too Hollywood—the jurors would focus on the machines instead of the testimony. This was the most important moment of the trial. The verdict hung on whether the jurors believed what he was about to say.

"I put my right hand on the bulge and I asked him, 'What is this?' And he is playing the machine. He turns his head and he goes, 'It's a gun,' but as he turns his head, he stands up straight. It's a real narrow corridor, and his buttocks are touching the other machine behind him. His hands are not touching the console now, but they are almost on the console.

"When he tells me it's a gun, I switch hands and I draw my service revolver. And I put my revolver between both of our faces and I go, 'Don't move.' " He barked the command, holding the gun between our faces, barrel pointed toward the ceiling.

Luis was handling this as a monologue. It was going well, and I didn't interrupt.

"And I tell him, 'All right. We are going to get out of here. You are not going to give me any trouble. You are going to do it slowly and quietly.' "

We were standing near the railing of the jury box—almost close enough to touch the jurors.

"He looks at me," Luis went on. "When he turned his head, he didn't take his eyes off me. We looked at each other for a second or two. And I tell Cruz to get the gun. I turned my head slightly to look at Cruz. I directed my voice towards him. He was standing close—right where Mrs. Hoodwin is."

Luis nodded toward one of the jurors, Mary Ellen Hoodwin, who beamed back a smile. What an extraordinary moment this was. Luis had mentioned the retired medical secretary's name casually, naturally, and that quickly made her his partner. The hundreds of hours he had spent working on his own case included memorizing the jurors' names. In this one unexpected moment the work had paid off.

Building on this success, Luis continued with the demonstration, showing that after ordering Cruz to take the gun, he moved his hand from the imaginary gun in my rear waistband to my left shoulder.

"What he does is he pulls and I lose the grasp of what I had. At the same time as I lose the grasp, I started to turn just automatically. When I started to turn, I start to bring my gun up."

We showed how Johnson spun around, with Luis reacting to the sudden movement. "He's a little tall. I'm looking up. When I see this man, I know he shot me at that time because there is nothing you can do. When I see his hand, that is coming across at that time, I believe I'm dead."

He had seen the top of Johnson's right hand move toward the left, across his body, as he spun left. Johnson was reaching for the gun. "That is where I got frightened. I got really scared there. They will tell you in training how fast things happen, and you got me. What went through my head was, He got me, I'm dead.

"At the same time, I started to turn. I thrust my gun into his head and my left hand is somewhere around here and it's awkward and I fired."

"What happens next?" I asked. This was the first question I had asked in fifteen minutes.

"The thing I think is, God, I'm shot. I just like froze and I look at myself." He showed how he looked at his chest for a bullet hole. "Then I realize I'm not shot and I knew that he fell. He didn't look twenty. He looked like a kid, and he was on the floor. There was blood all over the place. I thought, God, I've shot a kid. A gunshot to the head—I knew he wasn't going to make it. I kind of stayed in limbo. I was kind of dazed and I'm looking at him. Then it dawns on me. Wait a second. I'm a policeman. I got to do something. The very first thing that came to my head was get the squad."

Putting his gun back in its holster, he pulled out the portable radio attached to his belt, but amid the blaring jukebox and the clamor of the video machines he couldn't hear. He raced outside and made the call from the sidewalk "I turned around. Officer Cruz is right there, and I asked him, 'Did you get the gun?' He tells me, 'No, it's still on him.' "

Alvarez ran back inside and grabbed the gun. It was still stuffed in the waistband, but it had been loosened either by Johnson grabbing for it or because of the fall. "When I picked up the gun is the first time I realized he didn't get a shot off." He ordered Cruz to clear people out, and he himself shouted for everyone to leave. "There could have been four more persons armed in there. This man could have had a partner, I don't know." People stood, gawking, until he drew his gun again. Then they ran out.

"Do you remember what you said in that first radio transmission?"

"No sir. First time I heard it was in your office, four or five months after the indictment. And I don't remember asking for the squad. I was fading in and out."

"Has this affected you since then?"

"Yes sir, the first couple of nights I didn't sleep. Every once in a while I get a nightmare. It's always the same scene. I always remember him on the floor, you know, and the blood around him."

"Was this an accident?"

"No sir, this was not an accident. I didn't want to shoot. I shot because I had to shoot."

"Did you shoot him deliberately?"

"Yes sir. I shot him deliberately. When he turned around to shoot me, I shot him."

"Why did you shoot him?"

"Because he was going to shoot me."

"Did you ever cock your gun?"

"Sir, I *never* cocked my gun."

As I walked back to my seat, I saw the journalists looking at each other in surprise. Luis's direct testimony had lasted ninety minutes. Perhaps, because of the length of the trial and the importance of the case, they had thought my direct examination would drag on for hours. But I had wanted Luis to tell a simple story, focusing only on the essential facts. Why give Laeser a bigger target?

Laeser's chief investigator piled on the counsel table Luis's internal affairs file, academy records and personnel folders all tabbed and indexed. As I had anticipated, Laeser began by questioning Luis about the complaints made against him. Only two had been sustained. Both concerned minor infractions involving report writing.

"Do you recall," Laeser asked, "an incident at the jai alai fronton and you sort of intervened by claiming one of them was your aunt?"

"Oh yes."

"That person really wasn't your aunt, was she?"

"No sir." Luis explained he was working as an off-duty guard at the fronton when he saw a guy bothering a lady. "He kept following her and she was afraid of him. She kept changing seats and he kept changing seats. He would always sit right directly behind her." She complained to Luis that the man even followed her to work.

"Anyway, I went up to the individual where he was sitting. I told him, 'Listen, I understand you are harassing this lady.' I went through all the allegations that I had received and I told him, 'I really don't appreciate you doing that to my aunt.' I just said that to make him stop, you know. She was not my aunt. And he made a complaint, but there were four or five witnesses, and the complaint was all lies, and it was cleared up right there on the scene."

Several jurors were beaming at Luis.

About this time we broke for lunch. Shortly before court resumed, Wanda Gómez, my secretary, came over and said she had just gotten a call from someone who had threatened to blow up our office.

Back in the courthouse, Laeser's questioning jumped from topic to topic throughout the afternoon as he searched for a weak spot.

"Did you ever speak to the person who you had requested to work on your firearm?"

"I never met him. I never met him before."

"Didn't you meet with Mr. Rivera around November or December of last year, and he explained to you that he was the person that worked on the gun?"

"Never."

"He never met with you?"

"No sir."

As we would learn later, Laeser had set up this little exchange about the gun polisher for a bomb he was planning to drop during rebuttal testimony, but rather than telegraph his intentions he moved on, trying to get Luis's goat by suggesting that he had wanted a big-barrel gun as a symbol of his machismo. When Luis laughed off that idea, the prosecutor went back to talking about the alleged statements Luis had made at the arcade. At one point, Laeser scribbled the word "truth" on the blackboard, as if that gave him extra authority.

At 6:15 p.m. court was adjourned. Luis had held up under almost five hours of cross-examination without a mark on him. As he left the witness stand I gave him a hug and one piece of advice: "Don't be so hostile with Laeser." Luis protested: "What should I say, 'Thanks for ruining my life'?"

At nine o'clock the next morning, Luis was back on the stand. Laeser had come up with an idea overnight: Prove Luis was wrong by having him do a demonstration.

Laeser arranged the two of them in front of the jury box so that Luis was playing Johnson, with the .22-caliber revolver tucked into his rear waistband, underneath his suit coat. Laeser became the arresting officer.

Laeser's plan was to hang on to the gun through the suit coat, so that there was no way the suspect could get the gun and fire. This was what Sergeant Hill claimed Luis should have done. The trouble was that Laeser was trying to keep hold of the gun *through* the coat.

In one swift motion Luis swiveled, jarred Laeser with a sweep of his left elbow, reached under his coat, grabbed the gun and jammed it against Laeser's head.

Stunned, Laeser still clutched at Luis's coat. He said nothing.

"Sir," Luis said, "you ended up with a bullet in your head, and only my coat in your hand."

"That's because you were pulling with your hand on the other end of the coat," Laeser complained.

Precisely. With his left hand, Luis had opened his suit coat, allowing his right hand access to the gun. Laeser had a death grip on the coat, but he couldn't keep a grip on the gun.

Laeser and Alvarez kept staring at each other, the prosecutor still clinging to Luis's coattails, Luis holding the gun to his head. Three jurors in the back row were standing. This was a little too close for comfort. I complained to the judge: "This is getting argumentative."

Laeser exploded. "I'm not trying to be argumentative."

Luis, tugging at his coat, said, "Let go of my suit."

Gersten admonished the prosecutor: "Let's not have any arguments with the witness, Mr. Laeser. Let's get the gun back on the table unless you are going to use it. Now, Mr. Laeser, let's move on. I don't like this."

I liked it a lot more than the judge and certainly more than Laeser. The prosecutor's self-inflicted wound proved the sweater made it impossible to take a firm grip on Johnson's gun. Laeser had violated the rule of never doing a demonstration with a hostile witness.

This debacle left Laeser frustrated and it showed in each of his questions, turning the rest of his cross into an acrimonious argument that lost its effectiveness. Finally, at 4:58 p.m., he gave up, and I announced that the defense rested. Laeser said immediately that he planned to present rebuttal witnesses the next morning.

Laeser surprised even me when he announced Luis Rivera as the next witness.[8] I had a premonition that Rivera spelled real trouble. A fat man with a thin moustache, Rivera had cleaned and modified Luis's gun. We had tried

---

8. The Florida Rules of Criminal Procedure permit prosecutors to hide the identity of rebuttal witnesses. The power of surprise cannot be overemphasized. Trial lawyers quickly learn that defeat is the nastiest surprise of all.

very hard to get this man to testify for us about how he had modified Luis's service revolver, and he had repeatedly evaded us, claiming he might lose his job if he stepped forward.

Under Laeser's questioning, Rivera said he was employed at a Burger King and worked on firearms only on the side. Another officer, named Becker, had given him Luis's revolver. He polished the exterior and was paid $20. He denied trimming the trigger coil.

Rivera claimed that he had met Luis Alvarez once. It was shortly before the trial started, at Officer Becker's house. "He asked me that I had done the polishing on the gun, could I become a witness for him." He said Luis had made a vague reference about Rivera having done nothing wrong, but "when you go to court you take a toothbrush with you, or something." Implying that you're ready to go to prison. What's more, Rivera said, Luis's attorneys had once summoned him to their office and another time had gone to his home. I glanced at the jury and saw the quick intake of breath by two jurors. Others were frowning.

This was tough stuff. On cross-examination Luis had testified that he had never met Rivera. When Laeser was through, the judge ordered the afternoon recess. In the corridor a television journalist asked me if I thought Luis was going to be indicted for perjury. In the empty men's room I filled my hands with cold water and lowered my face into them. Then I stared at my reflection in the mirror. The months of missing sleep and the stress of the trial had taken their toll. My face looked gaunt, pasty white, and my eyes more red than white. Think, damn it, I said to myself. Concentrate.

Rivera had scored points where we were most vulnerable, not about the shooting, but about Luis's credibility. Few juries will acquit a liar. Rivera had seriously damaged our defense with a concoction of lies and half-truths. I knew that no matter what questions I asked him about his alleged meeting with Luis, he would stick to his original story. I could not allow him to score further points by just repeating his tale. I had only moments to decide on a strategy. What I needed to do was to show that this guy was a spineless little creep who would do anything to protect himself.

Back in the courtroom, trying to look more relaxed than I felt, I asked Rivera: "You and I have met before, have we not?"

"Yes sir, we have."

"I called you numerous times to try to get you to call me, didn't I?"

"I wouldn't say numerous times. You called me twice, I believe."

"I left messages to have you please call me, isn't that true, sir?"

"I suppose it was."

"You never called me, did you?"

"I never called you."

"Finally I got you at home?"

"Yes. That's the day I met you at your office."

"You told us you were afraid?"

"I was afraid that—I was worried."

"You said you had been lying awake at night?"

"Yes, I have."

"You said that you were afraid of getting in trouble."

"Yes, I was."

"You were afraid that you had done something wrong?"

"Yes sir."

"You were afraid because you did not have an occupational license?"

"Exactly. In this country you need a license for anything."

"And you did not have a gunsmithing license, did you?"

"Exactly, sir."

"And you did not have a license in the Bureau of Alcohol, Tobacco and Firearms?"

"No sir."

"And you know that you needed authorization to work on guns, don't you?"

"I didn't know that then. I assumed that as I was doing it as a hobby there was no problem. When this problem popped up, I was afraid."

"You have a buffing wheel, don't you?"

"Yes."

"It's a cloth wheel?"

"Yes."

"You buff up guns for people?"

"Not for people. I buffed, I suppose, a total of five or six guns, and believe me, those will be the last ones I do."

"When you came to my office, I asked you about the spring?"

"Yes, you did."

"You knew that was an important issue in the case, didn't you?"

"Yes."

"I asked you, 'Isn't it true that when you had polished the gun, you clipped the spring?' Do you remember that?"

"Yes."

"And you said that because of the problems involved in the case, you did not want to remember whether or not you clipped the spring?"

"No sir. I told you from the very beginning, okay, that I did not recollect doing that, being it was so long. You told me that I was afraid to admit it, and I said possibly there's fear of me saying so."

"Then you said that you wanted to have a couple of days to think about it, didn't you?"

"Yes."

"You said, 'I will call you back and tell you whether or not I clipped the spring'?"

"Yes."

"You never did call me back?"

"No, I didn't." He kept wiping his sweaty palms on his shiny pants.

"I had to find you again?"

"Yes, you did."

"Unable to get you on the phone, I had to come out to your house, didn't I?"

"You came out."

"About five o'clock on a Sunday afternoon?"

"Right."

"Mr. Seiden was with me?"

"Uh-huh."

"And you were polishing your Camaro on your front lawn, weren't you?"

"Yes, I was."

"I asked you about the spring again?"

"Exactly."

"And I said, 'Would you please tell the truth and testify about clipping the spring?' Do you remember that?"

"Yes sir."

"And once again you said that you were real worried about the situation?"

"I also said, 'Sir—I said I have stayed awake nights trying to remember whether I did it or not, and I said I cannot tell you whether I did it.' You said, 'Well, you have to come up with the truth. You have to be honest yourself and tell us the truth.' And I said, 'Sir, if I cannot recall it, I cannot recall it.' And you were imposing on me that I did do it."

"I wanted you to tell the truth."

"Yes sir."

"You said you were worried about losing your job?"

"Exactly."

"You were worried about your family?"

"The whole bit."

"Then after we talked on Sunday afternoon, you said, 'Give me a couple of more days to think about it again'?"

"Yes. That was when you said, 'Well, we'll give you maximum three days because we got to know what to do in this case.' "

"And finally you said, 'No, I just really can't remember, and I just don't want to get involved.' Isn't that right?"

"Yes, that's right."

With that I dismissed him. I had taken a risk by sidestepping his lies, focusing instead on his character. The cross was designed to expose him as a moral coward, one who could not be trusted to tell the truth. His job at Burger King was worth more than the truth.

The next morning, even the *Herald* made no intimation about Luis's committing perjury.

The State's final witness was George Kirkham, an associate professor at the School of Criminology at Florida State University. He was a tall, slender man with a moustache and a tweedy look. To Mark and Luis, he was a traitor, a former cop who took money to testify against other cops and was now trying to put one in jail. He was also crucial. As the last witness, he was the one whose words would ring in the jurors' ears as they started deliberations.

Cowart began by running Kirkham through a list of impressive-sounding credentials. His specialty was law enforcement, with a doctorate in criminology from the University of California at Berkeley, and he had the fancy title of "executive director of the National Academy of Police Specialists." He had co-authored a textbook, *Introduction to Law Enforcement*, and written

Signal Zero, describing six months that he worked as a cop in Jacksonville, Florida.

In Cowart's direct examination, Kirkham repeated the prosecution's theory of the case: Luis was wrong to leave his assigned sector; Luis should have told his partner what he was doing; he made a mistake by getting too close to Johnson; and, of course, an officer should not cock his gun.

Cowart described a hypothetical example that repeated the State's theory of the case, in which Luis "flinches." The prosecutor asked Kirkham whether he could tell if the gun was cocked.

I objected. There was no way that Kirkham or anyone else could conclude whether the gun was cocked. Gersten overruled me.

Kirkham answered: "My opinion is that weapon clearly was in a cocked or single action mode."

I heard snickers from the audience behind me. How could he know this? There was no evidence to back him up.

"In examining over one hundred police shootings," he continued, "I have only seen two accidental shootings where the weapon was fired in a double action mode." In each case, the officer had fallen over backwards and fired accidentally.

In this case, the professor maintained, "the shooting is not at all justified. I've seen so many times—it's a cocked gun. You cock that gun in tense field situations, it's very likely that it will go off."

As soon as I had seen Kirkham's name on the witness list, I began tracking down his academic record and all his writings.

Now I put all these documents to use. Under my questioning, Kirkham acknowledged that all his graduate research was not on police work, but homosexual behavior. Where was his original research and published articles about police procedures? He had to admit he didn't become a specialist in police procedures until he had briefly served as a cop.

As I probed, Kirkham grudgingly agreed that social scientists, like their physical science counterparts, must test their theories by developing hypotheses and subjecting them to rigorous testing. To accentuate that his opinion was a purely subjective view, unmeasurable, unprovable and supported by nothing more than anecdote, I drew out of him how little he knew about the arcade. He had visited it once, early in the morning, before it was open for business.

"So you had an hour to sit there, mull over your experiences, imagine what it was like with the noise and the tension and the things that were going on, and then in your own mind try to figure out what you would have done under the circumstances?"

"Tried to fairly consider all the possibilities, yes."

"In formulating your opinion you have referred to yourself as a scientist?"

"Yes, I've used that characterization."

"I take it as a scientist you consider yourself to be an objective person?"

"I seek to be objective."

"Of course, you have to be honest in an investigation?"

"Yes."

With that setup I picked up his thick doctoral dissertation. It was a study of men who wanted transsexual operations. In all of the three hundred-plus previous cases Kirkham had been involved in, opposition attorneys had never come up with this document. I asked, "When this went to the dissertation committee, did they require you to write a disclaimer?"

"Well, normally," he said, swallowing hard, "there's a preface written."

In fact, his professors had forced him to admit that he used "conscious deception" in dealing with the transsexuals. Because he was bothered that these men were seeking sex-change operations, he had given the notes of his interviews to the medical committee that would decide whether they should be operated on. He hadn't told his subjects he was doing that—an omission that angered his professors.

"Does conscious deception mean the same thing as lying?" I asked him.

"Well, you can semantically, I suppose, talk about it in a number of ways," he dodged. He claimed he was a victim of campus politics.

For the next few minutes I barraged him with questions, repeatedly using the words "conscious deception," "lying," "duplicitous" and "unethical." With this tone set for the jurors, I turned to his short police career that he had written about in *Signal Zero: The True Story of a Professor Who Became a Street Cop*. The book recounted how his field training officer had told him to forget 75 percent of what he had learned in the classroom.

Under my questioning Kirkham acknowledged that he himself had driven outside his assigned zone and had broken another regulation by using hollow-point bullets. According to his book, this infraction could draw a two-week suspension, but officers risked it because they wanted to make certain that if they fired at a suspect, the bullet would stop him.

When he claimed some details in the book were done for "purposes of character development" and were not strictly accurate, I read from his own introduction, in which he promised to "tell it like it is." Then I turned to a vivid description of his stopping a nineteen-year-old driver. To Kirkham, the young man seemed nice. Suddenly, his partner shouted, "Freeze!" Kirkham saw his partner cocking his .38 and pointing it at the youth's head. The partner had seen what Kirkham hadn't: The teenager was reaching for a gun down by the floorboard.

Now, Kirkham said the anecdote wasn't quite accurate. "There was no cocked weapon."

I didn't care what he testified to. The anecdote showed how unexpectedly a suspect could get to his gun. Either his partner cocked the gun to get the suspect's attention or Kirkham lied in the book. Either way, it was a plus for our side.

I read another anecdote, about Kirkham facing an angry crowd in an impoverished black neighborhood. People were throwing rocks and bottles at him. A woman tried to grab his service revolver. Kirkham knocked the woman down and drew his revolver. He called on the car radio for other officers to come, then pulled out a shotgun and racked a shell into the chamber.

"You pointed it at the people nearest to you?"

"In actuality," he replied, "I had the weapon in a port arms position." He claimed that in the book he had merely been using "dramatic license" about aiming the gun.

I read on: " 'I could see myself standing there with a shotgun. Scared. Cursing. Shouting. "Menacing an unarmed assembly with an offensive weapon," I once would have said disapprovingly. I had learned that night that the desire to remain alive and uninjured is the lowest common denominator for every human being—including professors of criminology. I had been ready to kill, would have killed, would have done anything I had to in order to survive.' "

This book was a powerful expression of what Luis Alvarez and all the other Miami street cops felt. I continued reading. " 'If I had fired it that night, if I had actually shot, even to save our lives—my God. The community, the newspapers, the civil rights groups, the department's own internal affairs division would have come down on me like a ton of bricks. It seemed so wrong to me, so consummately unjust, that we who so often found ourselves forced to make the gravest of human decisions in a matter of seconds should then be judged by outsiders, people who enjoyed the luxury of quantities of time in which to dissect and examine every action retrospectively. Outsiders who had never personally experienced the crushing grip of fear, the incomparable climate of emotional pressure in which a policeman must sometimes act. Outsiders for whom the differences between right and wrong were always so clear.' "

I paused to let the words sink in. "That's a pretty good summary of what it's like being a police officer, isn't it?"

"Well, I'm pleased that you think it is. I tried to make it be so."

By this time it was 6 p.m. The judge adjourned for the evening. As we were walking out of the courtroom, a television reporter said to me, "That was a great expert witness you had."

Back at the office we discussed Kirkham's testimony. We all agreed that by the time I was through with him, he was more our witness than the State's. What more was left to do? I could have challenged him directly about the absurdity of claiming the gun was cocked, but I would have run into trouble. He was a professional witness.

The next morning *The Miami Herald* had a bold black headline: "Professor: Cop's Shot Unnecessary." When court resumed, I announced that we had no more questions.

We could have gone immediately to closing statements, but Abe Laeser had the flu and the judge ordered a two-day delay. I worked on my summation. I figured I could get through the last day just on adrenaline. Being in a trial is like fighting all night in the foxhole and then looking up in the morning and seeing the enemy charging with bayonets. I don't care how tired you are—

you're going to keep going. I worked sprawled in a chair, making notes and constantly rearranging the outline for my remarks.

When the trial resumed, on March 15, everyone was prepared for the worst. The officers protecting the courtroom wore bulletproof vests. In black neighborhoods, hundreds of parents kept their children home from school.

The packed courtroom included reporters from the local media, all the television networks, *The New York Times, Washington Post, Los Angeles Times* and *Time* magazine.

I anticipated a polemic of the type Laeser was famous for and I was not disappointed. "What did Nevell Johnson do to deserve dying? He turned with his hands up. But Luis Alvarez wasn't paying attention. He had his gun on single action. He looked at his partner. His gun just went off."

He harped on Alvarez's first radio message. "He never said, 'I had to fire. I shot my gun I acted in self-defense.' He never said, 'I was in fear for my life.' Luis Alvarez's own words—out of his own mouth—don't have one single solitary sound that even resembles self-defense."

Laeser picked up Luis's police revolver from the evidence table. He called the gun "the most important piece of evidence in the case." He claimed that the gun had been modified "to become the most lethal machine for killing that a police officer is allowed to carry." He was making it sound sinister while acknowledging that it didn't violate regulations. Laeser leaned over the jury rail, waving the .38 police special and invited the jurors to take the gun into the jury room with them. "Put your finger on that trigger. There's almost no pressure. Just the tiniest of movements and that gun goes off."

He ran through all the errors that Luis had allegedly made in the game room. Then he slowly, dramatically took off his suit coat and picked up Johnson's stolen Saturday night special. He said the gun was not over Johnson's left kidney, as the defense was claiming, but in the small of Johnson's back. "Try it in the jury room all day. You can't get to the gun. The man who put it there, Nevell Johnson, knew he couldn't get it. Nevell Johnson wasn't insane. He wasn't a madman. He wasn't trying to commit suicide."

He blasted me for attacking Johnson's character. "We heard about bad Nevell, archenemy of the people, arrested once as a juvenile and returned to his mother. That's the depths to which the defense has sunk." I flushed with anger. But I knew I would soon have the floor to myself.

Laeser denied there was any political motivation. "There's a difference between a good cop and a bad cop. Even if he's a good cop, the police officer of the year, if he unlawfully kills someone he has to be prosecuted."

He ended with an ominous note to the jury, warning that the "community" wanted "answers." I heard them as code words signaling that if Alvarez was acquitted, the jurors could expect rioting.

As I walked to the podium, I decided I had to shift the jurors' focus from Laeser's argument about Luis's violating minute details of police regulations because the jury could easily decide, sitting a year later in a courtroom, that Luis could have waited another half a second, that perhaps he had misinterpreted Johnson's movements or that he hadn't been in actual danger.

Until this case, despite all my years dealing with cops, I hadn't fully grasped what they felt. How could I expect the jury to?

I stood before the jury rail, without a podium blocking me, and without notes to distract me, I quickly walked the jurors into the arcade: "Alvarez had no choice but to confront him. Imagine his emotion facing a teenage punk with a gun, the most dangerous animal on the street. Fear is just the beginning of your emotions. The situation quickly falls apart. He sees Johnson's eyes lock on his. This isn't going right. He senses it before he sees it, Johnson's arm is going across his chest, his hand reaching for the gun. With a sickening jolt he thinks it's too late, Johnson has the drop on him, he's dead. But his reflexes and training kick in, almost without conscious thought, saving his life.

"The decision made in less time than it takes to get out the fourth word of this sentence. As soon as the crack of the .38 police special fades, reality slams in, nausea hits him like a tidal wave. He loses sense of time, objectivity. All he can think, Get on the air, call for emergency, get me out of this. He had to force himself to pull out his hand-held radio. He kept thinking to himself, It wasn't my fault. That one thought keeps recycling through his head as he struggles to make sense of what happened.

"The law of self-defense requires you to put yourself in Luis's shoes, patrolling the ghetto of Overtown, walking into that game room, confronting a man with a gun who quickly turns, grabbing for his gun. The question you must answer: Would a reasonable person believe that under these circumstances he had a right to defend his own life?

"But in this case, because Luis was a police officer, *wearing our uniform and our shield,* you must look further. Under Florida law, police officers have an expanded right of self-defense. The law provides that a police officer may use as much force as he reasonably believes necessary to make an arrest and to protect his own life. The law makes a distinction between the self-defense rights of a police officer versus that of other citizens. If I see a man on the street with a gun, I have no responsibility to arrest him. I can simply turn around and walk to the nearest telephone, dial 911 and shift the responsibility to their shoulders.

"But a police officer doesn't have that luxury. He can't turn his back and walk away. No matter how distasteful, no matter how dangerous, he is required to confront that criminal, even if he has a gun. The law, using great common sense, says that since he's required to do that, he is entitled to special protection, granting him the right to use whatever force is necessary to protect his own life while arresting him." He has to confront knives, guns, burning cars, ticking bombs, landslides, earthquakes and floods, while we all seek shelter. Sudden and senseless death is a frequent companion in a street cop's life.

"The cops call it 'The Street.' It's a world full of predators and victims. It's thick with the expectation of violence. You are constantly alert. You know the criminals don't follow rules. They can shoot you just because they're having a bad day."

I went through all of Lacser's accusations about what Luis had done inside the arcade. All his actions—approaching Johnson quietly because he didn't want to alert everyone in the arcade, drawing his gun, having Cruz reach for the Saturday night special—were perfectly proper. "They descend so far as to even complain about the wording of his police commands. They say Officer Alvarez told Nevell Johnson, 'Well, let's walk out of the game room together,' and that's all Johnson was doing. Ladies and gentlemen, that is hogwash. There can be no doubt that when Officer Alvarez told Nevell Johnson don't move, showed him the gun, grabbed him by the sweater and held him there, that man knew he was not supposed to move.

"Mr. Johnson saw the revolver. He saw the uniform. He looked at the officer. He *knew* he's not supposed to move. Do you really believe that under these circumstances, knowing what's going on in that game room, the showing of the gun, the uniform, the commands, that Mr. Johnson, Mr. Snake, the man with the street-wise experience thought, Well, gentlemen, now we're going to stroll out of here nicely and hail a cab on the corner and we're all going to go down to the Dade County Jail?

"The prosecutors conveniently overlook time and time again that Officer Alvarez had hold of him, had grabbed on to him so he couldn't move. In order to break that hold he had to jerk his shoulder back to break the grasp of the hold. This is not someone casually strolling out of the game room to get into a cab."

I had to answer one of Laeser's main arguments: Johnson had placed the gun in a location where it could not be reached or drawn. If the jury believed that, they would also logically conclude that Johnson wouldn't be going for the gun. If he weren't, there was no reason to shoot him.

"Mr. Laeser claims that the best evidence Johnson wasn't going for his gun was that the gun was secreted in the small of his back where Johnson couldn't reach it. Mr. Laeser told you: 'The man who put it there knew he couldn't get to it.' That argument has some superficial appeal, but it is illogical and foolish once you examine it. How could Johnson place a gun where he couldn't reach it? And more importantly, *why* would he put a gun in a place where he couldn't reach it?

"Picture in your mind the scene. They are in the game room. [Alvarez is] confronting Johnson. He feels the gun in Johnson's waistband. The noise is deafening. The thunder-like percussion of fifty electronic machines blasting, exploding, banging, roaring, clanging in his ears. He is surrounded by children. He has to disarm this man, without endangering himself, and without endangering the children engrossed in their video games. Then, in a heartbeat, Luis feels Johnson jerking around and thinks: He's going to shoot me."

Then I turned to Laeser's argument that Luis's call to the dispatcher proved his actions were not in self-defense. Laeser had argued, "He never said, 'I had to fire, I acted in self-defense, I was in fear for my life.'" If it had been self-defense, Laeser claimed, Luis would have said so instantly on the radio. I wanted the jury to feel the shock, the confusion, the hurt that Luis had felt. The purpose of the call was not to create an alibi or an excuse. The only thought in Luis's mind was that this kid needed help.

The novelist Willa Cather claimed that only opera singers, novelists and doctors entered the skin of another human. She wasn't thinking about juries.

In the moments after the shot, I told the jurors, Luis was in emotional turmoil. I pointed to Dr. Fitzhugh's description of the "intense state of shock and confusion" that an officer feels after a shooting. It's the same thing that soldiers feel in war. Both cops and soldiers are subject to post-traumatic shock disorder. I reached back and replayed descriptions the jurors voiced in voir dire of confronting sudden danger and the almost paralyzing aftermath.

I moved on to the cocked gun theory. I made sure I framed it as Laeser's "theory" because the choice of words is important. Juries are not going to send a police officer to prison on a "theory."

"The major theory of the State's case is that the gun was cocked. But where is the evidence? Let us examine the alleged eyewitnesses' testimony. Bell claimed while Officer Alvarez is walking up to Mr. Johnson, he's drawing his gun and cocking it. We know that's untrue. We've heard testimony from Officer Alvarez, Officer Cruz and even Mr. Laeser admits that Officer Alvarez did not draw his gun until he felt the gun in Johnson's waistband and asked him what is it, and Johnson said it's a gun. *Then* Officer Alvarez drew his gun from his holster.

"The important part of Mr. Bell's testimony, the part studiously ignored by Mr. Laeser, is that Officer Cruz never got anywhere near Johnson. Bell claimed he could see right through the doors that Officer Cruz never approached or stood near Johnson, nor did Officer Cruz ever reach for Johnson's gun.

"If there's one fact you can rely on, it's that Officer Cruz was there, that he did reach for the gun, that his hand was only two or three inches from the gun at the time the shooting happened. Yet Mr. Bell, who the State tells you has acute eyesight, for some reason could not see a large man wearing a dark blue, distinctive police uniform, standing right next to Johnson. Mr. Bell's testimony is absurd. Could he see a hammer being cocked from thirty-four feet away, yet not see a man in a police uniform?

"You remember the multiple-choice tests we all used to take in school? Mr. Hoskins has a twist on that — he gives multiple *answers*." Answer no. 1: Officer Alvarez comes in and first grabs Mr. Johnson by the arm, swings him around against the other machine and shoots him. Answer no. 2: He grabs him by the shoulder, swings him around, and shoots him by the machine. And answer no. 3, my favorite of all, the one that he gave on his TV interview when he had his press conference, Mr. Hoskins says that Alvarez comes in, grabs him in a headlock, swings him around and shoots him, all while still holding him by the head.

I shifted the focus to Luis. "On December 28, what did he do when he got up in the morning, when he went to work, when he put on his uniform, when he put on his badge, when he put on his gun? Did he say, 'Well, I'm going to go out and kill someone today'? Did he say, 'I'm going to go out and commit a crime today'? When he put on that uniform, his only thought was going to do his duty as a police officer, and he was going to try to stay alive so he could go home at the end of his shift.

"Ladies and gentlemen, you are soon going to retire to reach a verdict in this case. But no matter what verdict you return, you can never undo the year of agony of what this man has gone through. You can never undo the fifteen months of vilification in the press that he has undergone. You can never undo the heartache that his family has suffered for the last fifteen months. You can't do anything about the civil suit that's going to follow this trial. But there is one thing you can do. You can reject this criminal charge and let Luis Alvarez walk out of this courtroom a free man."

When drafting the indictment, prosecutors had used the trick of over-charging in an attempt to frighten the defendant into a guilty plea to a lesser offense. Now it was payback time. "One final matter: The judge will instruct you that Officer Alvarez is charged with a crime of manslaughter with a firearm. We have a special statute in Florida which doubles the sentence for criminals who use a gun to commit a crime. Manslaughter usually carries fifteen years, but under this special statute Officer Alvarez can get thirty years.

"The last indignity of this case is that the prosecutor deliberately charged this officer, so he gets double the sentence. Can you imagine? Prosecutors charging a police officer who's authorized to carry a gun by us and saying we're going to charge him under a statute that's going to punish him double because he was carrying a gun. That's the ultimate slap, the ultimate vicious-ness, the ultimate insult to every law enforcement officer in this community."

My summation lasted two hours and forty-two minutes. Trial lawyers learn by sad experience that juries can be influenced by one seemingly insignificant fact. As a young lawyer I had studiously avoided discussing the difficult points of my opponent. I soon learned that was the path to disaster. Answer them all.

At 6:10 p.m. the jurors began deliberations. Gersten was expecting a long bout. He ordered dinner sent into the jury room and told us he would allow the jurors to deliberate until midnight before sending them back to the hotel.

We packed up our case files and returned to our office, escorted by a string of squad cars. Rumors were flying that there might be attempts to assassinate us if there was an acquittal. Back at our thirty-four-story office building, a SWAT team in full-body armor had taken up spots on the roof, in the main lobby and in the corridor in front of our offices. It was a besieged fortress. Less than two hours later we received a call: The jury had a verdict.

Escorted by armed guards, we set off for the courthouse. Mark had a bulletproof vest, two pistols and four extra magazines. We were driven through the dark, empty streets of Miami into a garage in the courthouse basement, where we were met by more guards and bomb-sniffing dogs. An escort took us to an elevator. When we stepped out on the fourth floor, a hundred reporters and cameramen were waiting. Blinded by the bright TV lights, we made our way to the courtroom, which by the judge's order was empty of spectators because he feared a violent reaction to the verdict. Not that anything was being kept secret: Miami's television stations were broadcasting the verdict live.

We waited a short time for the prosecution team to arrive. Mark was pacing. Luis lounged in a chair. "Aren't you nervous?" Mark asked.

"Of course I'm nervous," Luis said quietly. "But I'm not going to show it."

As for myself, the pressure was excruciating. My heart was pounding I felt an odd lightness in my head, as if I were about to faint.

Finally, Laeser and his associates arrived, and the jury was brought in. Mark whispered, "They're not looking at us. We lost." Luis groaned.

The clerk began reading the verdict sheet. "In the case of *State* v. *Alvarez*, we the jury find on this 15th of March, 1984, as to the charge of . . ."

When the clerk reached the actual words of the verdict, her voice cracked. Finally, she got them out: "Not guilty."

Luis leaped up. He raised clenched fists in the air, then embraced us. "Thank you, thank you," I shouted to the jurors as they filed out.

Now all we had to do was worry about our lives. We were led to a fire escape at the end of the corridor. As we dashed down the stairs, we saw an
armed guard on each landing. One of them gave Luis a thumbs-up sign.

In the basement, the jurors were being loaded into a bus. We banged on
the windows and waved thanks. Then the guards led us to an unmarked squad
car. There had been discussions about getting us out via helicopter or squad-
car convoy, but it was decided that an unmarked car would attract the least attention.

As we sped back to our office, squad cars blocked the intersections. An odd
clicking sound was coming from the police radio. Luis told me what it was:
Street cops all over Miami were sending secret congratulations. They knew all
their transmissions were taped. They were showing their feelings by clicking
the on-off buttons on their radios.

At our office building, we hurried past the guards in the lobby to our special elevator and then up to our offices. Soon, the place was filled with street
cops dropping by to congratulate Luis. Some were prepared for anything; they
wore bandoliers of shotgun shells crisscrossed on their chests. We opened a
couple of bottles of champagne, and Ralph brought out a bottle of Scotch. So
many officers and friends were dropping by that the liquor didn't go far.

Meanwhile, rioting was breaking out all over the city. Crowds were throwing rocks and bottles, setting fires, moving through the streets. This time the
police were prepared. A thousand city, county and state officers were ordered
to take control. Trouble spots were barricaded off. Field-force convoys of
twenty-plus squad cars moved through Overtown and Liberty City to discour-
age people from taking to the streets.

Sometime after 1 a.m. I headed home. The way I usually take down U.S. 1
was blocked by a barricade of squad cars, to keep motorists from running into
rock throwers and snipers.

The next morning Luis's acquittal and the riots made the front pages of *The
New York Times, Washington Post, Los Angeles Times* and *USA Today*. The
network morning programs showed scenes of burning cars and officers in gas
masks. "Alvarez! Alvarez!" black youths shouted at the cameras. Most of the

victims were black. As with every riot, there were photos of black shopowners forlornly staring at the wreckage of their burned-out stores.

Altogether, about four hundred were arrested. Twenty-four people were injured, including four police officers. This time no one was killed. In Miami, that's called progress.

The Aftermath: *The Miami Herald* and other news media expressed shock at the verdict and found it more convenient to place the blame on the jury.

Luis Cruz was still in his first year probationary period so the city could—and did—fire him without cause. He took the only law enforcement job he could, as a guard at Metropolitan Correctional Center in Miami, the federal prison in south Dade. He continued to show his courage by becoming a volunteer pilot for Brothers to the Rescue, a group that searched for Cuban rafters in the Straits of Florida. In 1996, four members of the group were shot down by Cuban MiGs.

As expected, the Johnson family pursued a civil suit against the city. Rather than risk another riot, the government settled for $1.1 million. With this windfall, Nevell Johnson Sr. bought a couple of Cadillacs and moved to a nice suburb. His grand life lasted less than two years. By 1986, his money was gone, and he was arrested for selling crack and carrying a concealed weapon. A judge sentenced him to three and a half years.

In March 1993, Janet Reno became the Attorney General of the United States. Several weeks later she ordered a tank assault on the Branch Davidian compound in Waco, Texas, killing at least eighty people, including at least seventeen children. While Luis Alvarez had been indicted for making a split-second decision that cost one life, Saint Janet's decision had cost eighty lives. She didn't indict herself for manslaughter. She didn't even resign. In fact her decision made her wildly popular.

In February 1998, Jeffrey Hoskins was indicted for buying votes at ten dollars apiece in the mayoral election scandal. Hoskins, in a newspaper interview, claimed votes cost ten dollars in Liberty City and Coconut Grove, but only five dollars in Overtown. He quickly turned State's evidence.

Under the Florida constitution, an acquitted defendant is entitled to prompt reimbursement of a limited number of trial costs. Soon after the verdict Judge Gersten ordered the county to pay $48,041.17. For the past twelve years the Fraternal Order of Police has sought repayment. Despite lobbying and a lawsuit, the county still hasn't paid a dime.

As for Luis Alvarez, he started a company of security guards. When he went around soliciting business, people recognized him and trusted him. Luis had a great business sense. He started a branch for security alarms, which by itself grossed $3.5 million a year. Eventually, he sold the guard business to Pinkerton for a huge profit. For a while he was a Pinkerton vice president. Then he became a security consultant, establishing guard and alarm businesses throughout Central and South America. In Mexico alone, he built thirty-two central-alarm stations, set up a nationwide guard company and helped launch a training program for Mexican police officers.

For me, the ending was more prosaic. The verdict was read on Thursday night. At 9 a.m. Monday, I was picking a jury in the frozen tundra of Hammond, Indiana, before a federal judge who twice tried to find me in contempt because he had to delay his trial due to the unanticipated length of Luis's trial. Only two appeals kept me out of jail.

Turning point: The prosecution's case began collapsing when we turned Laeser's main witness, Detective Buhrmaster, into our own witness. By the time he was through, the police detective had become the unwitting ally for our cause, the good-guy lawyers defending the police officer, while the prosecutors were defending the young man with the criminal past.

Still, the case could have collapsed on us if Luis had come across as a lying hothead on the witness stand. Instead, he was calm, charming a juror by name and impressing everyone in the courtroom with his sincerity.

Knight

EVERYONE WANTED THOMAS KNIGHT DEAD. THAT'S WHAT I WAS THINKING THE day in 1981 I picked up the phone and heard Susan Cary say his name. His number was just about up. The governor had signed his death warrant and only seven days remained until his execution. Cary is an attorney whose self-appointed task is to rescue men on death row. She was in Miami trying to keep Knight out of the electric chair, and she desperately needed help. I owed her for bailing me out in another death penalty case, so I told her to come right over. My stomach was burning with anxiety, as it always does when the State decides to kill someone.

As I waited, I reviewed what I knew about Knight. My first impression had been the same as everyone else's in Miami. It came from the same source, the news media: He was a mad-dog, cold-blooded criminal who had committed two gruesome murders in 1974. But I had one personal experience with him.

As an assistant public defender I was in court when Knight was arraigned. He was rushed in by a phalanx of grim homicide detectives. His dead, dark eyes swept the packed courtroom, then abruptly stopped at our table. He stared right into me. I turned away. You can't outstare a madman. When the judge looked to appoint a lawyer, it must have looked like a Chinese fire drill as we ducked for cover. I managed to dodge the bullet.

A young black man with a long rap sheet, Knight had kidnapped his employer, Sydney Gans, the wealthy owner of a paper-bag manufacturing company. On a hot July day, Knight forced Gans into his Mercedes at gunpoint. They drove to Gans's home, picked up his wife, Lillian, then went to the downtown branch of City National Bank. While Knight held Lillian at gunpoint, Sydney went into the bank. He told a manager what was happening, and the manager called the FBI. Agents rushed to the bank. Gans insisted on returning to his car with $50,000 in cash. The FBI set up pursuit teams to follow the car, but the agents lost it on the Palmetto Expressway.

Two hundred police officers fanned out to search for the Mercedes. They found it in a deserted field on the edge of town. Both Ganses had been shot through the back of the neck. Several hours later an officer discovered Thomas Knight in a nearby field. He was hiding in a hole, covered with dirt. Underneath him were a .30-caliber carbine and the bank's $50,000. The next day a half-dozen FBI men identified Knight as the man they had seen sitting beside Lillian Gans in the Mercedes. Knight was charged with two counts of first-degree murder.

Sydney Gans was a dedicated reformer who believed in giving ex-cons a second chance, and he often hired them. Thomas Knight was one of these ex-cons, and he had gone to work for Gans while out on bail for stealing roof tiles. The murders so enraged the public that Florida's attorney general called a press conference to plead that the U.S. Supreme Court immediately reject the constitutional challenges to Florida's new death penalty law so that Knight could be executed when he was found guilty.

A few months after his arrest Knight led a mass breakout from the Dade County Jail. The FBI put him on its nationwide Ten Most Wanted List. Three months later he was captured in a run-down motel in Central Florida. The court bounced the Public Defender's Office, saying it had a conflict because it represented another escaped prisoner who had been offered a reward if he led the police to Knight. The judge selected four attorneys in private practice to represent Knight. He was quickly convicted, sentenced to death and transported to Florida State Prison. The prison has a rigidly controlled death row where condemned men are housed in small, individual cells. One day, while being led from his cell to a shower, Knight killed a guard with a sharpened serving spoon. Governor Bob Graham signed the death warrant of the most unpopular man in Florida.

• • •

When Susan Cary called, I had no intention of signing on to Knight's case. I had just spent two months in a triple murder trial, and I could not afford another destitute client. At that time the State provided no funds for defending condemned prisoners after their automatic appeal to the state supreme court, and one of the certainties of our justice system is that no one on death row has any money. I figured I would offer Susan some advice and send her on her way.

She arrived at my office with Deborah Fins, a young attorney with the NAACP Legal Defense Fund who had rushed down from New York to assist in the case. As soon as they sat down, Susan explained the situation they were in. With only a week remaining, the Florida judicial system had trapped them in a Catch-22. The state supreme court was delaying action on their appeal, and that put Knight in limbo because no other court could touch the case while it was before the supreme court.

"They will sit on it until the last possible moment—then deny it," Susan predicted. Prosecutors were charging that Susan and Deborah were a "well-oiled legal machine," but in truth they were struggling on a shoestring. At one point the two women were so desperate for supplies that they had been reduced to rummaging through wastebaskets next to the University of Florida Law School's copying machines to find usable paper.

Because they were trapped in the state courts, I suggested that the only way out was to file a writ of habeas corpus in the federal court in Miami. Neither Susan nor Deborah had any experience making oral arguments in court, and they knew nothing about the federal system. They hadn't been able to find any lawyers in Miami willing to defend Knight.

"We really need your help," Susan pleaded.

Seeing my reluctance, Susan told me she had spent hours with Thomas at the prison. He wasn't nearly the monster he was made out to be. He was a human being who had grown up in the worst possible conditions. The whole basis of the State's case had been a fraud. The prosecutors' portrayal of Thomas as a brilliant, calculating killer was absurd. The truth was that Thomas was flat-out insane, and he shouldn't have been sentenced to death.

I wasn't impressed. "Susan, we all know insanity is a loser as a defense. Juries don't buy it. They think all state mental hospitals are built with revolving doors and the maniac will get a miracle cure and be right back on the street."

That wasn't true in Thomas's case, Susan insisted. A lot of crucial evidence about his insanity had never been presented at his trial. His four lawyers had blown it.

"Susan," I said, "every guy on death row claims he was screwed by incompetent lawyers. Besides, one of Knight's lawyers, Bill Meadows, had been both a circuit court judge and the United States attorney. No judge is going to find him incompetent."

"Even if he was competent," she retorted, "Knight didn't get a fair trial." Besides, we wouldn't challenge Meadows's competence as an attorney—only his performance in Knight's case. "But we need to work fast."

I knew how frustrating and chaotic death cases could become. In 1979, when Governor Bob Graham signed the death warrant for Bob Sullivan, the former University of Miami student convicted of killing a motel manager, Susan had waited with Sullivan at the prison, while I worked around the clock preparing habeas corpus petitions backed with voluminous exhibits. The pleadings had been carried to Eastern Airlines to be flown to a federal appeals court—only to be lost. I worked all night rewriting the papers, worrying that a man would die because my brief had ended up in lost luggage.

I told Susan I didn't want to go through this kind of frantic guerrilla war again.

"Oh," Susan replied, "there's one other thing." She pulled a thin document out of her briefcase and handed it to me. "This," she said, "is truly abominable." The document was titled *Thomas Knight vs. State of Florida. Submitted by William Hutchinson Jr. APPELLANTS BRIEF.* I noticed the missing apostrophe.

I flipped through it quickly. The first seven pages were a recitation of the facts of the Ganses' murders, but even here, in the simplest section of any appeal, there were incoherent statements: "The Ganses vehicle was splutter with blood, smugs and smears."

The actual argument, only six pages long, was a rambling stream of consciousness, laced with misspellings: "Where a statement was spontanenes, was made by one who witnessed the act concerning which statement was made, was made at the scene of the homicide in sight or hearing of the accused on victim and is relevant to a material issue in the case, the statement under such circumstances is part of res gestae and is admissible." This made no sense.

I kept reading until I came across the most obtuse section I have ever read in a legal brief: "Moreover facts provide evidence that someone other than the defendant was in the vehicle downtown and killed Mr. & Mrs. Gans: Black male in rear seat wore a brown shirt according to all FBI agents survilling downtown. The muzzle or barrel of the gun was at least 6 inches. The gun was very close to Mr. Gans at time of shooting. Blood through the vehicle, & would have appeared on gun. Swears of bolld were in rear seat."

Even if one ignored the misspellings and typos, Hutchinson seemed to be arguing that the evidence at the trial was not sufficient to convict Thomas Knight. Actually, the evidence had been so overwhelming that Knight's lawyers at trial had never contested that he committed the crime. Their position was that he was insane. Now, on appeal, Hutchinson was claiming the evidence wasn't sufficient? This wasn't a brief. How could the court make a life-or-death decision based on this document?

As I had finished reading, Susan pounded home the inadequacies of this document.

"All right," I relented, "but only until the execution is stayed."

That night we prepared a federal petition for a writ of habeas corpus. We sifted through stacks of West federal reporters, thick books of published legal opinions, searching for the right cases to back up each of our arguments. At 9:30 p.m. we called Sid White, the clerk of the Florida Supreme Court, and asked whether any action had been taken on Knight's case that day. He said that no opinion had been rendered and that he had no idea when the court would rule. We continued to work through the night, piecing the pleadings and their voluminous exhibits together.

The next morning we drove to the federal courthouse to file the petition. I knew that, despite all our work, the selection of a judge to hear our petition would be, literally, a life-or-death matter. Today, there's a formal ritual to death cases as they wind their way through the courts, but in 1981 we had no idea what to expect. Some judges might be receptive to our arguments; others would dismiss them quickly. Since an appeal was still in state court, it was possible the federal court would say it could do nothing.

In the clerk's office, a man behind the counter stamped DEATH PENALTY in big red letters on our petition, flagging it for immediate attention. Then he pulled out a large wooden box that rotated on an axle, like an old carny game of luck. The clerk spun the box. When it stopped, he pulled out a little ball with a number on it.

"Oh my God," Deborah said, staring at the wooden box, "it's the ghastly lottery." She recalled U.S. Supreme Court Justice William Brennan's statement that the death penalty was applied so capriciously that it was nothing more than a "lottery."

The clerk selected a tag with the name of Judge Joe Eaton, one of the more remarkable individuals on the federal bench. He had been a minor-league first baseman, a World War II fighter pilot with the Army Air Corps and a state senator in conservative North Florida, where he fought alone against the segregationists. It had destroyed his political career, and he had moved to Miami, where he became a prosecutor, then a judge. I told Susan that Eaton was a genius on constitutional law, that he asked questions as sharp as a razor blade. Our papers had to be first-class.

We went back to my office and pored over all the files on Knight's case. Late that afternoon Sid White, the court clerk, called. He said that by a vote of 6–0, the Florida Supreme Court had rejected a stay of execution. The justices had decided that Hutchinson's appellate brief, "while not a model of legal writing," did not fall "measurably below the performance expected of appellate counsel."

The next morning Deborah, Susan and I walked into the north courtroom on the second floor of the old Federal Courthouse and found reporters anxiously awaiting word of the execution. They had their own lottery—because of limited seating in the death "suite" not all of them could view the electrocution. In 1981 it was still a novelty, and newspaper readers were eager for each grisly detail. Periodically a condemned inmate would burst into flames.

Our adversary was Calvin Fox, an assistant attorney general who was a death penalty hard-liner. A huge man, six feet five inches tall and heavyset, Fox continually harangued judges to impose death sentences.

As I sat nervously awaiting the arrival of the judge, the questions kept coming. Had I covered all the bases? What if Judge Eaton dismissed our petition out of hand? Only five days were left.

Suddenly, the clerk rose, the room fell silent, and Judge Eaton took his seat on the bench. Without any introduction he addressed Fox: "Tell me what a judge should consider in deciding whether to stay or not."

"I think," Fox replied, "the delay by the defendant in this case is most material. There have been five years between the time of conviction in this case and the time of this petition." Our habeas corpus pleadings, he said, were "totally untimely and inappropriate."

"How could this be untimely?" the judge asked, frowning. "His death warrant is merely twenty-eight days old. It was Governor Graham who dallied these five years, not Mr. Knight. So let's put aside your accusation of deliberate delay while you answer a more critical question. Is it your position that Knight's petition does not even *state* a claim?"

"Yes, Your Honor."

With a sour look on his face, Eaton turned and stared right at me. "Mr. Black, give me a rundown of your claims."

It was my turn for a grilling. Fox's argument was preposterous, I argued. Our petition clearly stated constitutional claims. Quickly, I ran through our first ten points. Then I mentioned ineffective assistance of counsel, and the judge perked up.

"Have you ever," he asked, "had this matter considered by the state courts of Florida?"

"No, Your Honor."

Eaton had been waiting for me to raise this point. He had obviously read our brief. We had explained in detail the "ping-ponging" that had kept the courts from considering all of Knight's appeals.

"So," repeated the judge, "this has *never* been considered by a Florida court?"

"No, Your Honor."

"Mr. Fox, is that right or wrong?"

"We *have* to proceed," Fox said emphatically. "We want to have this hearing *now*. We want to argue this case on the merits. We want to argue it on the law, then it can be disposed of on the law, and Mr. Knight can be promptly executed next Tuesday."

For a long moment Eaton stared at Fox. "You would like this court to hear it *now?*"

"Yes," Fox replied.

"Has the Petitioner had any opportunity to subpoena witnesses to attempt to prove up his claim, or—"

"Excuse me," Fox interjected, "Your Honor, would you—"

The judge looked surprised. "Should we proceed without the opportunity to have witnesses?"

"Your Honor," Fox said, "they waited five years. If they are not ready right now, the petition should be dismissed. We can have an evidentiary hearing right now. We can have one immediately." He mentioned how much time the courts had wasted before the state of Florida had finally been able to execute John Spenkelink.[1]

"All right, sir," the judge said sternly. "What happened in Spenkelink, I do not care, counsel. You are not here to impress the public or these reporters. You are here to present a matter to this court in the interest of the United States constitutional system. Do you understand that?"

"I understand that," Fox replied.

"But," Eaton continued, "you're saying, 'Let's hear it immediately,' without the rights accorded under our Constitution just so you can execute him on your timetable, right?"

"Yes, Your Honor." Fox looked a little ill.

"This court," the judge announced, "isn't going to be stampeded by the fact that the man's sentence was death rather than forty years. We are still going to apply the law. I still have this terrible interest in due process, and therefore I am going to let folks argue, you see. This judge is going to hear this case on the merits. This court is more devoted to the law than it is any matters of

---

1. A drifter who killed a man in a motel room fight, Spenkelink was electrocuted on May 25, 1979, the first to be executed against his will since the U.S. Supreme Court threw out existing death penalties in 1972 and states had to pass new laws.

great public concern, because that is my job. So the stay necessarily has to be entered because if Mr. Knight wins but he is dead, that would be a rather peculiar way to operate the courts."

The judge rose and left the courtroom. The hearing ended so abruptly that Susan wasn't certain it was over. "What do we do now?" she whispered.

"We go home," I said.

Thomas Knight would be allowed to live while his case was fought in the courts.

After the hearing we trooped back to my office. The job I promised to do was over, but as we gathered up all of Knight's files I realized I didn't want to stop now. I no longer was thinking of reasons not to take the case.

Shortly after the hearing before Judge Eaton, Debbie caught a flight to Baton Rouge, where she was fighting another execution. Susan and I held a strategy conference. She said that she had spent a long time building a rapport with Thomas Knight and that she was the only person to whom he would talk. For reasons we were just beginning to understand, Knight felt comfortable talking only with women and refused to deal with men. Susan worried that if I tried to talk to him, he would refuse our help. Therefore, it would be best that she handle all personal contacts with Knight and his family. My job would be to coordinate the litigation and legal research, and handle the courtroom work.

My first task after that wasn't pleasant. Thomas Knight had formally changed his name to Askari Abdullah Muhammad, and he wanted the court papers to reflect his new name. Muhammad was not a name that I would choose for a defendant. Representing an unpopular killer was difficult enough without his adopting a militant-sounding Black Muslim name. I thought judges would be more sympathetic to Thomas Knight than they would be to Askari Abdullah Muhammad. I filed a notice of his new name in the federal case, but since Knight was the name on all the records of his state and federal cases, I continued to call him Thomas Knight.

Ever since he had killed the guard, Knight had been held in a special punishment cell located next to the execution chamber, in what is called Q Wing. Human Rights Watch described the place this way: "Cells in Q-Wing are six feet 11 inches by eight feet seven inches, with a cement bunk, a toilet and a sink. There is no window and no furniture. The front of the cell consists of a grill, in front of which there is an enclosed area about two feet wide with a solid metal door; the heat in the cell is stifling."

No window, no breeze, no air conditioning to get through the brutal Florida summers, no one to talk to, and only that solid steel door to look at. It was like living in a coffin. In this awful cell Thomas baked day after day in shorts and rubber-soled slippers, the only clothing he was permitted. He was allowed no television, no radio, no newspaper. The only time he was taken from his cell was for a five-minute shower twice a week. That was it. He was never permitted outside to exercise. Q Wing, Human Rights Watch concluded, "clearly amounts to corporal punishment, explicitly prohibited under the U.N. Standard Minimum Rules."

Q Wing was enough to drive anybody mad, and Thomas was mad to begin with. After the Eaton hearing I read a report by Dr. Brad Fisher, a clinical and forensic psychologist, who was astonished that prison officials were doing nothing to treat Knight's illness: "This is clearly a man with a major psychiatric problem in need of appropriate medication and treatment responses. I diagnose him as paranoid schizophrenic and only wonder why the medication and treatment previously given to him for this condition has not been continued during his incarceration."

While we were pursuing our case concerning the murders of the Ganses in state courts, Thomas went on trial in Bradford County for the murder of the guard. Just because he already had a death sentence didn't stop the State from seeking another one. Prison guards wanted revenge with their own day in court, and prosecutors thought that a second capital conviction might speed Knight through the appeals courts to "a final solution."

I wasn't involved in that case. Bradford County is a rural area where the main employer is Florida State Prison. This was the worst possible place for the Knight trial. Still, the story behind the guard's murder came out through bits of testimony.

The drama began when Thomas refused to shave, in defiance of prison regulations. Sometimes he cited his sensitive skin, sometimes his new Muslim religion, but whatever the reason, he was adamant about not shaving. The guards punished him for this, and he ran up more than two hundred disciplinary reports.

One day in 1980, Thomas's mother went to see him. She had been seriously ill for a long time, and it had been four years since she had made the two hundred–mile trip from her Fort Pierce home to visit her son. The guards ordered him to shave before going to the visiting area. At first he refused, but eventually he relented. He wanted to see his mother.

It was too late. Prison officials had already told Mrs. Knight that Thomas had refused to see her. She had left. In his cell Thomas went into a rage. Nearby death row inmates egged him on, saying he had to get even with the bastards. One of the inmates apparently passed him a sharpened serving spoon. Later, a new guard named Richard "Jim" Burke, who knew nothing of Thomas's recent rage, was assigned to take Thomas to a shower. In the corridor, Knight jumped him, stabbing him repeatedly with the spoon before other guards arrived to pull him off.

When it came time for sentencing, the courtroom was packed with prison guards in uniform. No one was surprised when Thomas Knight was given another death penalty.

Thomas's appeal of the Ganses' murders moved slowly through state courts for more than a year after the Eaton hearing. Finally, the Florida Supreme Court rejected it, by a vote of 4–2. Back in federal court, we had even worse news: Judge Eaton, the only judge who had taken Knight's rights seriously, had taken senior status and was no longer hearing criminal cases. Our appeal was transferred to Judge William M. Hoeveler, a Harvard-educated southern patrician who was a meticulous disciplinarian.

In the fall of 1983, while we were waiting for a hearing before Hoeveler, I found a new motive to keep battling for Thomas Knight when Governor Graham signed another death warrant for Bob Sullivan, the former University of Miami student. On November 29 the U.S. Supreme Court rejected Sullivan's appeal by a vote of 7–2. The Court blasted the delays caused by Sullivan's attorneys, who, of course, included me. After a decade of litigation, the Court stated, "there must come an end to the process of consideration and reconsideration." Chief Justice Warren Burger complained that Sullivan's case had reached the U.S. Supreme Court four times: "This alone demonstrates the speciousness of the suggestion that there has been a 'rush to judgment.' " But Justice Brennan wrote in a dissent that it was unfair that the justices had had only twenty-four hours to study the "voluminous stay application and exhibits. . . . The Court has once again rushed to judgment, apparently eager to reach a fatal conclusion."

A new group of Washington attorneys for Sullivan filed appeals, but they, too, were rejected.

The night after the Supreme Court decision, Susan Cary stayed with Sullivan for his death watch. In the morning the guards shaved his head. As Sullivan was led into the execution chamber at 10 a.m., November 30, a reporter noted that he had a "look of absolute mortal fear. He took deep breaths, trying not to cry."

Five hundred miles to the south, I lay awake in bed, an image of Sullivan strapped in the electric chair in my mind. I furiously justified all the steps taken in his appeals, seeking an absolution that was just out of reach. Had we done all we could? I wasn't so sure.

It took five years for Knight's case to grind through the courts after the day that Susan Cary first called me. All the time he was incarcerated in those miserable conditions of Q Wing. Finally, I received an order from Hoeveler's chambers scheduling a hearing for May 7, 1986, but it contained a nasty surprise. Hoeveler was limiting the testimony to one point only: whether Knight's attorneys had effectively represented him during the penalty phase of his trial, when the jury recommended death. Admittedly, this was not a minor point, since it focused precisely on how little the lawyers had done to fight for Knight's life. But it seemed that Judge Eaton's promise that Knight would get a full hearing had disappeared with his retirement.

Now we had to back up the academic arguments in our appeal with real evidence a federal judge would buy. I decided the only way to prove Knight's

lawyers had been negligent was to present before Hoeveler the case for mitigation of punishment that the trial jury should have heard.

But we had a client enshrouded in a schizophrenic fog and evidence
had been lost over the past twelve years. To find the material that should
have been presented to the jury, we needed to go back to the place where it
all began, to the workers' camps and shanty towns near Central Florida's corporate mega-farms. Susan traveled to Knight's childhood neighborhood in Fort
Pierce, a town that was home to many black agricultural workers, where she
tracked down his mother and sisters, former neighbors, police officers, a probation officer and even a priest. Finally, we had some live bodies to put on the
witness stand who could describe the horror of Thomas Knight's early years.

The rest of the story required testimony from his former lawyers. I could
hardly think they would admit their negligence, but the law gave me no
choice but to call them as hostile witnesses. We subpoenaed three of them.
The fourth one, James Matthews, had been the lead attorney at the trial, but
after Thomas's case, Matthews had been disbarred for stealing money from his
clients and had fled Miami in disgrace. We failed to locate him.

As the hearing neared I dug through every police report, hospital record,
trial transcript and witness interview. I also researched Judge Hoeveler. He had
a stellar reputation. In a poll of attorneys by the *American Lawyer* magazine he
was voted the most respected judge in the southeastern United States, with a
98 percent approval rating. But most of these lawyers had never defended a
criminal case in his courtroom. Hoeveler tended to be more forgiving of prosecutors' misconduct than he was of defendants'.[2] He saw the world in black and
white, and I was certain Knight's crimes would greatly disturb him. He probably remembered the sensational news stories about Knight's killing of the

---

2. An example involved DEA informant/Casanova Mario Portell and defendant/ beautician
Miriam Guzman. Portell romanced Guzman into bed and talked her into introducing him
to a drug dealer who later sold Portell cocaine. She testified: "I did it for Mario because he
was desperately pleading for help." A defense investigation turned up twenty other women
lured to bed, then wooed into cocaine deals by Portell. He made more than $250,000 in in-
formant fees and theft from the women's checks and credit cards. Guzman's lawyer, Steve
Kreisberg, moved to dismiss the charges due to outrageous government misconduct. Judge
Hoeveler found Portell's conduct reprehensible, but not enough to shock the conscience of
the court, and he denied the motion.

Ganses and his escape from jail. If he hadn't read the stories at the time, he certainly would have for the hearing: We had submitted copies of the articles to support our argument that Knight could not have received a fair trial in Miami.

I entered the Westlaw system and downloaded everything I could find with Hoeveler's name on it. I scrolled through his opinions, but found nothing of value. Hoeveler had no track record on our issues. I used the legal grapevine, calling lawyers, searching for unpublished opinions or orders, asking for advice on how Hoeveler might react to our claims, for anything that might shed light on his thinking. Again, I came up empty.

On the morning of the hearing, while I was setting up our files in the courtroom, Susan visited Thomas in his holding cell at the federal courthouse. A half-dozen death row guards had driven him down to Miami, leaving Florida State Prison at midnight so that they could complete the 350-mile trip just in time for the hearing. They had not wanted death row's most feared prisoner to be kept overnight in a local jail.

For the past nine hours Thomas's legs had been shackled and his arms handcuffed to a belt at his waist. He hadn't been able to go to the bathroom, wash his face or comb his hair. He looked awful.

Judge Hoeveler summoned us and Calvin Fox, still an assistant attorney general, into his chambers. Before I could complain about Thomas's condition, the judge expressed his fears about Thomas's reputation. "I want to finish this hearing today," he announced. "I am advised that the State Bureau of Prisons wants to have Mr. Knight, or Mr. Muhammad, on his way back as soon as possible. Apparently they are treating his movement very seriously. Any comment?"

"Are you serious?" I exclaimed. "This man's life is at stake and I am not going to be rushed. The length of the hearing should depend on the testimony, not the convenience of the guards."

Hoeveler explained that the U.S. marshals, who usually handle prisoners involved in the federal courts, didn't want to be responsible for Thomas overnight. He then mentioned that Bill Meadows, one of Knight's lawyers, had warned him how uncontrollable Knight was.

"Of course, you know Bill," the judge said. "There is no more honest, pure individual in the legal profession, I guess, than he." Great. Hoeveler liked

Meadows and thought Knight was too dangerous to sit in his courtroom for more than a day.

The judge said Meadows had told him that Knight was the only client he had ever been afraid of. "He had a conference with him one time in a cell and his mood changed so quickly that he became concerned, and he never went in the cell with him after that."

Hoeveler added that Meadows had made other comments about the case, including that Knight had refused to let the attorneys call his mother as a witness. That was a major issue in our petition. "I wanted you to know what was said before we went any further," the judge said.

Meadows had stolen a march on me by lobbying Hoeveler. The thought of demanding Hoeveler's disqualification shot through my mind, but I hesitated. If we bounced him off the case, we could get someone much worse.

I made a quick decision, one I would later regret, and did not seek his removal. Instead I tried my own spin. "Competent criminal lawyers know that mentally ill clients take more time and understanding to defend," I said, adding that Meadows was a vital witness because we had not been able to find the lead attorney. "Mr. Matthews, unfortunately, has disappeared."

Fox smiled. "I contacted his sister in Tallahassee and located him in Puerto Rico." Matthews was in the courthouse and ready to testify.

How the world changes. Thomas's former lawyer, appointed by the court to save him from the chair, now was cooperating with the prosecution to ensure his execution.

Trying to recover, I mentioned Thomas's wretched conditions. "I object to him being shackled during the proceedings," I said.

"That question," the judge responded, "was asked of me by the marshals: Did I object to it? I told them, frankly, I did not, because we were not before a jury. Unfortunately, he does have a rather heavy history."

The judge's sympathy seemed to be in short supply this morning so I tried another approach. I repeated to him the unbearable conditions Susan had described to me. The judge seemed shocked. "He has not been able to go to the bathroom?" he asked.

Fox quickly objected: "Your Honor, I would not accept that as evidentiarily valid."

Susan shot back: "Are we going to have an evidentiary hearing on whether he has gone to the bathroom?"

The judge ignored our squabbling and announced that we would start the hearing in ten minutes.

Susan and I left Hoeveler's chambers and walked down a narrow hallway to the small holding cell, where Knight was huddled on a bench. His feet shackled, his hands secured awkwardly to his sides by the belt, he stared at us intently. He had a short, army-style haircut and was wearing a prison uniform. On his right cheek was a triangular tattoo. On his left inner forearm was another tattoo: El Diablo. A tough-guy image. But at that moment, he seemed subdued. He appeared much smaller than the six-feet-one-inch height listed on his rap sheet. Like most men behind bars, Knight seemed diminished.

Trying to be pleasant, I said hello and explained what we would be doing that day. His sisters and mother were going to testify, but the guards weren't going to allow him any personal visits with them. There was nothing I could do about that.

He listened quietly and seemed to understand what I was saying. I noticed a urine stain on his pants. I asked him how he was getting along with the shackles.

He said he had at last been allowed to go to the bathroom, which he did with difficulty. The guards had given him some food, but he hadn't been able to eat because he couldn't lift his hands high enough. I told him we'd try to get the judge to order his hands released during the first recess.

Then suddenly, without warning, Knight exploded in anger, babbling and screaming things I couldn't understand. He grabbed the steel bars of the holding cell and began banging his forehead into them. For a minute or two he had seemed lucid, then this. His ranting fit what I had heard of him. I jumped back. Though I had had my share of violent, mentally deranged clients—one had tried to strangle me in a holding cell—I was shaken. I tried to continue the conversation, but it became apparent that Knight was responding to some violent inner voice.

As we walked back to the courtroom, I wondered what had triggered Knight's abrupt switch. Meadows, in his *ex parte* talk with Hoeveler, had described just such an episode, yet I knew he had never sought an answer, had never considered the accumulation of anger, rage and humiliation that boiled below the surface. Wasn't it the job of lawyers to find answers?

When considering punishment, the one question jurors want to know is why. Why did he kill? Was there any explanation other than that he was pure evil? Only Knight's attorneys could provide the jurors with an answer.

• • •

The new federal courtrooms in Miami were obviously designed for judges and not for attorneys. The judge sits up high, in the curved portion of a window-less, semi-circular room. The attorneys are cramped together at two small, im-movable tables that don't provide much room for documents. The place is chilly and stark, with bare off-white walls that have only one adornment: the large seal of the United States behind the judge. The lighting is indirect, and the small spectator area is kept in semi-darkness, which adds to the room's brooding atmosphere.

The phalanx of guards led Thomas Knight in, his arms locked to his sides, his ankle chains clanking as he moved. He was seated at the end of our table next to Susan. The guards sat behind us, within arm's reach, ready to grab Thomas if he made the slightest move.

After the judge had taken his seat, I complained about Thomas's condi-tion: "I think it is too much to ask to have his hands shackled to his side. This man has been in this condition since midnight. I think it is also proper during these proceedings that he be able to perhaps take notes or at least be comfort-able." I wanted to make certain that the judge looked upon him as a human being, not as a shackled hulk that could be ignored.

The judge said he would wait until the first recess and consult with the marshals. Obviously, he was buying the marshals' and Meadows's views that Thomas was a dangerous man, and somehow I had to make him see that there was another side to him.

I called Mary Knight first. Dressed in her Sunday best, she walked to the witness stand, clearly awed by the cold formality of the courtroom. I knew I had to start slowly with her because I needed to ask her about an incident in her childhood that she had never shared with even her closest friends.

"Ms. Knight, are you related to Thomas?"

"Yes. He is my brother."

"Where did you and your family live?"

"In Fort Pierce." Her mother, Anna, had fifteen children. Mary and Thomas were products of their mother's union with S. T. Knight. When they were growing up, there were usually five children in the home. Mary was a year older than Thomas, and they were quite close.

"What kind of house did you live in?"

"We had a house that was real old. A broken-down house. The floors were all torn in, and it was unlivable to live in."

"Was the house legally condemned?"

"Yes. We didn't have any water. Most of the time really, we didn't have any food or clothing, and the neighbors really is the ones who helped us."

I led her through a few more questions before I asked: "When you were ten years old, did there occur a very traumatic incident between you and your father?"

"Yes," she said softly.

"What kind of person was your father?"

"He was an alcoholic."

"Was he violent?"

"Yes."

"When you were ten years old, did your father sexually assault you?"

Fox jumped up. "Your Honor, I would object to counsel leading this witness."

"How else," I asked, "do we get to an incident unless you ask about the incident?"

"Well," Judge Hoeveler said, speaking directly to the witness, "did something happen when you were ten with your father?"

"Yes sir."

"What happened?" asked the judge.

"It did. My father, he had intercourse with me."

"When you were ten?" the judge asked.

"Yes sir."

"Now," I asked, "did anything happen during that time while your father was having sex with you? Did anybody come in to save you?"

"Yes. It was my brother Muhammad."

"Tell us what happened."

"My mother had been to work, and I was in the bedroom, and my dad came in and threw me on the bed and he attacked me, and I was screaming and hollering. My brother was at the window, and he seen what was happening. He came in and he tried taking him off of me, shoving him and pushing him away, and he helped protect me from him."

"Was your father arrested because of that?"

"Yes, he was arrested."

Mary was severely injured, and twice her mother had taken her to the doctor because she was hemorrhaging. Afterwards, Mary became a withdrawn, frightened child who rarely spoke.

"Did you and your brother Thomas testify as witnesses against your father?"

"Yes, we did in a court."

S.T. had threatened to kill her if she testified. Still, she did. So did Thomas, who had to endure his father yelling at him in the courtroom. Based on the testimony of his two children, S. T. Knight was sent to prison.

This was testimony that should have been presented eleven years before, during Thomas Knight's original trial. I was confident that, when we fit all the pieces together, it would be perfectly clear what had happened to this nine-year-old boy who had stumbled upon his father raping his sister. We would show how parental abuse, government-sanctioned racism and judicial insensitivity had sent Thomas Knight spiraling down into a life of crime and violence. None of this would have excused his murdering the Ganses, but I was certain that the information would have been powerful mitigating evidence that would have convinced judge and jury that he should not be sentenced to death.

"After this," I asked Mary, "did you notice any change in Thomas?"

"Yes, I did. He was always looking, like staring all the time and his reactions was different. He was always by himself. I feel like it really did something to him inside to see my father, because he wanted my father to be a perfect father, so it really did something to him."

She couldn't have known that she was describing classic symptoms of psychological damage caused by child abuse. Abused children lapse into a disassociative state in which they stare and seem dazed. They force themselves not to cry and to pretend nothing has happened.

Mary went on to describe the forms of torture S. T. had enjoyed inflicting on young Thomas. He frequently took Thomas's clothes off, tied up his hands and feet, then beat him. Sometimes he used iron cords. Sometimes fan belts. Sometimes prickly sticks taken from palmetto trees. Sometimes a heavy police blackjack.

After these beatings, Mary Knight told the court, Thomas wasn't the same.

"He would always jump a lot, as though someone was after him or someone was going to harm him." Meanwhile, the boy was creating a fantasy life about perfect parents. "He always fantasized it. He always would just build this wall around himself as though it was really true, that he had a perfect mother and father with a lot of love."

"Did you and Thomas," I went on, "ever have any problems eating?"

"Yes. When we were younger, many days we didn't have any food. We didn't have any clothes. We had to go to school one day, work the next day to try to get food, and the neighbors would have to sometimes feed us or clothe us, and sometimes Thomas would have to go and try to find food for us, because we didn't have it."

"Prior to your father's sexually assaulting you, had Thomas ever been in any trouble with the law?"

"No. He was never in trouble until my father went to prison."

I asked how Thomas changed after his father was sent away.

"He felt responsible for us as children. He felt like he should take care of us as though we should have—even though I am older than he, he felt as though he should help us with food and stuff."

"Did Thomas ever steal food?"

She nodded. "He would take food from other people so that we could survive because we had to eat. We had no food."

When S. T. Knight returned home after a year in jail, Mary was sent away, to live with an aunt. It was a horrible blow, but the aunt had led her into a religious life. "If it had not been for my aunt raising me and bringing me up in a Christian home, I would not have been the person that I am." She became a traveling gospel singer with church groups. Thomas, who had remained in the home with his father, had a tougher time.

"Ms. Knight, prior to you being contacted by Susan Cary, had anyone on behalf of your brother ever contacted you to be a witness for him or even to discuss with you any of the family's life?"

"No lawyers. No, nobody."

A final question. "Were you ever able to help your brother Thomas?"

"At the time when he came out of Raiford Prison [the state penitentiary], when I went to get him and he stayed with me, I tried to show him how much I loved him."

"Was it too late?"

Fox objected: "It is leading. That is leading."

"I have no further questions," I said. I was certain the judge knew the answer.

In his cross-examination Fox's major theme was that the abuse, if any had occurred, was irrelevant to Knight's crimes. "Was he arrested at any time before your father had sexual relations with you?"

"I am not sure," she replied.

Perhaps, he hinted, there was a plausible explanation for the beatings: S. T. Knight was disciplining his delinquent child.

"Did he ever beat him for stealing food?"

"Yes."

"Who were these other people that he took the food from?"

"He stole from a lady next door, Mrs. Durand, and from stores."

"Do you mean like shoplifting?"

"Like taking food from stores, so we could eat."

"He took food from other black persons?"

"Yes. That is the only community that we had, was black people. We weren't around any white people."

Fox shot his last question: "Do you believe that everyone should have perfect parents?"

"No," Mary Knight volleyed back. "But they should have love."

I walked back to the podium and read from a document that indicated S. T. Knight had assaulted her on June 20, 1960. "Are you aware," I asked her, "that your brother's first arrest occurred one month later, on July 19, 1960?"

"Your Honor," complained Fox, "I would object to Mr. Black testifying into the record as to facts."

"Sustained," said the judge.

I didn't mind. Other witnesses, waiting in the foyer, could describe precisely what happened.

Our next witness was another of Thomas's sisters, Doris Benjamin, who was a year younger than Thomas. She told how their small, two-bedroom house was in such bad shape that it was condemned. There were, she said, "plenty of times" when she and her brothers and sisters could not go to school because they didn't have any clothes. Whenever her father was drunk, he seemed to enjoy beating Thomas.

"How," I asked, "would you describe these beatings?"

"They were terrible," she said. "I remember one where he tied my brother to the bed and he beat him. He tied his hands up. He tied his feet up and tied him at the bed and just whipped him naked, you know."

"How long had he been tied to the bed?"

"Almost five hours."

"Are you aware of the rape of your sister Mary?"

"Yes, I know about Mary. I would like to get that out of my mind, but it stays there. My mother, she had gone one day and Thomas and I, we were at our grandmother's house. We came home. Thomas went inside the house, and he was very upset when he got back out to tell about this. He said I got to go and get mama, and he said that my sister, something had happened to her. He was very, very upset about this. *Very* upset."

"Did your father try to rape any of your other sisters?"

"Yes, my sister Edna, the baby girl. When my mother came home, she told her that my father had tried to rape her, and she was crying. My mother didn't do anything about it."

"Have you heard of any incidences with your sister Kathryn?"

"She had confided in someone else, but she never, you know, really discussed it, you know. I guess it hurt her so bad, you know."

"Your father, did he ever physically attack you?"

"Well, when he got out of prison, I was trying to speak up for my sister. He turned around and struck me on my mouth, and my teeth is still broken."

"Did he ever make Thomas sleep in an unusual place?"

"Yes. Under the bed."

"How often did Thomas have to sleep under the bed?"

"It was so many times, so many times."

"Did any lawyers other than us ever contact you to be a witness on behalf of your brother?"

"No."

In his cross-examination Fox focused on Thomas's brothers and sisters. "How did these other children turn out?"

"Some very confused."

"Have they ever been charged with murder?"

"No."

"You were beaten too, right?"

"That's right."

"Frequently?"

"Yes."

"Have you ever been charged with murder?"

"No."

I jumped on Fox's last question and asked Doris about whether her experiences traumatized her. In an evidentiary hearing the rules are less formal than in a trial, and the two sides often bounce back and forth with the questioning.

"It *did* affect me," Doris replied. "The only way I got over it, I tried to blot it out of my mind, but really it was still there, you know, and it stuck with me, and it stays with me now, you know, and it hurts so bad. It really hurts deep inside."

Fox wouldn't let her off the hook. He emphasized that Doris herself had turned to a life of crime when she was eight and Thomas nine. "You mentioned that you and Muhammad had taken food from a packing house?"

"Right."

"Was that given to you by the packing house?"

"No."

"You *stole* it?"

"We went in and we got it."

"You took it from the packing house without their permission?"

"Yes, it was sitting out. I guess anyone could take it."

"But they did not give you permission to take it?" Fox asked, expressing moral indignation. "Did you and Thomas do this a lot?"

"Yes, very often."

I looked at Thomas for some reaction, but he just sat, slumped in his chair, staring at the wall.

When Fox finished, Hoeveler announced a luncheon recess. Before we adjourned, I told the judge that we had an expert, Dr. Jerry Miller, who had flown down from Washington to testify. Before he did, he wanted to talk to Thomas and I hoped they could get together over the lunch hour. I said I was concerned also about Thomas's ability to eat with the shackles on. He had been sitting quietly all morning, making no fuss, and I thought the restraints were punitive.

The judge held a quick sidebar conference with the marshals, and then announced: "Mr. Black, there will be an adjustment to that situation so Mr. Muhammad can eat his lunch comfortably."

Thomas could eat, but I didn't. I sat in the courtroom, going over the questions for the next witnesses. At the end of the lunch hour, Jerry Miller came back to the courtroom, frowning. His attempt to interview Thomas had been a disaster. The guards had allowed him only eight minutes.

When the hearing resumed, I complained to Judge Hoeveler, who said Miller could come into the courtroom. "Sit him down beside the petitioner and let him talk." He said he would take a short recess so that could be done.

Ask Thomas to talk about his family's darkest secrets while there were guards and lawyers sitting a few feet away? I declined the offer and told the judge we would interview Thomas that evening.

That resolved, we entered into evidence documents that proved what we had been saying about Thomas Knight's early years. On June 20, 1960, S.T. had raped Mary and been arrested. Exactly one week later a distraught Mrs. Knight applied for welfare. She was unemployed, with six children at home, and was six months' pregnant with another. The welfare worker thought she looked frightened, sick and "older than her thirty-eight years."

To the social worker, Mrs. Knight complained that her bills were piling up and, since S.T.'s arrest, she had no money. She couldn't pay Mary's medical bills from the rape. Sanitation workers told her the house needed indoor plumbing or it would be condemned. The children had no clothes for school.

The social worker calculated that Mrs. Knight needed at least $229 a month to keep the family going, but the maximum that the welfare department gave out was $81 a month. The payments would start only the following month. In the meantime, Anna Knight was given $10 for groceries and told to go to the Seventh-Day Adventist Church for clothes.

Three weeks later, on July 19, Thomas Knight was caught stealing three checks from a mailbox. This was the beginning of his life of crime. On September 1 he testified against his father. On September 9 his father was sentenced to five years for the rape of his daughter. That same day Thomas was arrested for stealing a bicycle. Four days later he was caught stealing $30 from a mailbox.

Thomas Knight's life was miserable, and it was going to get worse. Thomas's depressed, frightened mother decided she couldn't deal with this little man whose testimony had put her husband in jail and who was desperately trying to feed the family. What could be done?

At age nine Thomas Knight was shipped off to the state "reform" school.

Another witness, Mary Sandlin, a neighbor of the Knights in Fort Pierce, described the children's treatment as "brutish." Many times neighbors provided food and clothing for the kids. She, too, would have been available to testify eleven years before.

In his cross-examination Fox asked why she hadn't come forward on her own to testify at the trial.

"Nobody called me."

"But you did not come forward on your own?"

"No."

How was this poor, uneducated woman to find out when the sentencing phase of Thomas's trial was, get all the way to Miami and then present herself to Knight's attorneys? It seemed as if the legal system was being turned on its head. Instead of the lawyers finding the witnesses, the witnesses were supposed to find the lawyers.

Next we called Thomas's aunt, Margaret Range, his mother's sister. She testified about how mental illness ran through the family. Her brother had been in and out of a state mental hospital. Her father—Thomas's grandfather—had killed two women and was then committed to a state mental institution. Another aunt had been hospitalized at various times for mental illness. We also had documents showing that one of Thomas's sisters had been committed to a mental institution, where she died at the age of twenty-four, and that two brothers were on psychiatric medication.

We called Howard S. Gilford, the superintendent of the Florida School for Boys at Okeechobee when Thomas was there. He testified that at nine, Thomas was the youngest child ever to enter the school. The average age was fifteen. Only the worst juvenile delinquents in the state were sent to the institution.

Gilford remembered Thomas as a "very frail, undernourished-appearing child. That is one reason that I can remember him so vividly. Thomas was one of the best kids I think I have worked with in the system. He was never a problem as far as discipline was concerned." Thomas had helped Gilford's wife, doing small errands and serving as office messenger. "Academically, he was one of the smartest children we had."

Gilford said no attorney had ever attempted to contact him before Thomas's trial in 1975. What an impressive witness he could have made. A juvenile-prison superintendent—certainly no lover of criminals—testifying what a terrific kid Thomas had been.

Because his behavior was so good, Thomas remained at the school less than a year. He was released on August 4, 1961.

That same day, according to welfare records, Anna Knight was visiting S.T. in the Fort Pierce Labor Camp. In a pathetic letter to prison officials, Anna wrote: "Please let him come home to me and the children because we need him home very bad. . . . My husband did take care me and the children when he was home."

S.T. was soon released. Thomas did ten months for stealing from a mailbox. S.T. did thirteen months for raping his daughter.

We ran quickly through other witnesses who knew the family or the Fort Pierce area. Parolee Ellington, a teacher in the segregated school that Thomas attended, testified that after Thomas returned from the reform school, he had changed, becoming "withdrawn and very quiet."

Charles Frank Matthews talked about being black in Fort Pierce. He had been executive director of the local poverty program for ten years, head of the human relations commission for the city and leader of the NAACP. He testified about how differently black kids were treated by the police and judges in Fort Pierce: He couldn't imagine a nine-year-old white child being sent to Okeechobee.

Our next witness was Father Frank O'Loughlin, a Catholic priest devoted to helping the agricultural workers of Fort Pierce. In his thick Irish brogue he testified that the area where Thomas Knight grew up was right out of the "Harvest of Shame," the famed 1960 Edward R. Murrow documentary about the life of farm workers. Nothing had changed there in a quarter of a century. He also said that the neighborhood where Knight had grown up, no more than a square mile, had produced six men who were now on death row.

Of the people Knight grew up with, the priest testified: "All of the studies characterize these people as not only the poorest people in the nation, but as the most powerless people in the nation, the most marginated and the most hopeless. . . . They are talked about as a Third World USA, as a separate nation."

Fox rose: "Your Honor, if I may object to this speech. Certainly there are social problems in the United States, but I don't think this is the forum here for it."

"The issue here," I responded, "is whether some of this should have been presented at Mr. Knight's penalty phase hearing. Unless the jury had any idea of where this man came from and what he went through, how in the world would they ever understand any of the mitigating circumstances?"

The judge allowed Father O'Loughlin to continue. The priest talked about starvation, about mothers working late in the fields, which meant that the kids had to fend for themselves. "They were without adult supervision from about two-thirty in the afternoon until nine-thirty to ten o'clock at night when their parents came home."

"Father," I asked, "would you have been able to testify about these matters back in 1975 and describe them to a court or to a jury?"

"Certainly, sir."

Our next witness was Everard Bedell, a probation and parole officer. When Thomas was a teenager, Bedell testified, he was constantly in trouble with the law. In 1966, Bedell conducted a pre-sentence investigation on him. He found that the home was a wreck. The kitchen sink didn't work. Dirty dishes were in the bathtub. S.T. was usually drinking and abusive toward his family. The father particularly enjoyed belittling Thomas.

On cross-examination Fox quarreled with Bedell, arguing that miserable homes and families were typical for criminal defendants.

"Bad home environments are not unusual," Bedell replied. "It is just that this particular situation was out of the ordinary. The house was in complete disarray. It was always filthy."

"Didn't other defendants you investigated also have dirty homes?" Fox disputed.

"Oh yes. This one was just not your usual filthy house. The house would reek of . . . urine. There were dogs hanging around the house and inside the house. The bedroom was separated by a sheet, torn and tattered, and you could actually see through the sheet into the bedroom. At one time there were two dogs resting there, and the dogs had gotten sick, and the mess was there on the bed."

Fox asked about S. T. Knight's punishment. He tried to make it appear as if the father had done nothing more than spank a disruptive child.

I asked the probation officer: "If a father tied a child's hands and feet to a bed or a couch and beat him with a fan belt from a washing machine, would you characterize that as a corporal punishment?"

"I would not call it corporal punishment, but an abusive criminal act."

It was time to call Thomas's former attorneys. First up was William Hutchinson. He had authored the incoherent and careless appeals brief. I had thought of using blowups of pages from the brief, but Hoeveler's order limiting the evidence foreclosed that avenue.

I got Hutchinson to acknowledge that the State had an almost ironclad case against Thomas. "So," I asked, "it was not a total shock to the lawyers when the jury found Mr. Knight guilty?"

"I don't think it was a total shock."

He admitted a penalty hearing had been expected. "So," I asked, "how did you prepare to save his life?"

"The specific preparation, I don't know."

"Can you tell us the defense strategy for the penalty phase hearing?"

"No."

"Did you or anyone from the defense talk to his family?"

"I don't know."

Next was James Matthews, the former chief defense counsel who was now cooperating with the prosecution. "Mr. Matthews," I began, "this is the first time you and I have met regarding this case."

"Correct."

To get the judge to understand who this man was, I drew out the details of his disgrace. Some years after Knight's case, he had been disbarred for stealing $34,000, the life savings of one poor client, and taking money from patients of the Veterans Administration.

After this setup I focused on Knight's trial. "What was your defense at the guilt phase?"

"Our defense was to make them prove the case in light of the overwhelming evidence that they presented."

"You mean you had no defense, right?"

"Objection," shouted Fox.

"Sustained," the judge said quickly. "Mr. Black, it's too early to get that sarcastic."

"So you admit," I asked, "that you knew you would most likely lose the guilt phase of the trial?"

"Yes."

"What, then, was your strategy for the penalty phase?"

"To save his life."

"And how did you intend to do that?"

"By presenting what I thought would have been sympathetic, if not legal, mitigating circumstances."

"Aren't lawyers supposed to raise legal defenses, not just beg for sympathy?"

"Perhaps."

"What was that sympathy?"

"His family background history."

"And how did you go about presenting it?"

"I subpoenaed his mother and had her brought to court. I proceeded to preliminarily question her as to matters that I knew factually from other sources. Subsequently, I visited with Thomas when they brought him over to the holding cell, and he prohibited me from calling her as a witness adamantly."

"Did he tell you why?"

"I don't think specifically, but he did not want his family history exposed publicly."

"Did he tell you what he did not want exposed?"

"No. I knew and he knew. He did not want the testimony that she would give, as I understood it from him, public information."

"What was your next step in your vigorous defense of this client?"

"I went and talked to his mother. They allowed her to go in the holding cell and see him, and his refusal was just as adamant, and I, therefore, did not proceed in that fashion."

"You must have reported this conflict to the judge?"

"No, I did not."

"You must have documented it in a memorandum?"

"Of course not. I discussed it, I guess, with my co-counsel and we tried to proceed as best we could with the information that we had."

What else had he done for the penalty phase? Matthews was forgetful. After I showed him the transcript, he conceded, "In fact, I don't think we called a witness at the penalty phase."

"Why not?"

"We didn't have anybody to call."

"Why didn't you call any witnesses?"

"He would not let his mother testify. That was the only person that could factually add anything to the trial, as I saw it."

Matthews's sole "strategy" had been to call Thomas's mother as a witness. He hoped that the jury would feel sympathetic toward her and that that sympathy would somehow save Thomas. Yet, even by his own admission, Matthews had never discussed with Knight the proposed evidence—the abuse of Thomas's childhood.

For my next witness I called someone who could punch holes in Matthews's claim of having had a strategy. Bernard Jacobs, an officer with the New York City Police Department for thirty years, had retired as a commanding officer with the detective squad. He had moved to Florida and started a private detective agency. He had been assigned by the court to assist in Thomas's defense.

Jacobs testified that early on he had learned that Thomas had once been mentally ill. He proposed to Matthews that he conduct an investigation in Fort Pierce, where he could question Thomas's friends and family. He wanted to know where Thomas had gotten psychiatric care and to get his records from the institution. This was all classic background investigation.

When Jacobs called Matthews's office to ask for an advance for the trip, the attorney didn't return the call. Two days later Jacobs called again. Matthews didn't respond.

"How many times did you try to get in contact with him?" I asked.

"Well, I would imagine, out of pure stubbornness, at a minimum of twenty to thirty times."

"Did you ever hear from him again regarding this?"

"No sir, I did not."

"What did you finally do?"

"I finally sent him a letter which stated—as far as my recollection serves me—that if I did not hear from him within a specified number of days, that I would have to resign and withdraw from the case because it was impossible for me to conduct an investigation under his auspices."

"And did you subsequently resign from the case?"

"I never got a response."

When I finished with Jacobs, it was well into the evening, and Judge Hoeveler announced that we would resume the hearing in the morning. I told him that I was still concerned about our expert, Dr. Miller, getting time to talk with Thomas.

"You take it up with the marshals," the judge said, "and I am sure they will advise you so that you can make whatever arrangements you need to make." Then, indicating that the evidentiary hearing was taking longer than he had anticipated, he added, "I do look forward to finishing this in an hour and a half to two hours."

Great

As soon as the judge left the courtroom, we tried to get Jerry Miller together with Thomas. Miller, who had a doctorate in social work, was a specialist in researching mitigating evidence and had testified dozens of times about why defendants' pasts suggested reasons they shouldn't be executed. We started with the marshal in the courtroom. He said he couldn't help us. "Our supervisor has to arrange it," he said. "You have to go down to the second floor."

We went to the second-floor marshal's office. In the anteroom, we pressed a button—and waited. Eventually, a marshal arrived to see what we wanted. We asked to speak to his supervisor. Impossible, he said. We told him what we wanted. Sorry, he said. Thomas was already gone—he had been sent to the Metropolitan Correctional Center.

MCC was a forty-five-minute drive away, in the far southern suburbs. The marshal said we could talk to Thomas there, but from experience I knew that officials at MCC could be uncooperative, and I figured it would be best to call first. We reached a lieutenant who grumbled, "I'm going to have to check into this and call you back."

A half hour later I called again. This time the lieutenant was too busy to talk to me. Susan drove Jerry down to MCC, on the slim hope that he could examine Thomas, and I settled down to study the documents we would submit to the judge the next day. They were our primary evidence to prove that the attorneys' omissions were due to negligence. I had reread them several times in preparation for this hearing.

I began with the news clippings. A kid who lived next door to Thomas at the time of the Gans murders told a reporter that he was "nuts and dumb." Thomas's common-law wife, Beatrice, had left him shortly before the murders. "When Beatrice left," a neighbor told a reporter, "my Lord, something must have snapped inside him." His mother was quoted as saying: "I think there's something wrong with his head." No one on the defense team had bothered to find these witnesses.

As I examined records of Thomas's life from before the Gans case, I was struck with how often I came across mentions of his mother. When he was a child, he apparently viewed her as the one good force in his wretched home life. It was to support his mother that the nine-year-old boy had shoplifted food and stolen from mailboxes. Twice while confined to a mental hospital, he had escaped to go see his mother. And it was after she was turned away from the prison in 1980 that Thomas killed the guard.

I found the staff reports from the mental institution, Northeast Florida State Hospital. "The patient's speech," a staff member wrote, "betrayed his dependency upon his mother. He says that no one is going to separate him from his mother." Why had he been admitted? At the age of nineteen Thomas had been arrested for waving a gun at a woman and then throwing a ht in the courtroom. The judge noted that Thomas seemed to "fly off the handle" at the slightest provocation, that he appeared "homicidal" and "wants to see blood." The judge signed an order of commitment.

Upon admission, Thomas was diagnosed as schizophrenic. Hospital records indicated that Thomas told doctors he sometimes took eight to ten tabs a day of LSD. I had seen psychiatrist reports that Thomas, trying to self-medicate his schizophrenia, had used marijuana, barbiturates and even intravenous heroin. This type of behavior is hardly unusual. Studies show that 29 percent of mentally ill people abuse alcohol or other drugs.

Art Wells, a hospital psychologist, concluded that Thomas was "a latent schizophrenic who could decompensate under environmental stress or under the toxic effects of certain drugs." Another psychologist decided he was suffering from a "psychosis with drug or poison intoxication. In addition, he displayed a personality disorder with strong paranoid features." Three months after he was admitted the hospital released him with a warning that he might become "psychotic again, perhaps being dangerous to others."

Thomas was a grown man—twenty-four years old—when the Ganses were murdered, but he clearly hadn't been able to deal with his past. He had difficulty talking to the psychologists who had been appointed by the Public Defender's Office to examine him shortly after his arrest. When one had gone to see him, Thomas told him he didn't feel like talking. The psychologist said he would come back the next day. Before the man could return, Thomas escaped from jail.

These reports indicated that Thomas had been medically insane for years before he killed the Ganses, but did he meet the standards of the 150-year-old M'Naghten Rule? The rule states that a criminal will be relieved of responsibility for his actions only if, as a result of a disease of the mind, he does not know the nature and quality of his act or he does not know that what he has done is wrong. This archaic formula has been criticized for failing to take into account the complexity of the human mind, but that failure is not surprising considering the test was invented by English judges in the 1840s, when witches were still chained to Bethlehem Hospital's walls. What is surprising is that the M'Naghten Rule is still the norm. Even more surprising, I soon discovered, Thomas's lawyers didn't seem to be aware of the rule.

I waded into the thick court files of Knight's trial. Sitting at the prosecution table were Richard Gerstein, the state attorney, making one of his rare courtroom appearances, and his chief assistant, Ed Carhart.[3] They were backed by a team of prosecutors, investigators, police detectives, FBI agents and paralegals.

Stacked against them was Knight's disorganized band. James Matthews had been appointed by Judge Gene Williams to defend Knight on January 9, 1975—three months before the trial. Matthews then requested the judge appoint a former U.S. attorney in Miami, William Meadows, William Hutchinson and Harold Culmer. It was a close-knit group, or should have been. Matthews had worked for Meadows in the U.S. Attorney's Office, and Hutchinson had interned for Matthews.

At the beginning of a big murder case, the defense team usually enters a flurry of motions, seeking a change of venue, demanding discovery from the prosecution, trying to suppress whatever evidence the police have found. But in Knight's case, there was not one pre-trial motion.

The next document I came across was the transcript of a pre-trial conference, six weeks after Matthews's appointment, in which Matthews asserted that he wasn't ready for trial. The judge gave him an additional six weeks. Another month went by with the defense producing nothing. Finally, four days before the trial, Matthews filed a request that Thomas be examined to see if he was mentally competent to stand trial. The rules required such motions to have been filed months before.

Matthews stated in an affidavit that, after spending more than ten hours with Thomas, he had concluded: "That the defendant appears to have lost

---

3. Carhart was Richard Gerstein's long-time top assistant. An outstanding trial lawyer, Carhart was the odds-on favorite to become state attorney when Gerstein retired in 1977. He was outflanked by Janet Reno, who never prosecuted a case but had powerful political friends who convinced then-governor Reubin Askew to appoint her instead.

contact with reality, and is of no assistance in the preparation of his case for trial. That the defendant and close members of his family have a long history of emotional disturbances, and the defendant himself has been previously found to be incompetent." Attached was the judge's order that had committed Thomas to the mental hospital five years earlier.

Judge Williams appointed two psychiatrists, Dr. Charles Mutter and Dr. Albert Jaslow, to examine Thomas to see if he was competent to stand trial.

On March 31, while the jury panel was sitting in the hallway outside the courtroom, the competency hearing began. The defense team then sprang another surprise on the court: It wanted to pursue an insanity defense.

Prosecutor Ed Carhart called this last-minute tactic "unconscionable." The judge was also upset. The competency hearing was one thing: It was held only to decide whether Thomas was lucid enough to assist his attorneys in his defense. Whether he was insane at the time of the killings was a separate matter. Insanity claims are supposed to be entered long before trial because they require that both the defense and the prosecution find experts to conduct in-depth interviews with the defendant.

Meadows explained that he had just discovered that Thomas had been examined by a psychologist hired by the Public Defender's Office. Only on Friday, the last business day before the trial was to begin, had Meadows learned that Dr. David Rothenberg had tested Knight and found him insane.

The judge recessed until the afternoon so that the defense could find Rothenberg. They brought him to the courtroom, where he testified, without any preparation, that his four sessions with Thomas shortly after the murder had convinced him that Thomas was insane.

Prosecutor Carhart said it was too little too late. How could the defense raise an insanity defense on the first day of the trial?

Pressed by Judge Williams, Meadows admitted that "it may have been that we didn't pursue [an insanity defense] as strongly as we should have. Maybe we were lax in that regard. Nevertheless we did not have any knowledge of Dr. Rothenberg until last Friday. I could not reach Mr. Matthews on the phone the rest of that day because his office was closed. Frankly, I did not make any attempt over the weekend to get in touch with Mr. Rothenberg. That's the way it happened."

Judge Williams said his hands were tied. If he refused to allow the lawyers to raise the insanity defense, such a clear violation of the rules of procedure would be proof of the lawyers' incompetence, and an appellate court would reverse the verdict. "The court is under severe limitations as to what sanctions can be enforced against court-appointed counsel." This was the first of what would be many decisions in which the judge tried to cover up the defense lawyers' blunders.

Finally the competency hearing began. The two psychiatrists, Charles Mutter and Albert Jaslow, had gone over to the Dade County Jail and spent fifty minutes with the defendant. Knight claimed he had never been in a mental institution and insisted that he was perfectly sane. Because the psychiatric interviews were done at the last minute, the defense lawyers had not prepared Knight for them. No one supplied the psychiatrists with Knight's medical records or a social history of his child abuse. Having received no evidence to the contrary, both doctors bought Knight's assertions that he was competent. Worse, they also concluded that he was not insane at the time of the shooting.

I kept going through the transcripts. During jury selection the defense team lost track of the most fundamental fact—how many challenges they had left. It didn't even get through the opening remarks without another major blunder. "The evidence," Meadows told the jury, "will show that early in his life he was in trouble with police authorities, and that he was confined in prisons, in jails. The evidence will show that at the age of fifteen he was imprisoned in the state penitentiary for a considerable period of time." Then he mentioned that Thomas had escaped from jail. Had the prosecution announced this, it would have been grounds for a mistrial. Prosecutors are not allowed to mention a defendant's previous crimes, out of concern that jurors may conclude that a person who has committed other crimes would be more likely to be guilty of the present charge. What's more, a judge would never have permitted a prosecutor to talk about a jail escape—another clear suggestion to jurors.

The State's case began with a series of eyewitnesses who saw Thomas in the Ganses' Mercedes. On cross-examination the defense attorneys fumbled

around, uncertain what questions to ask. It was clear to me they weren't prepared.

When court wasn't in session both the prosecution and the defense were
scrambling to prepare for an insanity defense. Each night, after an exhausting
day in court, Thomas was put through neurological and psychological exams.
A paranoid, surly inmate was questioned by experts he saw as enemies, in a
solitary confinement cell, during his murder trial.

The first days of the trial moved so slowly that the judge complained about
the defense's dawdling. Prosecutor Carhart agreed: "Judge, it is becoming very
apparent to me something very strange is going on. This is like a slow-motion
movie. It takes five minutes to ask a question. Then we reask the same question. It is getting ridiculous."

Carhart suggested this was a stall tactic, but I was certain it was not: The
defense simply didn't know what it was doing. It was drifting through the trial,
filling up time.

In one such instance Meadows waved some papers and claimed he had
discovered a report from a Fort Pierce doctor who considered Thomas insane. The attorney complained to the judge that he hadn't been able to talk
to the doctor. Carhart, the prosecutor, responded that he had tried to help
out by giving Meadows the phone number for the area's public defender; he
wanted to know if Meadows had called. "That is not important," Meadows
said

At 10 p.m. Susan Cary called from the Metropolitan Correctional Center to
report on our attempt to get Jerry Miller in to see Knight. The guards had "flat
out refused."

I phoned the duty marshal and demanded that he contact the judge. A few
moments later the marshal called back and said he had been unable to locate
the judge. He promised that Thomas would be back at the courthouse at 7:45
a.m.; that was the best he could do.

I called Susan back and gave her the news.

I went back to the transcripts. During one interchange with the judge,
Matthews admitted that he had taken only four depositions, though the State

had given him a list of sixty witnesses. All four witnesses had been deposed after the trial began.

In a bizarre switch Hutchinson claimed Knight had been hiding in the Mercedes trunk when the Ganses were murdered. Hutchinson's reasoning was that Knight had been wearing a black shirt, and several witnesses had said the kidnapper's shirt was brown. He explained the drops of blood on Knight's clothing by saying "the blood skeeted back" into the trunk.

"I think," Hutchinson told the judge, "that the jury ought to hear ten more people were in the trunk. This may be part of a kidnapping gang." So at this stage of the trial, Matthews was looking for reasonable doubt, Meadows was admitting that Knight committed the murders but was insane, and Hutchinson was claiming it was a case of misidentification.

Thomas apparently hadn't liked his attorneys' performances any more than I did, for he kept complaining about their behavior. The judge told him to be quiet, that complaints should come from his lawyers. "You have four of them," Judge Williams reminded him.

At this point Gerstein popped up with a vigorous defense of his opponents: "As Your Honor knows and as I know from more than twenty years' experience, this case is being as vigorously defended and as articulately defended as any case I have. The fact is there are no lawyers anywhere who could do a better job for him than is being done here." The judge quickly interjected that he, too, thought the attorneys were doing an excellent job.

Thomas was not mollified. In one of his lucid moments he told the judge, "I only had two public defenders," referring to his previous lawyers, "but what these two public defenders did for me, legal work, it surpassed the work of these four attorneys. I am charged with, you know, capital charges. I am not charged with minor offenses. If I lose, there is no comeback. So since this is the case, I feel that I am not to fight my best fight later, but my best fight is to be fought now, because I might not get a chance later on. So that is why I am asking for competent counsel to assist me." The judge quickly denied his request.

I made a note of Thomas's comments. Many times the State complains that appellate attorneys in death cases raise the issue of incompetency of counsel because it's a quick, cheap shot, but it was clear from the transcript that the quality of lawyering in Thomas's case had been an issue from the be ginning, raised by the defendant himself, at least during those moments when his mind was not "somewhere else."

But what did that prove? I had submitted all the trial transcripts as exhibits, and our papers highlighted the key points for Judge Hoeveler to read. Would he think that if Thomas was making lucid criticisms of his attorneys, that he was clearheaded and sane?

I had to locate whatever evidence I could to rebut Matthews's last-minute claim of trial strategy. I soon found them in the defense portion of the trial. The main witness was Dr. David Rothenberg, who had seen Thomas four times shortly after his arrest. Rothenberg was the one expert who had concluded that Thomas was insane. It was the belated discovery of his opinion that had led the defense to make a last-minute request for an insanity plea.

Rothenberg had tape-recorded his lengthy interviews with Thomas. In court, Meadows announced that he was going to play them. Thomas immediately objected. He said he hadn't heard the tapes. Neither, as it turned out, had his lawyers. They were wandering into dangerous territory—playing the defendant's voice to the jury without a clue as to what the tapes contained.

The tapes began innocently enough, and they contained material that might have been useful if it had been presented within the context of Thomas's childhood:

"You want to hear about my whole life? My whole life has been hell, man, you know. I'm not lying, you know. . . . When I was nine years old, these bastards, man, instead of sitting me down, talking to me, you know, like, hey, I'm nine, you know. Now, I'm a kid, you know. . . . I was playing hooky from school, you know. I shoplift, you know, and I fight, you know, and things like this and, you know what they do to me? . . . They throwed me in a fucking boys' school, man, for doing this. Ninth grade. Ninth. When I'm in the ninth grade ninth grade. I was fourteen. Yeah, I was fourteen. They sent me to Raiford. Talk about shit, man. You just don't know about my life. I had a hell of a fucking life."

If a foundation had been given for this, if Matthews had told the jury about the horrors Thomas had been subjected to, this could have been a sympathetic statement. Matthews's job was to link Thomas's behavior to a mental disorder, but without the background, the tapes were a disaster.

In one spot he admitted he had been before a judge "a lot of times." In one instance he said, "I took a pistol and stuck it in front of a girl's face. . . . We was at this bar, . . . I was doing a lot of acid, you know, LSD."

The next part of the tape caught my attention. Rothenberg was giving Thomas a word-association test. When he mentioned the word "father," there were thirty seconds of silence. When Rothenberg said "boyfriend," again there was thirty seconds without a response. The same for "homosexuality" and "penis."

This wouldn't have meant much to the jurors because they were given no explanations for the silence, but to me they were hints. Had Thomas been sexually abused? Is that why he refused to talk about his past? His sisters had been victims of incest, so why not Thomas as well? The truth was trying to come out. The psychologist had seen a glimpse of it. Even without knowing anything of Thomas's background, Rothenberg had hit on the right diagnosis: Thomas was mentally ill, with the roots of his schizophrenia going back to the age of nine. It was startling that he picked nine because he didn't know that was Thomas's age when his sister had been raped and he had been sent to reform school.

If Rothenberg had had Thomas's history, he could have made a powerful witness. Without it, he was an easy mark. Prosecutor Carhart kept demanding proof that Thomas had gone insane at the age of nine. Rothenberg replied that he couldn't really explain it.

The next witness at the trial might also have been a good one. Art Wells had been the chief psychologist at the mental hospital where Thomas had spent three months. Wells knew nothing about Thomas's childhood, but he too had glimpsed his problems. Wells had stated that a "stressful situation might provoke a psychotic reaction in this patient. Some schizophrenics are extremely violent and can go into a rage in which there is absolutely no rational control or rational perception."

Wells noted that Thomas's "deep underlying paranoid fantasies seem to represent a fear that his father will kill him because of the patient's love for his mother, and in a psychotic state this patient could kill a male in delusional defense from the murderous onslaught of the father represented by the male." What a powerful statement that could have been if the jury had known the full story of Thomas's past.

All of this could have been put together by a competent defense team into a coherent portrait of a diseased mind.

• • •

The next witness had been Pat Duval, a police lieutenant from Fort Pierce. Carhart objected as soon as his name was called because the defense lawyers hadn't put his name on the witness list. The judge sent the jury out of the courtroom and asked what Duval would testify to.

Duval stated that he knew about the Knight family. Once or twice a month he would be called to the Knight house to control the drunken father. He had heard stories about S. T. Knight being arrested for incest when Thomas was a small boy. He thought S.T. was an abusive drunk. Later, when Thomas grew up, the lieutenant testified, he had encountered him often: "As he grew older, he became more irrational, up until the time that he was sent to the mental institution."

Carhart objected: "The testimony about Mr. Knight's father is clearly irrelevant to the issues in this trial, since we have not accused him of anything."

Duval didn't know the full story, but his statement might have been important. A police officer was willing to testify for the defense in a death case, with proof of the defendant's insanity. The jury never got to hear him. Duval was dismissed by the judge.

Duval was Matthews's last attempt at an insanity defense. The prosecution came back with rebuttal witnesses, all of them experts willing to attest that Thomas was sane.

Carhart got right to the heart of the matter with Dr. Charles Mutter: "Doctor, could one be schizophrenic and still know the difference between right and wrong?"

"Yes sir."

That was the basic point the prosecution needed to make to refute Rothenberg.

Then the defense took over. Instead of a hammering cross-examination, with the attorney making statements and the witness forced to reply with a simple yes, Matthews asked vague, open-ended questions that allowed the hostile witness to lecture to the jury.

When Mutter said that there were different kinds of schizophrenia, Matthews asked: "And will you distinguish for us, if you will, the differences?"

The psychiatrist talked about that for a while, then said he had concluded that Thomas had only a "sociopathic personality disorder." If Matthews had consulted a medical dictionary, he would have quickly danced away from that diagnosis. Sociopaths cannot, by definition, be insane because they are not suffering from a recognized mental disease. Instead, Matthews asked: "Will you tell us specifically what you mean by that?"

Mutter obliged: "A sociopathic personality disorder is characterized by an individual who conducts himself in an anti-social way under certain circumstances, does not benefit from previous experience, does not have any emotional ties for any prolonged period of time, is usually considered to be a con artist. He has an ability to rationalize his behavior so that when he is caught many times he can show a great deal of remorse and cause individuals to feel sorry for him and to give him another chance, but when he's off the hook, he's off and running again. He has a very poor superego or sense of conscience. In other words, he knows right from wrong, but he doesn't care."

Matthews waded in deeper: "Are there any stages of progression from that?"

Instead of directing the witness to helpful admissions, Matthews was letting the psychiatrist ramble. Mutter's whole analysis of Thomas was completely wrong, and Matthews never attacked it.

The prosecution then called another psychiatrist, Arthur T. Stillman, who thought Thomas was psychiatrically disturbed but legally sane.

Matthews violated cross-examination rule no. 1: Don't ask a question unless you know the answer or don't care what the answer is. "Would you explain for us, please," he asked, "what you have in mind?"

"In this state," the psychiatrist announced, "we follow the M'Naghten Rule."

"M'Naghten Rule?" Matthews repeated, apparently unaware of Florida law.

When the psychiatrist mentioned that prisoners sometimes fake bizarre conduct, Matthews should have asked that the statement be stricken as prejudicial. Instead, he invited the doctor to explain what he meant.

Stillman's testimony nonetheless presented an opportunity to bring out

some important points. He had concluded that Thomas was psychotic, "with
what I diagnose as a paranoid condition . . . but legally speaking, he is not insane." A lot of questions could have spun off that statement if Matthews had
done his homework. All he had to do was consult a pamphlet called the *Di-
agnostic and Statistical Manual of Mental Disorders—DSM-II* [4] The DSM is
the bible for psychiatrists. It catalogues three hundred mental conditions and
their symptoms. When a psychiatrist testified that Thomas was psychotic but
still knew right from wrong, Matthews had merely to open up *DSM-II* and use
the definition of psychosis to impeach the testimony.

Psychosis is the most severe mental illness known to man. Patients "lose the
capacity to meet the everyday demands of life." They have a "serious distortion
in their capacity to recognize reality." Their "capacity to respond appropriately is
grossly impaired." They experience hallucinations and delusions. If the doctor
denied that any of these conditions applied to Knight, all Matthews had to do
was open the book and read him the definition. Better yet, he could have had the
definitions blown up for a large exhibit so that the jury could read along. The
doctor would have had to admit that the definition applied to Knight. For a couple of dollars, Matthews could have seriously hurt these experts

Two defense witnesses might have helped Knight's case, but they had nothing
to go on. Stanford Jacobson, a psychiatrist, testified: "I have no definite evidence of any psychotic behavior in the past."

Norman Reichenberg, a psychologist, was fascinated by a stick-figure drawing that Thomas had done for him: "If everything else is consistent, you can
interpret it in terms of anger toward the father I would look for other material
for disturbances involving the father figure."

Reichenberg didn't know anything about Thomas's background, but once
again, he was close to understanding Knight's pathology. He was read the quo-

---

4. *DSM-II* was the edition current in 1974. Since then the manual has been revised several times. Any competent lawyer, faced with a psychiatric opinion, would have a heavily
dog-eared and highlighted volume.

tation from the 1971 hospital report about Thomas's paranoid fantasies involving his father and said, "I would agree that this served as an underlying basis for much of his difficulty with authority figures." Again, the truth was trying to break out.

Each of the prosecution experts theorized that Knight was legally sane because he had been able to plan the kidnapping, drive a car and shoot a gun. The defense let this theory go unchallenged, even though it is a fallacy to think that the mentally ill can't plan carefully. The insanity is not in the planning but in the reasoning behind it.

As the trial neared its end, Meadows asked the judge for the jury instructions for an insanity defense. To Meadows's meek question, the judge replied: "It is the standard instruction that is in the book." The judge was referring to the Florida Standard Jury Instructions, used in every case.

"I don't have those, judge," Meadows admitted. "I'm sorry to say, I'm just not that well equipped."

Exhausted and angry, I read the defense's final arguments. The worst was Hutchinson's. He ignored the insanity plea and claimed Thomas was innocent. He stated "only three drops of blood" were found on Thomas's shirt. What about being caught with the $50,000? Maybe he had just happened across it, lying in the field. "If you came across $50,000, I think you would pick it up, too." Why would $50,000 in cash be lying in an open field near two dead people? Why would someone pick it up and then go hide in a hole in a field? Hutchinson didn't tell the jury.

Prosecutor Carhart concluded with an ironic twist. "You have seen his four attorneys. They have obviously left no effort undone to protect every single one of his rights, but all that is at an end now. I think that Mr. Hutchinson, Mr. Matthews, Mr. Meadows, Mr. Culmer have worked very hard and done a fine job in this case, but they have said some things that I think insult your intelligence and insult mine. And I'll tell you why they've done them. They have said them because they are buried by a mountain of evidence against this defendant just as this defendant buried himself in that pile of grass and dirt to try to evade detection that day." Carhart turned the lawyers' incompetence into a powerful weapon to convict Thomas.

The verdict came in on a Saturday after only an hour of deliberation: Guilty of two counts of first-degree murder. The judge announced that the jury could take Sunday off, then return on Monday to decide the sentence. Matthews was worried about the timing: "What time, judge? We would like to start late for the simple reason that our witnesses are going to be coming from Fort Pierce. And as opposed to having them come spend Sunday night, we would like to start at eleven-thirty."

In other words, with their client facing a death sentence in forty-eight hours, Matthews planned to take Sunday off. He wasn't even planning to prepare Anna Knight, Thomas's mother, who was supposedly going to be his only witness on Monday. In fact, as he admitted on the witness stand, he subpoenaed her to court, without a prior interview, intending to talk to her at the courthouse for the first time.

I turned to the penalty hearing. The transcript was a slender document. The defense team had done no work to prepare for this phase, which they must have been certain was going to come. They should have started long before the trial.

I skimmed the final arguments. I could envision the defense lawyer standing to speak the last words on behalf of a man facing death—one bold, defiant moment, throwing aside caution, speaking from the heart, in a supreme effort to rescue his desperate client against all the odds. Clarence Darrow brilliantly argued for three days to save Leopold and Loeb from hanging. Matthews argued for one and a third pages of transcript. I read his "speech" aloud. It took me one minute, forty five seconds. To save a man's life.

The jury deliberated fifty minutes before coming back with its verdict: death.

By the time I had finished with the files, a pale light was gathering in the east. I was back at the courthouse at 7:45 a.m.—the time the marshals had assured us that Thomas would be available for Jerry Miller. We were told that Thomas was back in the building, but we still couldn't talk to him. After heated discussions Jerry was allowed to talk to him in a holding cell for thirty minutes. He came back, saying the time hadn't been nearly enough.

As soon as the hearing began I complained to Judge Hoeveler: "I could understand people have all kinds of concerns, but I have a man who is entitled to have a hearing. We are entitled to have witnesses interview him, but under these circumstances, it is impossible to operate as counsel when you cannot talk to your client." I told him Dr. Miller was not ready to testify.

The judge frowned. He was obviously not pleased that the hearing was being further delayed. I called Jerry to the stand to explain what had happened. He told the judge about the thirty-minute session that morning and the eight minutes he had seen Thomas the previous day during lunch. "It is not sufficient time to do a thorough examination," he stated. "It should be a number of hours."

Hoeveler asked why we hadn't flown Dr. Miller down long before the hearing to interview Thomas. We explained it was a question of money. While Dr. Miller was interested more in justice than money and had agreed to be a volunteer, I couldn't ask him to do more than one trip. We were operating without a budget, and I was paying all the expenses.

The judge offered Jerry "a few extra minutes."

"I don't really think that 'a few extra minutes' will be helpful," Jerry responded. "I really should have hours. I don't think I would gather that much more in fifteen minutes than I already have."

"Then I think," the judge stated, "Mr. Black, under the circumstances, we probably ought to proceed."

"If there is no time available now, let's adjourn until there is," I replied. "We move for a continuance. Why should we rush to execute this man? I don't understand the rush."

"Well," said the judge, "I don't either, frankly, but we have the pressures. You know better than I."

This was an astonishing bit of honesty on his part, acknowledging all the politicians who were demanding quicker responses on appeals so they could execute people faster.

"If they want to take a human life," I said, "at least they must let us argue our case first. That was the mistake the first time around."

"You do not have to argue the point too much. I understand what you are saying. I am sympathetic to what you are saying. On the other hand, there comes a time when we simply have to conclude. I will give you an hour. If you think the doctor can do something with an hour, we will take an hour."

I sensed that the judge had gone as far as he was going to, and Jerry Miller, a veteran of many courtroom negotiations, sensed it, too. He hesitated briefly, then said, "That would be helpful, Your Honor."

We arranged for Jerry to talk to Thomas during a recess. With that, Fox announced suddenly that he was recalling Matthews to the witness stand. I was startled. I had assumed that the attorney had gone back to Puerto Rico. But here he was. I wondered what Fox and Matthews had cooked up.

Fox began by showing Matthews a stack of subpoenas that the defense had issued for witnesses. They had sought records from Raiford Prison and the mental hospital in Northeast Florida, and they had subpoenaed a bunch of witnesses who never appeared at the trial.

I had seen copies of these subpoenas—most of them had been sent out in the middle of the trial. It was a blizzard of paperwork issued too late and had produced nothing.

"I request," I told the judge, "that we get certified copies of the return of service of these subpoenas. Just having subpoenas does not mean anything, unless they were served."

Fox offered to have Matthews explain the documents from the witness stand, but he began by returning to the issue of Thomas not wanting his mother to testify.

Matthews repeated that he had tried to persuade Thomas, and that the defendant had been adamant. "If I attempted to do that, you know, he would make it unbearable, so to speak, disruptive. It was just something that he had not been able to face in his adult life."

Of course, these outbursts might have proved a point, and in any case, they would have been better than what they actually did.

"Was there any way during this proceeding in 1975 that you felt you could convince the defendant otherwise?" Fox asked.

"Absolutely not."

Matthews then went on for quite a while about how carefully he had thought out his actions at the trial. He was now coming up with explanations about how the defense team had done everything based on a concerted trial strategy. "Trial strategy" were two magic words that could be used to justify just about anything. Appellate judges rarely questioned attorneys' trial strategy, meaning that attorneys' incompetency, no matter how egregious, was conscious decisions not to do something, rather than negligence. Of course, the trial transcript proved they had never prepared for the trial and had no effective strategy. Because I read the transcript several times, I had the ammunition to destroy Matthews's attempt at self-justification.

"Mr. Matthews," I asked, "when did you begin preparing this case for trial?"

"Whatever day I was appointed."

"You were appointed on January 9, 1975, were you not?"

"If the record so reflects. I don't recall the date."

"That is when you began preparing for trial?"

"Yes."

"You're sure about that?"

"Yes."

"Why didn't you file your witness list until April 1, the second day of the trial?"

"I perhaps did not know who they were going to be. I don't recall specifically."

"Why wasn't the insanity defense filed prior to April 1?"

"I think my motion will reflect that we did not have knowledge that there would be an insanity defense until March 31, I am not sure."

"Why?"

"I have no idea."

I went to the defense table and picked up a transcript of the pre-trial hearing of February 24, 1975, six weeks after he had been appointed to the case. I asked Matthews if he recalled confessing to the judge he had done nothing yet in Thomas's defense.

"Not that I recall."

"Did you tell the court that you had not even seen the State's evidence as of February 24, 1975?"

"Absolutely not."

"Did you tell the court as of that date, despite the fact you had obtained a witness list from the State of sixty-five witnesses, you had not yet taken a single deposition from any of them?"

"That is possible," he said. "I don't have any recollection of it."

Fox challenged the document, trying to give Matthews a moment to collect himself.

To make sure the judge understood the point, I read from the transcript what Matthews had said at the February hearing: " 'We have a list of some sixty-five witnesses, and we have not deposed any of them at this time. Once we receive copies of statements, if they are material, we do intend to depose them.' " I looked back at Matthews. "Do you remember making those statements?"

"No, I don't remember, but I don't deny making it."

"Do you remember Mr. Carhart saying that the statements have been available at least two weeks before that, when they got a call from Mr. Jacobs, your investigator?"

"Excuse me?" Matthews asked.

Fox jumped in with an objection, giving Matthews another chance to compose himself. It was no small question that I had asked Matthews. The prosecutor is required to release statements of all the witnesses in a case. These statements are the most important background information a defense attorney can have. That the statements had been available for two weeks and Matthews had not picked them up was the most egregious example of neglect. I repeated my question to Matthews.

"I don't recall it," he answered, "but if Mr. Carhart said that, he was in error because no Mr. Jacobs ever has done any investigation for us in this case."

Rule no. 1 of trial practice is never show surprise, but this was so far out of the blue I couldn't stop my jaw from dropping. Jacobs had given testimony about Matthews's indifference, and eleven years earlier Carhart had mentioned in an on-the-record hearing about talking to Mr. Jacobs, the team's investigator.

"So," I said, "when Mr. Carhart said he got a call from your investigator, Mr. Jacobs, he was incorrect?"

"He was totally incorrect."

Why would the prosecutor have told a lie in court a decade before? Matthews was sinking under the weight of his own story. I hoped the judge was paying attention.

Again, Fox rushed in to rescue his witness: "Your Honor, I object. The witness said he did not recall." The assistant attorney general for the State of

Florida was trying to rescue James Matthews, Thomas's former attorney, from a morass in which he had called a State prosecutor a liar.

I forged ahead: "Do you remember Mr. Carhart saying that he had been holding copies of the statements since the eighteenth waiting for some pleading from you?"

"No, I don't."

I let him read the transcript, but his memory didn't improve. I turned to the documents he requested in the blizzard of subpoenas. I got him to admit that he couldn't recall a single document that all these subpoenas had produced.

I noted that Dr. Wells from the state mental hospital had been subpoenaed on April 11 — in the middle of the trial. He had been asked to bring Thomas's records with him. I asked Matthews if he had ever shown these records to any of the psychiatrists who examined Thomas. Matthews said he wasn't sure.

"Well, was there any strategy in keeping this information from the experts?"

"No."

Why hadn't he mentioned the problems with Thomas's home life to the experts? "Dr. Mutter, for example, in his report finds that there was a good family relationship. Why didn't you give Dr. Mutter the information you had?"

"I don't have any specific recollection."

"Was there any trial strategy on your behalf to keep this information from these doctors?"

"No."

I quoted from the testimony of Mutter: "I asked him about his father, and at that time he did speak for a number of minutes describing his relationship with his father, which he said was a very good one."

I looked at Matthews: "Did your investigation show that Mr. Knight had a very good relationship with his father?"

"Just to the contrary."

"Why didn't you confront Dr. Mutter with the truth?"

"Our attempt," Matthews replied, "was to not discredit medically, but to show bias on his part because of what he said was some threat that Thomas had made to him on an occasion of an interview."

This was like having the winning lottery ticket and not cashing it in. Instead of selecting a win, his "strategy" was to prove Knight was so dangerous that even a forensic psychiatrist who spends every day in maximum security jails was terrified of him.

I hesitated a moment. To say "our attempt was to not discredit medically" was to imply a trial strategy, but it made no sense, If the State puts an expert on the stand, it's up to the defense to discredit his opinion.

"So you thought Dr. Mutter's misconception of Knight's relationship with his father was not an important point?"

"I did not at that time."

I reminded Matthews of his previous testimony admitting that he thought it was important, but that Thomas hadn't wanted it brought out. "Didn't Dr. Mutter testify that one reason he found Mr. Knight competent was because while he was suspicious and hostile, this warm and close relationship with his father showed that he was competent?"

"I don't recall that as being the exact wording in the report."

I read Mutter's description of them speaking about his father "in a very tender manner," and of how that had made Mutter conclude that he was sane.

"Yes, but . . . there were many factors."

"Well, Dr. Mutter says here that if his affect was inappropriate—I am talking about his father—he would have used that as a basis for finding him incompetent, but since it was a warm and tender relationship, this showed a proper affect."

"My recollection is that he said that would have been a factor, not the basis."

"But you knew that Mr. Knight did not have a warm and tender relationship with his father."

Matthews asked to see the transcript I was reading from. I handed him the document. After he had read it I asked, "If what you say is true, you had facts in your possession to prove that the doctor's conclusion on that point was factually incorrect?"

"Correct."

"Why didn't you use it?"

"I really have no recollection."

Matthews sought to escape in a lack of memory. He knew there was no strategy for not discrediting the psychiatric opinions. A false history results in a false diagnosis.

I asked Matthews about S. T. Knight's incest and his beatings of Thomas. "Did you find that this was consistent with a warm and tender relationship?"

"Not personally, but some disciplinarians who love their kids do this."

"You demonstrate love by tying him to a couch and beating him for five hours?" I asked.

"For what?" He seemed surprised.

"Five hours."

"I didn't know about the five hours."

"Did you know how the father cared for and fed the children?"

"Not very well. I understand that he drank a lot and abused not only the children, but the mother."

"What evidence did you have of the warm and tender relationship then, if any?"

Fox objected: "Your Honor, I think Mr. Black is assuming a fact not in evidence: a warm and tender relationship. I don't think anybody said there was a warm and tender relationship."

"Except," the judge noted, "the psychiatrist."

I shifted to a new subject. "Was there any attempt to locate any other witnesses?"

Matthews mentioned the Fort Pierce police officer, Pat Duval, whose testimony had been rejected by the judge. I asked why Duval hadn't been called back for the penalty phase.

"It had been ruled on, and it would have been the same hearsay."

This is not true. The rules of admissibility are much looser in the penalty phase. "Did you feel," I asked, "that the same rules of evidence applied at the penalty phase as did at the guilt phase?"

"Of course not."

"Then why didn't you try to recall Lieutenant Duval?"

"I did not think that this testimony would have been effective or sympathetic."

This was another disingenuous response. The use of the word "effective" meant Matthews was citing "trial strategy" once again. But what strategy? If Lieutenant Duval's testimony would not have been effective or sympathetic during the penalty phase, then why would it have been effective during the guilt phase?

"Well, can I ask you if it was not going to be effective or sympathetic, why did you try to call him at the trial?"

"Because I could not call his mother, and I was desperate."

"I take it," I responded, "you lost your desperation by the penalty phase."

"No," he replied. "I just accepted the ruling and went ahead and concentrated my time and energies on something else."

"Please advise us which important matters you concentrated on."

"Well, I probably went to the office and sat up until ten or twelve o'clock at night going over doctors' testimony trying to find any little items of hope that had been given by the two who were most sure about his sanity."

"Was any of that presented in the penalty phase?" I asked.

"No."

I relinquished the floor to Fox, who tried to rehabilitate his witness: "Did Mr. Knight prohibit you from calling any of these family members?"

"We did not discuss it, as I recall. Because of the very adamancy about his mother testifying about their family history, I just knew that was out. He would not stand for it, so we did not waste any energy on it."

"How would you characterize Knight's participation in his defense?"

"Some days he was alert and participating by making suggestions and asking questions. On other days he was verbally disruptive and non-caring, and other days he seemed not to even be in the courtroom."

Not even in the courtroom! Matthews went on to say that in his conversations with Knight, his client at times talked about "something totally irrelevant."

I rose: "Mr. Matthews, Knight wasn't 'there' because he lived in a schizophrenic fog."

"I really don't know, but I think his mind was going, coming and the stress of the trial perhaps had something to do with it."

The stress of the trial. Close but not quite up to admitting that Thomas was not competent. I took a risk. I asked, "Do you think that at times he was not competent in the courtroom?"

"No, I don't think that." Matthews saw where I was going. If he admitted that Thomas was incompetent, how could he agree with his incompetent client's demand that his mother not take the stand?

I tried a little sarcasm to cover up my disappointment: "Well, the days that he was not in the courtroom, as you phrased it, what do you think he was doing?"

"Do you really want my answer?"

"Yes."

"Just psyching himself to eliminate from his mind—because of the many conversations that we had, I don't think he ever recalled or remembered even committing—the acts that he was charged with."

"Do you think there were days that he sat there and did not know what was going on?"

"No."

I walked back to our desk and retrieved an affidavit he had signed shortly before the trial began.

"Didn't you file an affidavit saying, in your opinion, he had lost contact with reality?"

"Yes."

Then why had he obeyed this person who had "lost contact with reality" when it came time to put his mother on the stand?

"I don't know whether at that time I had that opinion. If you recall, that affidavit was made several days prior to that."

"So, in 'several days,' during the stress of a murder trial, Thomas had gone from a man who had lost contact with reality to an astute member of the trial team able to direct strategy?"

"That is asking for a legal conclusion. I cannot assist you," Matthews replied.

I glanced at the judge, but it was hard to read Hoeveler's face.

I decided to close by returning again to Knight's father. Why hadn't Matthews bombarded the psychiatrists with questions when they testified that Thomas told them he had a "warm and tender relationship" with his father? Why had Matthews given the jury no evidence of the father's cruelty? The attorney fidgeted in his seat as I persisted with this line. I asked question after question.

Finally, his anger boiled over. "What you have known as a child about a warm and tender relationship is probably quite different from what Thomas and I have known. My father was a very strict disciplinarian, and at the time that he was beating me, I could hate his guts, but after that passed, yes, I had a warm feeling for him because he was my father."

There was an embarrassed silence in the courtroom. It flashed through my mind that Matthews had superimposed his own denial mechanism on his psychotic client. But this wasn't a therapy session for Matthews. The question was what he had failed to do, not why. All I could prove was that Matthews had failed to raise the subject of Thomas's brutal childhood as a reason to save his life.

Our next witness was William Meadows. I went right to Knight's eruption that he had described to Hoeveler immediately before the hearing.

"I do not remember specifics," he responded, "of what we were talking about, but obviously I am pretty clear that we were talking about his personal life and his likes and dislikes, and also talking about the case itself. We were getting along very fine, and all of a sudden he became belligerent. I cannot remember anything that he said, but he was saying things that made no sense to me; kind of like bouncing thoughts off the wall, and I became afraid." Meadows never tried to talk to Thomas again.

"So this was a disturbing interview, to say the least?"

"That latter part of it was disturbing to me, and it also indicated to me that—I am a layman, and I speak strictly as a layman—but certainly it struck me that this was a symptom of schizophrenia."

"Do you think that it would have been worthwhile to put on the fact that Thomas had been beaten?"

"Well, when you say worthwhile, I am not sure what to say to that." He said he hadn't known about the abuse at the time. "But I certainly—it should have been put on. I would have put it on."

Meadows's admission demolished Matthews's claim that he knew about Thomas's past but declined to use it at the client's direction.

Our next witness was Harold C. Culmer, Thomas's fourth defense attorney. I asked him why the defense team hadn't prepared for the penalty phase. Culmer said the death penalty was "utmost in our minds," but he said he couldn't recall why there had been no preparation. When I pressed him, he admitted that "the death penalty phase was something that was essentially put on the shelf unless and until there was a guilty verdict."

• • •

Next I called the defense team's chief witness, David Rothenberg, a board-certified forensic psychologist for thirty-seven years. He had been allowed to twist in the wind during the playing of the taped interviews with Thomas. He stated that Meadows had called him for the first time the weekend before the trial.

"Did Mr. Meadows give you any background information regarding Mr. Knight?"

"None whatsoever."

He had not been told of the beatings, the incest, Thomas being forced to testify against his father or his later stay in a mental hospital where he was diagnosed as schizophrenic. If he had known these facts, Rothenberg said, "it would have corroborated the findings of the psychological testing, so that my testimony would not have hinged solely upon my expert opinion."

"Would a history of mental illness in the family have assisted you?"

"Yes sir."

"How would that assist you?"

"There is an abundance of research data to indicate that schizophrenia has genetic components, and that when there is a history of schizophrenia in a family, there is a strong possibility that other members of the family will also become involved in that kind of an illness."

I read him the list of mitigating circumstances, including being "under the influence of extreme mental or emotional disturbance." I asked him if that might have applied to Thomas.

"Yes. At the time of the offense, he was, indeed, under the influence of extreme emotional disturbance, and he was mentally ill."

Rothenberg said that he was never given a chance to listen to the tapes of his interviews with Thomas, which had been made a year before. He and the jury were hearing the tapes for the first time. "It would have been very helpful," he said with understatement, "if I had been allowed to review the tapes."

It was clear from Rothenberg's testimony that Matthews had been stumbling about in the dark. None of the four defense attorneys could explain why the information about Thomas's background hadn't been given to the medical experts.

• • •

After Rothenberg's testimony the judge ordered a lunch break of an hour so that Jerry Miller could interview Thomas. While Jerry was talking to him in the holding cell, the guards brought in a tray of food. Thomas asked if one of his shackled arms could be loosened so that he could eat. The guards agreed, but only if he skipped his interview and went to a more secure room. Jerry realized it would not be productive to ask a hungry man tough questions about his childhood, so he told the guards to forget the interview.

When the break was over, I put Jerry on the witness stand and asked him how he went about gathering mitigating evidence in a death case.

"We generally put a great deal of investigation into developing a very thorough and corroborated life history of the person," he replied. "We pound the streets, find neighbors, find family members, review relevant medical documents, educational documents, talk to teachers, review any history of various medical treatments, any history of trauma, any history of child abuse."

All of this should have been done in Thomas's case. Jerry said his talks with relatives had gleaned useful information that Thomas's court-appointed investigator could have found if he had been allowed to look. Knight's siblings described times when Thomas couldn't remember how he had gotten where he was. There were reports that Thomas's father had sometimes beaten him about the head with a blackjack, and Jerry thought that an investigator should have pursued the idea that "severe head trauma" might be one explanation for Knight's mental illness.

Jerry said he had checked on the Okeechobee reform school and found that at the time Thomas was there, kids were sometimes hog-tied. Shortly after Thomas left, Okeechobee stopped taking boys under the age of fourteen, partly because of reports that younger children were being sexually assaulted. It was possible that the nine-year-old Thomas was assaulted there, but in the short interview time Jerry was allowed with Thomas, our mitigation expert couldn't develop the rapport necessary to ask Thomas what might have occurred at the reform school.

One final question: "When children are subjected to abuse by parents, are they very likely to tell people about it?"

"No."

• • •

Our last witness was Anna Knight. I had saved her so that she would appear only after all the attorneys had talked about how much they had been relying on her.

Mrs. Knight was a large woman who had suffered a stroke and was blind in one eye. Susan had to assist her up the small step to the witness stand. When she sat down, she glanced around the room as if she was not sure where she was. She had endured a life of grinding poverty and abuse; it was on her side of the family that most of the mental illness was found. Susan had told me that although Mrs. Knight didn't understand what this hearing was about, she wanted to do what she could to help her son.

Thomas stared at his mother on the witness stand. His expression didn't change. Was he on his good behavior because she was there? Or was he "not even in the courtroom"? I had no idea.

I tried to put Mrs. Knight at ease with a simple question: "What kind of work did you do during your life?"

"I work farm work. I work at Saint Lucie County School. And also I worked in a laundry. I did most all kinds of work."

"Did your son Thomas Knight have any problems as a child?"

"Well, I can't exactly tell you the problems he had, but I know one day he was crying. He come to me and throwed his arm around me, and he told me—he say, 'Mama, I just ain't satisfied.' It looked like there was something hurting him. He was going through problems, and, see, I was the only one, you know, that I talk with him, because his daddy wasn't there at the time."

"Did your husband ever abuse your son Thomas?"

"Thomas? Well, when he do wrong like that, or not do wrong, he be drinking and he beat him, and he be crying. I used to not go with him."

"Was your husband a violent man?"

"I don't do that, no."

The judge leaned forward, straining to understand her.

"Did he ever hurt you?" I asked.

"Once, he jumped up and kicked me, and I lost a baby. I had a serious operation. He was a mean man, and I'm scar't of him."

I got her to acknowledge that S.T. had raped their daughter Mary and that Thomas had pulled his father off. S.T. threatened to kill Mary if she told anybody, but because Mary was hemorrhaging, Anna took her to the hospital, and the authorities found out what had happened.

When I asked about her children, she said that her eldest, Willie Mae, had died in a mental hospital. Several others, she reported, had gotten into trouble with the law, and one was presently in prison for violating parole.

"Has anyone ever come to you and asked you to be a witness in court?"

"Hutchinson was a lawyer, one of them, and he came to my house and told me that Thomas didn't do that. It was just like a glass of jelly he picked up and he said, 'He is coming back. He is coming back up there to start the weekend and carry me up there,' and I ain't seen him no more."

This answer made no sense to me. The judge looked puzzled. "Well," I said, trying to clear things up, "what did you two talk about?"

"No more than he just told me about the glass. He didn't do it."

"I am not picking it up," said the judge. "What is she saying?"

I asked her to repeat, and she rambled on about the glass of jelly. She was a confused, sad woman. We had put her on not so much for her testimony, but so that the judge could see that she would have been a poor witness at her son's trial. Matthews had called her his "only hope" and had planned to make her his sole witness during the penalty phase. Clearly, Thomas's sisters, the parole officer, the reform school superintendent would have been better witnesses than his mother.

I asked Mrs. Knight whether anyone had talked to her about testifying.

She said she had come to a hearing in Miami, but she never said anything because "the lawyer and the judge didn't want me to talk and didn't want Thomas to talk."

"Do you mean the judge and the lawyer did not want you to talk?"

"No. He didn't allow us to talk."

"Your Honor," Fox interjected, "that is not what she said. She said the lawyer and jury."

"She said the judge," I responded.

"I thought she said the jury," the judge said.

"That is the way she pronounces judge." I turned to Mrs. Knight: "Are you talking about the judge or the jury?"

"The judge," she replied.

I told her she could step down. The evidentiary hearing was over.

• • •

Hoeveler ordered us to file post-hearing briefs, but he also gave us a few minutes to sum up our case. I said, We are not "second-guessing" the legal strategy of lawyers because they lost a case, nor am I asking you to substitute my ideas for theirs. I am saying there was no strategy because no thought was put into this case.

Justice Hugo Black wrote, in *Gideon* v. *Wainwright*: "Lawyers in criminal cases are necessities, not luxuries." Just like the pilot of a plane. If this team of lawyers were flying a 747 we'd all be dead.

Two months later the judge's secretary called: Pick up the order. I rushed a courier over to the courthouse and he came back with a thick document. I flipped right to the last page: Denied.

The word hit me like a sledgehammer. Slowly I read the uncommonly long, 123-page memorandum. I was stunned at its easy dismissal of my charges. For some of our claims—that pre-trial publicity had required a change of venue, that Judge Williams had wrongly prohibited the testimony of Lieutenant Pat Duval and given incorrect jury instructions during the penalty phase—I hadn't held out much hope. But how could the judge think that Thomas's attorneys had represented him competently?

As an example of the defense team's competence, the judge noted that three attorneys had presented closing arguments, apparently finding quality in numbers.

What about not raising the insanity defense until the first day of the trial? Judge Hoeveler said it wasn't the attorneys' fault that they hadn't seen Dr. Rothenberg's report. "The Court is fully cognizant of the fact that there was more that the defense counsel could have done in preparing for the insanity defense and that additional preparation would probably have helped the Petitioner at trial. However, the Court is also mindful that defense counsel were burdened, through no real fault of their own, by the late discovery of the psychological reports."

Hoeveler was not disturbed by the fact that the medical experts hadn't been given any background material on Thomas. He noted that Dr. Rothenberg and the other experts had not complained during the trial that they lacked any information. Of course, they didn't know what they were missing. "Although Petitioner's defense counsel did not render perfect assistance in preparing the psychiatric experts," the judge wrote, "the Court notes that perfect assistance is not required."

In his conclusion Hoeveler observed that Matthews had said he had based his decisions on a trial strategy. As I had feared, this claim killed us. "When an attorney makes an informed choice between alternatives," the judge observed, "his tactical judgment will almost never be overturned on habeas corpus." Besides, he added, "even if the mitigating circumstance of diminished capacity or mental disturbance were found in this case, the aggravating circumstances would still outweigh the mitigating circumstances."

At the end he threw us a sop by saying that allegations of ineffective counsel required "close and difficult decisions," but that was it. Not even Hutchinson's "swears of bolld" appellate brief could shift his opinion: "The Court finds that the brief, while not a model of legal writing, does not sink to the level of unconstitutional ineffectiveness."

I was profoundly depressed. I had put years of work into preparing for that hearing and been rejected on every front. Judge Hoeveler had found the performance of Matthews & Co. constitutionally acceptable. What had happened to the great calling of the law? I couldn't find it in the 123 pages of Hoeveler's opinion.

One court stood between us and the chair, and I didn't feel good about it. The Eleventh Circuit Court of Appeals in Atlanta was decidedly unfriendly to criminal defendants, and Hoeveler's 123 page opinion certainly wasn't going to make it any friendlier. I figured this court was our last chance. The Supreme Court's conservative majority would be unlikely to consider our case.

The circuit court gave us a strict thirty-day deadline, and we went into a crisis mode to finish the brief. Three bright young Miami lawyers volunteered their help. Marcia Silvers, Richard Strafer and Marisa Méndez each staked out an issue to research and draft. We pored through the transcripts, reread the death penalty opinions and brainstormed the legal arguments. Wanda Gómez from my office worked all night with us to get it out on time.

Our eighty-five-page brief carefully presented the facts of fifteen years of litigation. I took to heart the story of a lawyer who, criticized by an appellate judge for spending too much time on facts which the court already knew, said: "Your Honors, that was the mistake I made in the court below."

We backed up each of our accusations with supporting material: transcripts, exhibits, prior appellate decisions, books, even newspaper articles.

Culmer's admission that all work for the penalty phase was put "on the shelf" until after Thomas's conviction furnished the architectural keystone connecting and explaining all the blunders. A brief is advocacy in words designed to persuade. I searched for vivid adjectives to describe the defense's performance. Matthews's ignorance of basic death penalty law demonstrated the limits of a legal education. He was unable to describe Florida's death penalty statute or recognize the leading Supreme Court cases. I quoted Justice Hugo Black: "There can be no equal justice when the kind of trial a man gets depends on the amount of money he has."

The one last point I had always seen as our salvation if all else failed was Hutchinson's "swears of bolld" brief. Our grammatical analysis of the thirty-two-page brief showed six hundred errors of grammar and syntax and over sixty non-functioning sentences.

We filed on January 6, 1987. A month later we received a copy of Fox's brief. His office continued to maintain that Thomas's four defense attorneys had done an adequate job. In particular, Fox wrote, "Matthews conducted an extensive background investigation of Petitioner."

In our reply brief we disputed Matthews's "extensive background investigation" with an analysis of the twenty-six subpoenas that Matthews had produced at the evidentiary hearing. None was issued prior to trial. Eight were addressed to psychiatric witnesses who testified for the State. Two were addressed to defense psychiatric witnesses. Seven were not served ("whereabouts unknown," "no such hospital," "moved"). Four were for current jail or prison records. One was for psychiatric records from Thomas's stay at the mental hospital, which the defense already had.

As we were polishing the reply brief, eight days before it was due in Atlanta, the U.S. Supreme Court overturned the death sentence of James Ernest
Hitchcock because of a faulty jury instruction. In an opinion written by conservative Justice Antonin Scalia, the Court ruled that Florida's jury instruction
had limited the trial jury from considering favorable evidence about the defendant's background when deciding whether death was the appropriate sentence.

I believed this instruction was at best a side issue in our case: The fundamental injustice was that Thomas Knight had been denied a fair trial by his attorneys. In our reply, we devoted only a page to *Hitchcock*, outlining how that
case applied to ours.

A few weeks later we received word that three appellate court judges had
been assigned to hear our appeal. They were a tough lot, not known for siding
with defendants: Paul H. Roney, sixty-six, the court's chief judge, was appointed by Nixon in 1970; Gerald B. Tjoflat, fifty-seven, appointed by Ford in
1975; and Thomas A. Clark, fifty-six, appointed by Carter in 1979.

Tjoflat had a reputation as a brilliant conservative who specialized in un-
earthing technical errors to reject an appeal. That's why I was perturbed when,
two days before our oral argument, a clerk at the Eleventh Circuit called to
say I should be prepared to answer questions about why Knight's *Hitchcock* argument should not be procedurally barred. Fox had argued in one of his briefs
that we should be precluded from raising complaints about jury instructions.
His reasoning was that we had not raised the issue in state courts and therefore
should not be allowed to do so in our federal habeas petition.

During all the "ping-ponging" that Susan had endured in the state courts,
she had not raised a *Hitchcock* claim. But there were other briefs in state court
in which she had cited the *Lockett* decision. *Lockett*, like *Hitchcock*, said that
jurors should be allowed to consider any mitigating circumstances. Scalia had
relied on *Lockett* in reversing Hitchcock's sentence, so it seemed to me that
we should not be procedurally barred from citing *Lockett*.

Our argument was set for 2 p.m. on September 1, 1987, in an old-fashioned
and majestic Atlanta courtroom, with high ceilings, wood-paneled walls and a

massive carved bench that the three judges sat behind. The looming and fore-boding atmosphere reduced our small talk to a whisper.

We had a new opponent, Susan Hugentugler, a young Florida assistant at-torney general. Calvin Fox had gone into private practice.

"The question in this case," I began, "is whether equal justice is more than just an empty promise. Thomas Knight was a poor black man who couldn't af-ford an attorney. The Constitution promises people like him competent and vigorous advocates. Instead, he was saddled with lawyers who didn't care, who wouldn't work, and whose negligence allowed him to be sentenced to death. If there was ever a case for you to find ineffective assistance of counsel, *this* is that case."

"Counsel, that's fine as an abstract concept," Judge Roney interjected, "but what proof do you have this Petitioner didn't get it?"

I answered by describing in detail Thomas's wretched life. "How," I asked, "could his lawyers have failed to present these facts to the jury?"

"Okay, he had a hard life," Roney said. "How does this excuse two murders?"

I was ready for the question. I cited specific examples to show how the psy-chiatric testimony would have explained Knight's conduct by reference to his childhood brutality.

"But," interjected Judge Clark, "the issue is not how much more you could have done, but whether, under *Strickland* v. *Washington*, the lawyer's negli-gence caused a different result." He was citing the Supreme Court's ruling that a lawyer's incompetence wasn't enough, you had to prove prejudice. The standard was so vague that the only way to deal with it was by detailing the facts of the case. So I presented examples of the lawyers' failure to find and present the mitigating information.

Roney and Clark challenged every fact I raised concerning the *Strickland* standard. I turned to *Hitchcock*, changing the subject as softly as I could be-cause my claims that the lawyers had been negligent in not presenting miti-gating circumstances and the claim that the jury hadn't been permitted to consider mitigating circumstances were in contradiction. If the lawyers hadn't presented mitigating material, how could the jurors have been denied the chance to consider it?

Sidestepping that question, I explained how close our case was to *Hitch-cock's*. In each, the judges had told the jurors in almost identical language that they "may consider" factors that were read straight from the Florida statute.

Then I referred to Judge Hoeveler's lengthy opinion, in which he himself had found that Thomas's attorneys had mentioned some non-statutory factors during the course of the trial.

"Although the attorneys didn't develop it," I said, "there were *some* non-statutory mitigating circumstances.[5] The jurors could have considered these if they had been permitted. At least, the jury had a vague idea of Thomas's poverty. There may have been some compassion for the underdog. They knew that the Ganses' deaths were instantaneous. Judge Hoeveler found several non-statutory factors that could have been considered. One was the claim by the defense that no one had ever proven that the death penalty was a deterrent. Another was the idea that society had failed to deal with the underlying causes of crime and that people failed to give Thomas guidance when he was a young man. The focus of Judge Hoeveler's order was misplaced, but at least he found that this evidence was in the record."

I spoke carefully because I was walking a tightrope. In fact, I thought that these factors were clichés that wouldn't have swayed any juror. But I had to argue that some mitigating circumstances had slipped into the trial because if there were *no* non-statutory mitigating circumstances to consider, then it didn't matter that the judge had ordered the jury to consider only certain factors: There wasn't anything else for the jury to ponder. This would be a "harmless error." On the other hand, if I argued too strenuously that there was information the jury hadn't been allowed to consider, I would undercut my main argument, that the lawyers had bungled by not presenting mitigating evidence—statutory and non-statutory—during the penalty phase. I couldn't let

---

5. The Florida Statutes provide criteria for determining whether a convicted capital defendant should be sentenced to death. The jury must consider a list of ten aggravating circumstances and eight mitigating circumstances. If there are one or more aggravating circumstances that are not outweighed by any mitigating circumstances, the defendant is sentenced to death. The Florida Supreme Court originally held that the statutory lists were exclusive, so the jury could not be informed of and consider any other circumstances that might bear on the penalty. The United States Supreme Court overruled that decision in *Lockett v. Ohio* (1978), holding that the jury must be able to consider any circumstance that might mitigate the penalty. These unlisted mitigators are called non-statutory because they are not enumerated in the statute. Therefore, a lawyer may use any event in a defendant's life as a possible reason not to sentence him to death.

the Eleventh Circuit judges forget that there was a wealth of information that Matthews had overlooked.

I suggested to the judges that the mitigating material had slipped into the trial unintentionally; there was evidence for the jurors to consider, but they hadn't been given a chance to hear the additional information we had presented during the evidentiary hearing.

Hugentugler, the assistant attorney general, argued that the effectiveness of Thomas's attorneys didn't matter. He would have been found guilty and sentenced to death in any case. There was no question of his guilt. And at the penalty phase, there were so many aggravating circumstances—a calculated, heinous murder of truly innocent people, committed while the defendant was trying to carry out another crime for pecuniary gain—that it didn't matter what mitigating circumstances the lawyers had not presented.

Furthermore, she said, it was clear from the trial record that Thomas's trial attorneys hadn't raised any non-statutory mitigating circumstances. It would be absurd to count their clichés as "non-statutory mitigating circumstances." Therefore, Knight's case was clearly different from Hitchcock's. If there was an error, it was harmless.

Hugentugler had zeroed in on our weakness—she used the words "harmless error" a half-dozen times—and made her points quickly.

I was given ten minutes to respond. As I walked to the podium, my mind was racing about how to rebut her "harmless error" argument.

"You can't ignore the facts by invoking the cliché 'harmless error,'" I told the judges. "If the truth had been known, there were many legally acceptable reasons why Thomas Knight should not be executed. Despite the ugliness of these crimes the jurors might have had compassion if someone had guided them to the truth."

Immediately, all three judges peppered me with questions. I no longer had the luxury of following a prepared outline. The judges had taken control. Replying to their questions was the most difficult part of the argument—but also the most important. If I couldn't give satisfactory answers, we would lose.

Judge Roney went straight to our weak point: It was difficult to find in the trial transcript any authentic non-statutory factors that had been presented to the jury. So what was the error?

That was a tough question. I mentioned the horrible tape recording of

Thomas talking to Dr. Rothenberg. "Knight in the tape recording described his life as 'hell.' What he said was rambling, incoherent and only a small part of the story. This jailhouse conversation with the psychologist was certainly no substitute for a proper penalty hearing. But it did contain some non-statutory mitigating circumstances that the jury could have considered, if the judge had allowed them."

I had been convinced that this tape was the worst garbage the jurors could have heard, the best proof of how bad his trial attorneys had been. And here I was, citing it as a positive example of things the jury *could* have considered.

I had to tread carefully because some of the information was more aggravating than mitigating. I was walking a fine line between competing arguments. I hoped it made sense.

Now Judge Tjoflat took over the questioning. "Why aren't you procedurally barred from raising *Hitchcock* since it wasn't included in the state court petition?"

I was ready for this question. Briefly, I explained the "ping-ponging" that Thomas's case had been through in the state courts. It was true that there was a time when we had not included a *Lockett* claim in the papers, but that was only when we were asking the Florida Supreme Court for a new appeal to replace Hutchinson's incoherent rambling. Later in state court, the *Lockett* issue had been raised, so we could not be procedurally barred from raising it here.

I could not tell from the look on Tjoflat's face whether this statement satisfied him or not, but there was no time to go further because Judge Clark had a question: If the aggravating circumstances outnumbered the mitigating circumstances, as Ms. Hugentugler claimed, what difference did it make if there was a faulty jury instruction?

I pulled out the opinion in *Dixon* v. *State*, and read the section criticizing a life-or-death decision based on pure numbers. "Your Honor, even just *one* mitigating circumstance could outweigh several aggravating circumstances. We don't execute people by arithmetic."

Didn't Matthews's testimony that he knew he wasn't limited by the judge to the statutory mitigating circumstances prove there was no *Hitchcock* violation?

I told the judges that Matthews's statement was "a purely self-serving excuse for his incompetence." To find the truth, don't look at what he said, but at what he did at the trial. He failed to elicit from the witnesses a wealth of non-statutory mitigating evidence. In his summation, Matthews did not tell the jurors they could consider mitigating evidence that was not listed in the statute. He did not explain to the jury the meaning of mitigation and did not identify *any* non-statutory mitigating evidence. What's more, he never objected to the judge limiting the jury to the statutory list of mitigating evidence. The best proof of what he really believed was what he actually did.

The questions kept coming, all of them focusing on the *Hitchcock* case and "harmless error." My red light, which signaled the end of my turn, had flashed long before, but no one paid any attention.

Judge Tjoflat picked up my brief and asked, "Do you claim that in the testimony of the psychiatrist and psychologists, there was mitigating material?"

I said that was so, even though the lawyers hadn't really developed the information.

The judge then sprang a trap: "But didn't you prove that the experts really hadn't known Mr. Knight's background, and so they were mistaken in their diagnoses?"

"That's right," I said.

"So how could their testimony have included *accurate* mitigating factors?"

Good question. Tjoflat had turned my argument around on me. I hesitated a moment. "You're right," I said. "The psychiatrists got it all wrong. But at least we have Thomas Knight's voice on Rothenberg's tapes, telling the jury something about his miserable life." I prayed that satisfied him.

The judges' questions continued for thirty minutes after my time was up. Such a long exchange was unusual for the Eleventh Circuit, and it showed that the judges were captivated by the legal dilemma presented by this case. But what did that mean for Thomas Knight? The Eleventh Circuit had ruled against Hitchcock by the narrowest of margins, 7–5, before the U.S. Supreme Court overturned its decision. Perhaps the Eleventh's judges were looking for a way to narrow the *Hitchcock* opinion. Perhaps Thomas Knight would serve as their first example of "harmless error," as some of the judges' questions intimated.

Before I sat down, I made a last plea. "My time is long up, but I want to say one personal word. I've tried very hard to argue this case dispassionately, as a lawyer should, but I don't want you to think that I'm not personally affected by what happened in this case. None of us can afford to ignore the principles we discussed today. Thomas Knight stands convicted of brutal and senseless crimes. He is of no importance in our society, he certainly is poor and friendless, but he has the same constitutional right as anyone else to a decent defense."

I have many times left an appellate court with a sense of how the judges were going to rule, but in this case, neither Susan nor I had any idea.

Months went by without a word on Thomas's case from the Eleventh Circuit.

Finally, on December 8, 1988—fifteen months after the trip to Atlanta—I received a call from the court clerk: Thomas Knight's death sentence had been vacated.

The Eleventh Circuit's unanimous decision was based strictly on the *Hitchcock* jury instruction. After seven years of defeats we had finally won.

While the court spared Knight's life, its opinion left much to be desired. Despite all the injustices that occurred at Knight's trial, the outcome of this case had hinged on a seemingly insignificant jury instruction. The irony was that the Hitchcock decision had come down in 1987, twelve years after Thomas Knight had been sentenced to death. It was only because of all the elaborate maneuvering that we had done over the years—getting the stay from Judge Joe Eaton, then bouncing back to state court, then back to federal court for the long buildup to the two-day evidentiary hearing and finally the appeal to the Eleventh Circuit—that we had managed to keep Thomas Knight alive until the *Hitchcock* decision arrived to justify the vacating of his sentence.

What's more, twenty-six judges joining in six published opinions had allowed Hutchinson's "swears of bolld" brief to go unchallenged. While "not a model of legal writing" it was good enough for the likes of Thomas Knight.

The system fiercely resists change and refuses to admit the sad litany of our defense incompetence in capital cases. The judges are afraid such honesty would staunch the flood of executions, but unless the credo of equal justice is just a myth, how can we remain quiet and let the killings continue? As Professor Charles Black said: "Though the justice of God may indeed ordain that some should die, the justice of man is altogether and always insufficient for saying who these may be."

• • •

I sent Thomas a copy of the opinion, and after a while Prisoner #017434 sent me a nice note: "I'm thankful you sent me the opinion. I appreciate the hard work you have done and are doing in my case. I've been grateful these many years to have you to work on my case."

One final irony: The same jury instructions given by Knight's trial judge were also given by the judge presiding over the case of Robert Sullivan, the death row inmate I represented in the early 1980s. Both juries were limited to considering the statutory mitigating circumstances. But Sullivan was executed because his case wound its way through the courts quicker than Knight's. Dissenting from the U.S. Supreme Court's rejection of Sullivan's final appeal in 1983, Justice Brennan complained that "the Court has once again rushed to judgment." If Sullivan had still been alive at the time of the *Hitchcock* decision, his death sentence would have been vacated. As it was, he was executed after a trial that is now considered unconstitutional.

Should Robert Sullivan have died and Thomas Knight live only because of the timing of their death warrants and the length of their appeals? Is it fair to have a judicial system in which luck determines who lives and who dies? I remember reading that it's impossible to define justice, but everybody recognizes *in*justice when they see it. I'm convinced that when it comes to the death penalty, if you look close enough, you will always see injustice.

Turning point: The Supreme Court's ruling in *Hitchcock* gave us the opening, but that wouldn't have mattered if I hadn't been able to walk that fine line in my oral arguments in Atlanta. The irony became clear when I desperately had to search for any mitigating circumstances that Knight's bungling lawyers had made in their brief, vague pleas to the judge and the jury.

The Eleventh Circuit judges stated that they were ruling in our favor because of *Hitchcock*, a very small point, but judges oftentimes think bigger than the fine points of the law. Perhaps in this case they sensed that a fundamental injustice had been done and they looked for a way to rectify it, even if that way was a jury instruction that had virtually nothing to do with our main complaints.

Hicks

FORT LAUDERDALE IS LAND SHARKS WITH BLOND PONYTAILS DRINKING COLD Coronas on a snow-white tropical beach, eying beauties in G-string bikinis. It's Shooters, a waterside bar where the young and the beautiful arrive in sleek Cigarette boats. It's singles bars filled with rich kids with straws up their noses. It's overpriced art and antique galleries lining Las Olas Boulevard. It's miles of faux-Mediterranean mansions along the Intracoastal Waterway. It is a neon-washed Federal Highway packed with strip clubs where suckers buy hundred-dollar bottles of carbonated grape juice for exotic dancers. It's no longer the mecca of the colleges' spring break, the land of *Where the Boys Are*, of adolescent fun and innocent sex. It's a place to lose your soul.

Steve Hicks had moved effortlessly through the nocturnal world of Fort Lauderdale, cruising its seedy bars and dancing to its disco bands. When I met him, however, he was sitting in the city's downtown jail, and he wanted me to represent him.

His brother, Mark, had come to my office. The owner of an electrical supply company, Mark told me that the day before his twenty-eight-year-old brother had been charged with first-degree murder for shooting his live-in girlfriend. Mark was certain that Steve was innocent. Their grandfather had been sleeping in a room in the same apartment when the shooting occurred. How could anyone deliberately kill someone when his grandfather was in the next room?

Before Mark left my office I phoned the police and was told that detectives had finished examining Hicks's apartment. I ordered Mark to bolt the apartment door and keep everyone out until I could have it thoroughly searched. As soon as the police yellow tape in a murder case comes down, I want to inspect the place myself.

I made two other calls. The first was to the Medical Examiner's Office, to see if I could watch the autopsy. I was too late—the body had already been released for burial. I also phoned the prosecutor and asked for copies of all the police reports. He replied: "File a motion and perhaps in a couple of weeks I'll get around to it."[1]

With these preliminaries out of the way, I drove to see my new client at the jail. Steve Hicks was movie-star handsome—with long eyelashes, pouty lips and the edgy, pretty-boy look of Rob Lowe—but he was already taking on the appearance of most prisoners after a few days behind bars: puffy eyes, pale complexion, a slight tremble in the hands. He looked me in the eye and said that the shooting had been an accident. He had given the police a taped statement explaining that Betsy Turner was in a jealous rage and that she put a gun to her head. He made a desperate grab for it, and in the tussle the gun went off. "I didn't shoot her. It was just a horrible accident."

His explanation sounded reasonable, so I didn't press him too hard on the details. There would be plenty of time for that later. First, I had to try to get him released on bail.

Bail is rarely an option in a capital case with a prosecutor seeking the death penalty. Still, the courts have ruled that even capital defendants are eligible for bail if it can be shown that the evidence of premeditation is weak.

Our judge was Robert Carney, who had been on the bench for only a few months. His grandfather had been an admiral and chief of naval operations under President Eisenhower. Carney was an ex-marine who had been a platoon leader in Vietnam. People with military backgrounds are generally not liberals when it comes to defendants' rights. Moreover, for years Carney had been a colleague of our adversary in this case, prosecutor Tom Kern. They had been part of a four-man team that prosecuted the major homicide cases in Fort Lauderdale. Kern was a tough, veteran prosecutor in his mid-fifties who had put several men on death row. Carney himself had put his share of

---

1. This conversation was not with Tom Kern, the eventual prosecutor on the case, but with someone in the filing section of the Broward State Attorney's Office.

men on death row. His sympathies would seem to be with his old colleague.

At the bail hearing Kern argued that there was overwhelming evidence that Hicks had planned and carried out the murder of Betsy Turner. He put on the witness stand a detective who testified that Hicks had transported and abandoned the body in an attempt to make it look as if the dead woman had been the victim of a robbery. He had then called police to report her missing. When detectives came to talk to him, he lied repeatedly. This testimony not only destroyed my flimsy argument for bail, but worse, it meant that Steve had lied to me. Not a good start to our professional relationship.

There wasn't much I could say in response. The judge decided the State's evidence was strong. The death penalty was a serious likelihood. Steve Hicks was going to remain a prisoner until trial.

Immediately after the hearing I went to see Steve at the jail. Pointing my finger at his face, I said: "I don't like being embarrassed like that. I can't operate in the dark. I need to know *everything.*"

I was furious, but not with Steve. I was angry with myself because I hadn't dug deeply enough. It is human nature for a client to withhold harmful facts until he feels comfortable with his lawyer.

Steve said something I couldn't hear. I leaned forward to catch his words in the noisy jail. Raising his voice slightly, he said it had been an accident. He had panicked when the shot went off. He had wanted to tell me all this, but it had seemed too complicated to go into when we first met. He said he had tried to take Betsy to an emergency room but couldn't find one. When he realized she was dead, he left her in the car at a bank and walked home.

"I was scared and confused. I didn't know what to do with her body. I couldn't take her back to the apartment. I was terrified of calling the police. Why should they believe me, a bartender living off this woman? All I could see was them railroading me into prison." At first, he tried to cover up his actions, but later he made a formal, taped statement. Everything in that last statement, he insisted, was the absolute truth. Tears flooded his eyes.

Steve's explanation was so unbelievable that it had the ring of truth. Who would make this up? Still, I knew his conflicting statements to the police were going to be a huge problem in court. I could imagine Kern asking the jurors devastating questions in his summation: If the woman's death was an accident, why the cover-up? Why the lies?

Afterwards, I checked out a key aspect of Steve's story. He said he had driven Betsy, moaning and badly wounded, to Doctor's Hospital at 4 a.m. He claimed that the front doors of the hospital had been locked, and that he hadn't been able to find the emergency room. That seemed odd, but a guard at the hospital told me that the front doors were locked at midnight, and I saw for myself that the emergency room was in an obscure location in the sprawling complex.

I went to Steve's apartment in the suburb of Plantation with Bill Venturi, a retired Metro-Dade homicide cop turned private investigator. I told him to search every drawer, every piece of clothing. "Vacuum it and I want an inventory of the lint." He worked at the apartment for several days, examining it far more carefully than the police had.

I figured that the Plantation cops had looked no further than Steve's pretty-boy face and his lack of a job. They had quickly concluded that he was a killer. When he gave conflicting stories, the detectives assumed he was as good as convicted. So, naturally, they had looked for only those pieces of evidence that proved his guilt. They ignored a lot.

On a coffee table Venturi found Betsy's résumé and a cover letter seeking work in Atlanta. I couldn't know it at the time, but this letter would have provided Kern with a motive. Steve had been thinking of returning to Atlanta, where his estranged wife and his child lived. It looked as if Betsy had been planning to follow him.

There were also letters that revealed her intimate thoughts. One was particularly interesting, a card Betsy wrote to Steve in June 1985—a year before the shooting. On the front of the card was a plaintive Ziggy saying, "I'd follow you anywhere—so try not to go anywhere expensive." Inside, in plain, almost childlike handwriting, the twenty-four-year-old Betsy had written:

> To Mr. Stephen N. Hicks:
>
> Upon your request, I am composing a letter regarding my attitude and the changes I must make to remain with you.

She wrote that she knew they weren't getting along and she wanted them to be happy together. She promised to change her attitude and correct "my short temper and smart mouth."

From then on, she said, she would be "sweet and loving. I will be willing to do anything that is *asked* of me by Steve. . . . I will try to do something with my fat ass and legs. And yes, I'll even try to quit smoking." She also vowed to keep the house clean "even if it means getting up at 5:30 a.m." Right before her signature, she added this: "No matter what happens between us, I do & will love you for a very long time."

The card didn't prove anything about murder, but I could imagine Kern reading the words "I'd follow you anywhere" to the jury. He could build a story of desperation, of Betsy pleading to stay with Steve while Steve wanted to get away. A good narrator could weave that letter seamlessly into a tale of how murder was the only way this young man could rid himself of this young woman.

The detectives had left behind many other things as well. In the closet were dildos, vibrators and other sex toys. On a table was a receipt showing that Steve had purchased $119.91 worth of liquor at 5:14 p.m. the night Betsy died. On the kitchen counter were half-empty bottles of vodka and Kahlua. In Steve's Thunderbird, Venturi found a glass with the dried residue of liquid and a strong odor of alcohol. If the police wanted to emphasize Steve's drinking, all of that would have come in handy.

Venturi made the most problematic discovery in the nightstand. He listed the items in his report: "Two film containers with suspect marijuana and roaches, one metal container with Zig-Zag papers and a stone pipe, one glass tray and straight edge razor blade with possible cocaine residue on them and two clear plastic bags with traces of suspect marijuana."

These materials presented us with a dilemma. Only in fiction do criminal defense lawyers break into apartments and destroy evidence to hide a client's guilt. In real life we adhere to the law and follow the ethical code of the legal profession. It would be a crime for us to possess even the smallest amount of an illegal substance. Did that mean we should turn the discovery over to the Plantation police? Of course, the police would try to use this evidence against Steve. Can a defense attorney's own energetic work be used against his client? I told Venturi to leave the materials where he found them. I had no ethical obligation to inform the police that they had left this behind.

As soon as Venturi had finished his investigation, I went to the apartment to try to visualize how the shooting had occurred. I paced the rooms, sat in the living room, then the bedroom. I made notes of my impressions and added them to my notes from several lengthy interviews with Steve. Venturi had taken several rolls of photographs of the apartment, of Betsy's car, of the hospital and of the bank. And finally, after the State had responded to my written demand for discovery, I had all the reports of the police and the medical examiner, the police photographs and copies of Steve's statements. I was amazed when I read these statements. He had lied to the police not once, not twice, but *four* times concerning the death of Betsy Turner. We had our work cut out for us.

I lugged the case files into the library of my office at five o'clock one beautiful Miami morning and attempted to put together the pieces of the puzzle. I turned up the volume on Tchaikovsky's Piano Concerto No. 1 to just below the pain threshold and let the animal ferocity of its crescendos clear my mind. I began by taping the apartment floor plan to the wall and arranging the 8 × 10 crime scene photos around it. On the big library table I set out the lab reports, the police reports, Steve's statements, a street map, aerial photos of the hospitals and all the evidence I had gathered from his apartment.

By now, I had interviewed dozens of Steve's and Betsy's friends. I had initially assumed that Steve, with his good looks and sharp attire, was a resourceful, magnetic ladies' man, the kind who was sexually aggressive and liked to be in charge. The reality was the opposite. Betsy was the aggressor. She was intelligent, ambitious and had a scalding temper. It was she who had the good job, who made most of the decisions. I studied photographs of her. A long mane of blond hair framed dark eyes that were street-hard yet exuded sexuality.

Steve was softer, one of those charming young men who floated around the bars, pools and beaches of South Florida. Women fell for him, and he had a life of ease, drifting along without a real commitment to anything or anyone—the happy, superficial life of a bartender. He had married young and had a son, then separated from his wife. He wasn't accustomed to dealing with hard decisions and messy situations. Why worry? Betsy or someone else would handle them. As soon as Betsy was dead, he took the path of least resistance and simply abandoned the body.

Take a hammer to a mirror, smash it into a thousand pieces, then try to piece it back together, and you get an idea of what it's like to reconstruct a circumstantial case. Knowing something of Betsy's and Steve's personalities helped me frame the case, but I was a long way from understanding what happened that night. On a poster-sized pad I sketched a time line of the events of that evening. I then took several sheets of paper and diagramed a matrix, to place facts on a grid, so that each fact could be analyzed separately and in combination. I kept crossing out and redrawing lines and moving boxes around like a kid's board game.

Facts kept combining and recombining, but always in patterns that ran against our case. If the shooting was accidental, why didn't Steve call 911? If he was panicky, where did he find the poise to call in a missing person's report? How could I prove he was really looking for a hospital? How could I convince a jury that an innocent man would abandon his lover's body at a bank teller's drive-up window? For hours I jotted down tentative answers to each of these questions.

One huge problem was Steve's gun. According to the police reports, Steve had told the detectives that there was only one bullet in the gun because it had gotten stuck in the chamber. A State firearms expert had tried many times to see whether a bullet would stick. It hadn't.

I kept running strategies through my mind. Under Florida law, prosecutors could charge Steve with first-degree murder and risk nothing because the jury is allowed to convict the defendant of a lesser charge, such as second-degree murder or manslaughter. These alternatives presented us with a dilemma. Earlier in the evening of the shooting, Steve had gone to a bar by himself and had quite a bit to drink. One way to disprove premeditation was to hit hard on the alcohol because it took away intent: He was too drunk to plan a murder. But making that argument would almost guarantee a manslaughter conviction: If he had been drunk when he grabbed for the gun, he would have been criminally negligent for handling a firearm while under the influence of alcohol. I decided that I could defend against the charge of premeditation without emphasizing alcohol. That was a calculated risk, but I thought the facts justified my going for a complete acquittal. If the prosecutor emphasized the drinking, he'd be arguing against his first-degree charge.

Another problem was the detectives' indifference to the gathering of evidence. Venturi had uncovered gems that a team of Plantation's police hadn't found. Even when the police had found something, they hadn't bothered to examine it. Example: Two months after the shooting we discovered a roll of undeveloped film while looking through the Hicks evidence at the Plantation police station. The property custodian told us the police would have it developed for us—if we were willing to pay the cost. I mumbled something to avoid a direct answer and looked engrossed in another piece of evidence. From the station, I immediately went to Steve in the jail and with great relief heard the roll had only shots of Betsy and him at the zoo.

While my work went on, Steve Hicks sat in a cramped cell with nothing to do but worry about his execution. Prosecutors like to win without a fight, and many prisoners in such situations decide to give up, settling for a second-degree murder charge that can put them in jail for twenty years. Steve toughed it out.

Seven months after the shooting, we went to trial. Because it was a death penalty case, the law required twelve jurors rather than the usual six. That's both good and bad. Getting twelve people to agree to a guilty verdict, of course, is more difficult than getting six to agree, but in a capital case jurors are required to believe in the death penalty, and that means that they are more likely to favor the prosecution.

Because the newspapers had published only a few articles about Betsy Turner's death, we didn't have to worry about pre-trial publicity prejudicing people's minds. But I still took my time in questioning the jurors.

Steve asked me why I was asking such detailed questions. "What difference is there between these people?" I told him no two people see things exactly the same way: "We unconsciously view the world in patterns based on our past experiences. We don't see things as they are; we see things as *we* are." I wanted people who were interested in details, not big-picture thinkers. People who balanced their checkbooks, who made to-do lists, would be more likely to pay attention to the details of our case rather than dwell on the larger picture of Steve's conflicting versions.

As with any twelve-person panel, we ended up with a mixed cast. A woman who directed a maintenance department said she firmly believed in the presumption of innocence. If it were her son on trial, she said, the State would have to prove its case beyond all doubt. A forty-year-old widow owned a handgun for protection and I thought understood enough about guns to accept the possibility of an accidental discharge. On the downside she believed that the death penalty should be mandatory for all first-degree murders. I took a calculated risk, figuring that she was more likely to find Betsy's death an accident rather than a premeditated killing. We also allowed a woman who said she was anti-alcohol—not good because of Steve's occupation and his drinking—but we liked her because she was a sixth-grade science teacher, which meant she would understand why the police's unscientific handling of the crime scene was so important.

We also selected a young, newly married woman who was a second-grade teacher and a woman who had run a neighborhood tavern for twenty-three years. The bar owner described how three men with a shotgun had once burst into her place. "This is a holdup," one of the men shouted. Panicking, she burst out: "Hold up, my eye." She ran into the back room and phoned the police. She admitted that she had handled the situation foolishly. Perhaps she would be able to understand Steve's bizarre behavior after Betsy was shot. The woman also said that she thought young people deserved another chance. I was surprised when Kern allowed her to remain on the jury. These choices fit my strategy of targeting strong women who would have a healthy distrust of witnesses like a jealous ex-girlfriend of Betsy.

With my peremptory challenges, I rejected an accountant who seemed too dogmatic. He was a man of numbers. He saw things in black and white, not shades of gray, and I thought he might decide the case as soon as he heard the prosecutor's opening claims. I also dismissed a nurse who, like many in her profession, saw shooting victims in the emergency room and had close associations with the police. I struck another who seemed deeply disturbed by Betsy's death; he said he kept thinking of his daughter. I left on a man who said Steve looked like his son.

By far the most remarkable member of the panel was Gerald Klein. In his forties, he had master's degrees in education and political science, and had worked toward a doctorate in political science. He said he read widely in the physical and social sciences, and he had served on the board of a life insurance company in Massachusetts.

Klein didn't own a gun and appeared to be anti-gun, which wasn't good for us, but I was impressed with his intellect. He could understand all the scientific points that I wanted to make, and because of his educational background, he would be a natural leader.

Of course, natural leaders can be a problem if they're against you. Just before jury selection ended, I had a twinge of doubt: Klein was such a standout that I might be picking a one-person jury. Sometimes you get someone whose personality is so dominating that he or she can dictate what everyone else will think. You see that when a lawyer gets selected for a jury. That's fine—if the guy is on your side. If he's not, none of the other jurors matter. You're dead.

My overriding criterion in selection is that jurors have brains. The smarter they are, the more they're willing to look for reasonable doubt because they're capable of thinking critically and won't be swayed by a police uniform. That's why I felt confident in Klein. If the jurors looked only at Steve Hicks's statements to police, they might find him guilty. I decided Klein was a plus for us. I was surprised when the State left him on the jury.

In his opening statement Kern hammered on all the lies that Hicks had told. He claimed the evidence would clearly show that Hicks had murdered Betsy Turner in cold blood, and then had abandoned her in her car at a drive-up bank teller's window to make it look as if she had been killed in a robbery. Kern asserted that Hicks was planning to return to Atlanta, to move back in with his well-to-do wife and take over the business she owned. He alleged that the wife knew nothing about Betsy. Hicks had to get rid of Betsy, Kern claimed, so that she couldn't mess up Hicks's plans. The prosecutor hinted that a major piece of evidence was Hicks's false claim that a bullet had become stuck in his gun. He promised to explain this later.

Contrary to my usual strategy, I kept my opening statement short and gave a deliberately vague description of the shooting. I painted a tragic case of two lovers struggling over a gun in their bed with fatal consequences. The forensic evidence, the only reliable evidence, would prove it was an accident, I said.

I discussed the lack of a motive, then concentrated my hardest blows for the botched police investigation. "I know a few things about how cops think. They are cynics, never believing anything a suspect says unless it's a confession. Cops jump at the first solution to a crime. Usually they are right; as Occam's razor suggests, the simplest answer is most always the correct one. But life isn't always so simple. Cops are under immense pressure to make an arrest, then move on to the next case. They committed the cardinal sin of reaching a conclusion before all the facts were in. In no time, they arrested Steve, filled out their time sheets and went home. No sense in looking any further. Open and Shut."

We were working in a small, plain courtroom. The audience consisted of a couple of journalists and a handful of spectators, the most notable of whom was Kathy Hicks, Steve's wife. It struck me that she looked a lot like the Betsy Turner I had seen in photographs. Kathy and Steve had been separated for two years but had reconciled during his incarceration. As I walked back to our table after finishing my opening remarks, I saw her beaming at Steve like a woman in love. She looked as if she would do anything for him. In fact, she had paid for a couple of rather expensive Italian suits for Steve to wear during the trial. I hoped she wanted to pay the rest of my fee.

On the other side of the courtroom, Kern had his supporters. Directly behind the prosecution table were Betsy's father and sister, who had come down from their South Carolina home to attend the trial. No one introduced them to the jury, but I was sure the jurors could guess who they were. They attended every minute of the trial. Betsy's mother was also in Fort Lauderdale, but since she was going to be a witness she was not allowed to listen to the testimony of others and had to remain outside the courtroom.

Stanley Stake, an officer with the Plantation Police Department, set the scene by testifying that at 4:20 a.m. on a Saturday he spotted a young white male walking north on Pine Island Road. Stake stopped to question the man because he was searching for a burglar who had just fled a nearby apartment complex. The white male had no identification but said his name was Stephen Hicks. He claimed he was out for a walk. This was Hicks's first lie. He had just parked his girlfriend's car containing her corpse at the Barnett Bank two blocks down the street.

"I asked him what he was so sweaty about. It appeared he had been running. He said it was just a hot evening," Stake said.

A patrol car had come by with a relative of the burglary victim. She took one look at Hicks and said he wasn't the burglar. She was certain because the burglar had been wearing shorts, and Hicks was wearing long pants.

"I mentioned in my report," Stake went on, "that the only thing that seemed strange to me was that he had two—about a foot, foot and a half in length—dark stains on his dungarees. They were like grease stains or something. They were about six inches wide." He said Hicks seemed nervous.

On cross-examination I mined the lone possible bright spot by pointing out that Steve had given his correct name and address.

"He could have given almost any name at all?"

"That's correct, sir."

"You wouldn't have any way of verifying it, would you?"

"No sir, I would not."

A small point for our side.

The prosecution's next witness was Michael J. Mann, a uniformed police officer. At 10:32 a.m. on Saturday, June 28, he was dispatched to the Barnett Bank on South Pine Island Road for a "possible Signal 7," the code for a dead body. "When I arrived," he stated, "I observed a light Mustang vehicle with a white female in the passenger seat slumped over with an apparent gunshot wound to the right lower torso." The car had South Carolina license plates.

Through Mann, Kern introduced several photos of Betsy's body as it lay in the car. The body had slid between the front seats and the head was at an unnatural angle, with the facial skin pulled askew by a seat belt. Her blood had run onto the rear floor in a thick, dark stream. When shown the photos, one juror covered her mouth, another took a deep breath, and others shook their heads. Violent death is ugly. I tried to look calm, but I knew these graphic images had an impact on the jury.

Officer Mann said he remained at the bank for two hours while the crime scene technicians, detectives and an assistant medical examiner gathered evidence. At about 12:30 p.m. he returned to the police station. A few minutes later he was asked to take a missing person report by phone. A man who identified himself as Stephen Hicks said his girlfriend was missing. This was Hicks's second lie. Officer Mann wrote down the information: Martha E. Turner, a twenty-five-year-old white female. She usually went by her nickname, Betsy. The caller said she had left home at 1:30 a.m. wearing a gold necklace and carrying a purse. She was driving a cream-colored 1984 Ford Mustang with South Carolina license plates.

Officer Mann did not let on that he had just seen a body in a Mustang with South Carolina plates. "Mr. Hicks stated that they arrived home last night at approximately one-thirty after having a few drinks out. He said Martha Turner left the premises in an upset state. I asked him why and Mr. Hicks stated that he surmised that she was upset because he had been drinking. She was wearing blue jeans, a T-shirt, carrying her purse."

On cross-examination there wasn't much I could do but lamely point out that Steve hadn't tried to hide the body: "I mean, it would be pretty hard for either the customers or the employees at the bank to miss the car?"

"That's right."

With that, we adjourned for the day.

It was an inauspicious start: two officers, in full police regalia, reporting Steve's lies. The lies and the chilling photos were a powerful one-two punch.

The next morning began with more of the same. The first witness was Michael Price, who, Kern repeatedly reminded the jury, had been recently promoted to sergeant in the Plantation Police Department. With six years of experience, Price was initially the lead detective. He testified that at ten-thirty on Saturday morning, he was summoned to the Barnett Bank. He could see a bullet hole in Betsy's T-shirt, near the waist. Around the hole he noted "fibers of some type of material that I could not identify. They were white in color."

The police ran the license plate number through the computer and came up with the name of James C. Turner of South Carolina. Shortly thereafter, Officer Mann called saying that a Stephen Hicks had reported a Betsy Turner missing. Price and another detective, Nick Ranieri, drove to the Hicks-Turner apartment, which was a mile from the bank.

"Was there anything out of the ordinary when you walked up to the apartment?" Kern asked.

"We did spot what appeared to be dried blood spots on the stairs, yes. We observed what also appeared to be small droplets of blood just in front of the doorway."

Hicks had welcomed the officers. "He offered us a drink. We sat down in the living room and we began going over the entire missing person's report. He stated that they had somewhat of an argument over his drinking habits and that she got very upset. She was wearing just a robe prior to her leaving. She went in the bedroom and changed clothes, grabbed her purse and left the apartment directly." Lie no. 3.

Price said that Hicks described her handbag as being beige. "He was calm, cool, kind of jovial. He showed some concern, but in good spirits." This is the kind of spin that many detectives put on their testimony from the witness stand. Suspects are invariably described as "calm" or "cool."

Hicks showed the detectives a photo of Betsy. Price realized that she was the dead woman at the bank, but he didn't reveal this. Instead, the two detectives received Hicks's permission to look around the apartment for clues that might explain where Betsy had gone. While searching her dresser drawers, Price noticed "small circular blood droplets" on the wall by the bed. "I then told [Hicks] we're going to have to ask him a few questions. I informed him at that point that Betsy had been killed, what appeared to have been a murder. He put his face in his hands and looked up immediately and asked me if it was a robbery."

"What did you reply to that?"

"I said, 'Well, from everything you've told us, it is very possible. We did not find a purse.' "

"And what was his response to that?"

"Just sort of disbelief. He just said, 'God, how did it happen?' That type of thing."

While they were still in the bedroom, Price advised Hicks of his Miranda rights. Hicks still kept talking.[2]

"I told him, 'There is some disturbing evidence that needs explaining. I am hoping you can help us out.' He stated, 'No problem.' I stated, 'On our way over we did find evidence of blood on the stairwell. We also just observed some blood on the wall. Can you explain this to me?' At that time, Mr. Hicks looked at me, and he stated, 'I guess we better talk.' "

The detectives and Hicks went into the living room. Hicks sat on the sofa.

"He stated that he had shot his girlfriend and that it had been an accident," Price testified.

I made a note. Price had embellished his account. Even in his incriminating statements, Steve did not say he shot Betsy, only that both were groping for the gun and it had gone off.

"He stated that he had gone out drinking that night and he had come home, and Betsy Turner was a little upset about his drinking habits. He stated that they had an argument, but he said it wasn't an argument, just more or less a conversation. But she had sometimes raised her voice.

"I said, 'What happened?' He said, 'Well, she got upset and she went into the bedroom to lie down.' I said, 'Fine.' And he said, 'After a while I went into the bedroom and I had a cigarette. I wanted to find a lighter for the cigarette.'

"Betsy at the time was lying on the bed. He went to the nightstand beside the bed and looked for a lighter. He said while he was looking, he removed a .357 Magnum gun and placed it on the bed. It was wrapped up in a handkerchief. He said he did find the lighter and then he went to the bathroom, leaving the gun on the bed.

"He said as he was in the bathroom he had heard Betsy playing with the gun. He told Betsy to put the gun down. That it was loaded. He then went into the bedroom and stated that Betsy still had the gun in her hand. It was wrapped in a handkerchief and as he was standing at the corner of the bed he

---

2. Though the Miranda ruling requires that police inform a suspect of his right to talk to a lawyer before making a statement, many suspects don't invoke their rights because, like Steve, they fear it wouldn't look good to refuse to cooperate with police. Price used this emotion to let Steve play right into his hands.

reached over to grab the gun from her and as he pulled the gun away from her, he said he heard the gun discharge. He then heard Betsy cry out, 'Get me to the hospital.'

"He stated that he didn't even think about the telephone or 911. He said he took Betsy into the car and drove her to Doctor's General Hospital. He said the hospital was closed for the evening. So he said he remembered a hospital at Oakland Park and I-95. So he continued to drive there. Obviously there's no hospital there. He said he couldn't find one. So he started driving back. As he was driving back, he said Betsy collapsed and he couldn't get a pulse anymore. He said he then drove her to the bank and parked the car there and then walked home."

Price said he then asked Hicks where the gun was. "He stated at that time that he had driven out to the Bonaventure area, which is ten miles west of that location, and threw it into the canal." Lie no. 4. As the detectives would later discover, the gun had been hidden in the apartment's storage room. Price went on: "I asked him why he couldn't think of 911. He said he just didn't have an answer for me."

At this point, the detective said, Hicks showed him what had happened when he and Betsy wrestled for the gun: "He demonstrated in the living room. . . . He made a mannerism with his hand. He went to grab it, pulled away, it went off. He was unable to show exactly the way she was handling it or exactly the way he pulled it away." When he grabbed for the gun, it was still wrapped in the handkerchief. "He grabbed for the handkerchief. It fell off and he grabbed the gun from her. He said he grabbed it away from her and he heard a shot."

Price said Hicks agreed to go down to the police station, where Detective Ranieri took a sworn, taped statement from him. This time Hicks signed a form waiving his Miranda rights. A few hours later the detectives obtained a search warrant and returned to the apartment. At this time they found the gun in the storeroom, where Hicks had told them he hid it. In a bedroom wall they noticed a large hole. Price said, "It appeared the hole was made by a fist. There were fresh droppings of plaster on the rug below the hole."

In the bedroom, detectives found three .357 Magnum cartridges and several lighters in the nightstand. Then they removed the bed cover and turned over the mattress: A blood-soaked towel was between the mattress and the box spring. Obviously, someone had turned over the mattress because all the stains were on its underside. There were no sheets on the bed. The two pillows showed no signs of blood, but in a closet the detectives found a blood-stained pillow on the top shelf. Also in the closet, they found a folded sheet with a square cut out of it.

Kern slowly unfolded the bed sheet and held it in front of the jurors. He had Price point out how the hole seemed to have been carefully cut out, while glancing frequently at the jurors to make certain they understood how important this piece of evidence was. Why would there be a hole in the sheet? he asked the detective. I objected that the question called for speculation, and the judge agreed, but I knew it didn't erase the question from the jurors' minds.

"Are you familiar with the noise of a discharge of a .357 Magnum?"

"Yes sir, I am. It's like a cannon. Extremely loud."

The prosecutor asked how Hicks appeared during their interview at the apartment.

"He was very much in control, just as if we were talking as now. I saw no remorse on the man's face."

I objected. "No remorse" is one of those loaded phrases that prosecutors sneak into testimony. The judge agreed: The jury was instructed to disregard the answer.

That was Kern's last shot. As he walked back to his chair I slowly re-arranged my notes for Price's cross-examination. I decided to begin by raising doubts about the detective's memory.

"You do a lot of cases, don't you?"

"Quite a few, yes."

"And that's one reason why police officers like yourself carry notepads to take notes?"

"Yes sir."

"Taking a statement from a suspect in a homicide case, I imagine, would be pretty important, wouldn't it?"

"Yes sir, it is."

"Did you take notes as you were talking to Mr. Hicks?"

"I believe I had taken some notes, yes."

I asked to see them. As the jury stared at him, Price spent several minutes rummaging through a thick file folder that contained his material on the Hicks case. "Probably not in the file," he stammered.

"I take it, then," I said, "the notes that you took of the initial interview with Mr. Hicks do not exist?"

"I can't say they don't exist," Price responded quickly. "They're not here."

"But all the important matters in the case would be included within the detective's file?"

"Yes sir."

"And those notes are not there?"

"No."

"I would have assumed, being just a lawyer, that a demonstration as to how the shooting occurred would be important?"

"Yes sir."

"Something this important would surely be included in your report?"

"Well, the response that we had, Mr. Hicks wasn't clear enough to even indicate a possible way the gun was held."

"Let me see if I fully understand you. This demonstration was so important that you were able to describe it in detail for the jury, yet it was so vague that it wasn't even worth putting in your written report. Do I have that right?"

"Objection!"

"Sustained," bellowed Judge Carney. Judges don't appreciate sarcasm.

I waved Price's eight-page typed report in his face and asked: "Could you please examine your report and show me where you state in there that Mr. Hicks demonstrated at the apartment how the shooting occurred?"

He flipped through the report, hunting among the pages for something I knew wasn't there.

"Okay," Detective Price said at last with a sigh. "In my report I have stated here exactly what Hicks replied to my questions. As far as the demonstration— there's no reference to the demonstration, no."

"No mention at *all?*"

"No sir, there's not."

"According to your report," I said, picking it up, "and please correct me if I'm wrong, you say, 'Hicks informed the undersigned and Detective Ranieri that he shot the victim accidentally and after failing to get Turner medical treatment, abandoned the victim in her car at the bank parking lot.' The next sentence states: 'Hicks stated he discarded the gun in a canal in Bonaventure, Florida.' "

"Right."

"That's the *entire* description of the statement in your report, is it not?"

"Right."

"So you have given us a lengthy description of an interview that happened seven months ago. Yet all you have as proof are two sentences in a typed report, right?"

A meek yes was his only response.

My plan was to chip away at what the detectives had done and not done. Each fact might not seem important at the moment, but I needed to establish points I could assemble into a coherent picture in summation. Before jurors send someone to jail for life, and even more to the electric chair, they like to think they have all the bases covered. Little gaps in the story can grow into reasonable doubt.

I had to tread cautiously. Although the jurors needed to understand that the detectives had failed to do many things, I didn't want to transmit the impression that "my client's guilty, but the cops blew the investigation and so they didn't prove it." If the police had really investigated their case and found out what happened, Steve wouldn't have been charged—that was the message the jury needed to hear.

I began by getting Price to acknowledge that, as the lead detective, he was responsible for coordinating the work of everyone else involved in the case.

I asked about the crime scene technician. "You were aware that she was inexperienced."

"Yes sir."

In fact, this was Liz Hartman's first homicide investigation. "You directed her photographing of the scene?"

"Yes sir."

"I assume that you told her that she ought to be careful to bag the hands as soon as possible so we don't lose any evidence?"

Price bristled. In the bank parking lot, Hartman and the assistant medical examiner had removed Betsy's shirt, but they had not followed the standard procedure of first bagging the corpse's hands. All well-trained homicide detectives know that a corpse's hands should be bagged, so that they can later be examined for residue that would indicate that the deceased had recently fired a gun. There was no way of showing whether Betsy pulled the trigger. Nor could it later be proved whether she scratched Steve in a fight.

Price hesitated. Finally, he came up with an answer: "That we leave up to the professionals. They bag the hands."

"Leave it up to *whom?*"

"The professionals."

"You mean the ambulance drivers?"

"Whoever the medical examiner uses."

"You left it to them to decide how to preserve evidence in *your* case?"

"They are usually the ones that bag the hands, yes."

"So you decided it wasn't necessary for you to give any orders?"

"Dr. Ongley gives them instructions, yes." Dr. James Patrick Ongley was the assistant medical examiner who had come to the bank.

"Did you check with Dr. Ongley to be sure this evidence was preserved?"

"I don't recall."

I asked about removing the clothes from the corpse. "You had to be aware that this pulling motion is like wiping off her body?"

"It wiped off her body?"

"Yes."

"Possibly."

"Did you talk to Liz Hartman, this inexperienced crime scene technician, to be sure the hands were preserved so the evidence could be retained?"

"I don't recall saying that, no."

I moved to a detail which would appear unimportant to the jury at that moment but which I knew was going to be a crucial point for my summation.

"What did you do to preserve the white fibers on the shirt?"

"We collected a few of them and then we just folded the shirt inward."

"Where did you send the white fibers that you collected?"

"I believe to the sheriff's lab, but I couldn't be sure of that."

"Can I see their report regarding these fibers?"

Again, he shuffled through the file. Again, the jury watched as he searched for something that should have been there. "No sir," he said at last, "I don't see a lab report on it."

"Could you show me a transmittal letter that you sent to the lab asking them to do some work on these fibers?"

"No sir."

"Well, *did* you send these fibers to the lab?" I already knew the fibers had not been tested. I had the answer in a manila folder on the podium right in front of me, but I allowed Price to fumble through his papers. In my file was every relevant document carefully indexed and cross-indexed for quick retrieval. I needed to show the jurors that I had a better grasp of the evidence than he did. Not testing the fibers was a major blunder. Steve had told the police that the handkerchief was wrapped around the gun. A fiber test would have proved that he was telling the truth. Without the test, we had no way of backing up Steve's story on this crucial point.

The detective responded by passing the buck: "I had Liz Hartman collect them and have them sent. I instructed her to send them to the lab to be analyzed."

"I assumed you followed up on that to be sure the lab analyzed these fibers?"

"I didn't myself, no sir."

"Are you familiar with the Wayne Williams case in Atlanta?"

"No sir."

For forensic scientists, this was one of the biggest cases in years. Atlanta detectives had nailed down Williams's guilt in the murder of two black youths by matching fibers found on the boys' bodies to fibers found on rugs and other items in Williams's home.

I picked up the handkerchief from the evidence table and showed it to him. "What kind of material is this?"

"Appears to be cotton."

"Did you ask anybody to take a look at this handkerchief and to examine the fibers found on the T-shirt?"

"I don't believe so, no."

"Isn't it your job to coordinate these aspects of the case?"

"Yes sir. But let me make one point clear. As soon as Mr. Hicks was placed under arrest, okay, I was assigned and transferred to another case. Detective Ranieri was in charge of the follow-up work on this."

Price's statement was the first of many, from various witnesses, indicating that no one took responsibility for the investigation. Everyone pointed fingers. After the police had gotten a statement from Hicks and put him in jail, they all assumed that that was the end of the case.

"So," I said, "you take *no* responsibility as to what happened after Mr. Hicks's arrest?"

"Only that I knew of stuff had been collected, evidence, and hopefully taken down to the lab."

"*Hopefully* something would be done?"

"Instructions are given to the technicians, yes."

"And . . ."

"Ranieri followed the results up."

"Did you tell Ranieri to properly follow up the case?"

"I didn't explicitly. I am sure the supervisor did."

"How many homicide cases had Detective Ranieri worked on?"

"I don't know. Two maybe. One or two."

"Did that give you any pause turning over this case to somebody who really didn't have any homicide experience?"

"That's not my decision, sir."

I turned to the blood spatters. Experts diagram the positions of the spatters so that they can determine patterns. "Did you ask that somebody diagram those stairs and put in where this blood was found?"

"We had them photographed."

"Taking photographs of individual steps doesn't tell us where those steps are, do they?"

"No sir, they don't."

I showed him the photographs. Each showed a couple of steps. There was no way to tell which were the top steps, which were in the middle, which were at the bottom. Most of the photos were out of focus. They showed only blurry, discolored splotches—useless to a bloodstain expert, who needs to examine the tiniest streaks and spots. "Is there blood shown in this photograph?" I asked, handing him the fuzziest one in the bunch.

"Well . . ." He pondered the photo. "It's not very clear but this is it, yeah. This is what she was attempting to photograph, yes."

Attempting to photograph. I took the photo back. It was impossible to tell even which way was up. An experienced forensic scientist would have drawn a diagram and taken overlapping photos so they could be sequenced in the proper order. Kern had claimed in his opening that the photos would show Steve carried the body down the steps in a deliberate fashion, contradicting our case of rushing her to the emergency room. The photos had to be discredited.

"Does the photograph go like this?" I asked, turning it one way. "Like this?" I turned it upside down. "Or like this?" I turned it sideways—or what I guessed was sideways.

Sheepishly, Price bowed his head: "That I couldn't tell you."

I picked up another photo from the exhibit table. "What does this show?"

"I have no idea. It appears to be a stair, but obviously it is a bad picture."

"Well, it's introduced here as a State's exhibit. I assume it has some significance. Do you have any idea what significance this photograph has?"

"Only there might be some blood on the stair. You'd have to consult Liz Hartman exactly what the picture represents."

"In fact, any photograph we have to take it on faith this is blood?"

"Okay."

"You are *hoping* that Liz Hartman took the photographs of the blood and not just some stains on the stairs?"

"Right."

"These bloodstains in the apartment or the stairs show no evidence that someone was being dragged?"

"No sir."

It was a key point. "In fact," I said, "your evidence that you found of blood droplets and absence of dragging is consistent with somebody *carrying* her out of the apartment?"

"That's hard to say."

I glanced at the jury box. Gerald Klein was looking directly at Price. I showed Price a photo of the mattress. "Were you able to determine from this photograph that the bullet went into the mattress at an angle?"

"At an angle, yes."

"And that's because if we measure the bullet hole it's larger than a defect that could be caused by a .357, isn't it?"

"I don't think I'm qualified to answer that."

"The diameter of a .357 bullet is .357 of an inch?"

"Uh-huh."

I attached the photograph to the blackboard and then, from my briefcase, pulled out a pair of calipers. I was confident that my attention to detail would not be lost on Juror Klein. The detectives hadn't measured the bullet hole. A meticulous homicide man would have inserted a dowel through the mattress to trace the bullet's path, and then photographed the dowel in the mattress to solidify the finding. A homicide case is made or broken on the crime scene investigation. If your defense doesn't fit the facts gathered at the scene, then you don't have a defense—unless you can show that the detectives screwed up the evidence.

"If," I said, "we take a pair of calipers and measure one end to the other and use this, we find that the hole in the mattress is almost an inch on the photo?" This photo included a ruler so distances could be demonstrated.

"Okay," the detective nodded. "That's what it says."

"That tends to show, does it not, that the bullet's going in at an angle?"

Kern objected. He said the answer would require an expert, and he had not presented Price as an expert. I was glad to hear that admission. A homicide detective should not interpret evidence. In fact, I knew that my questions were close to the borderline. If Price had been giving expert opinions in answer to Kern's questioning, I would have been objecting, but part of the adversary system of justice is pushing the other side as far as you can.

"If, for example, you took a .357 bullet and fired it straight down into a mattress, you would expect a hole approximately a third of an inch?"

Kern objected again: "There is no way in the world anybody could testify to this accurately unless they ran experiments on the particular mattress."

The judge overruled him: "If the witness knows the answer, I will permit him if he knows it."

"I really don't know the answer," Price confessed.

"That's very interesting," I said. "I think Mr. Kern brings up a very good point. Did you run experiments on the mattress using a .357?"

"I myself?"

"Yes."

"No."

"Did you ask Patrick Garland, the State's firearms expert, to shoot practice rounds into a mattress?"

"Not that I know of, no."

"Did you make any attempt *whatsoever* to determine the angle of the trajectory of the bullet?"

"No."

"By the way, there's no blood in the bullet hole, is there?"

"No sir."

"The blood is over here?" I pointed to the stain in the photo, a few inches from the hole.

"Yes sir." Price nodded.

"So that tends to show you—"

"Objection," Kern shouted.

I insisted on finishing: "—that the person was not lying on the mattress?"

"Objection," Kern repeated. "Conclusion."

"Sustained," said Judge Carney.

Defense lawyers use different tactics than prosecutors. Our first line of attack, and many times our only defense, comes in cross-examination. So I felt justified in seeking the same type of speculation that I successfully blocked Kern from getting on direct a few minutes earlier. Any competent forensic expert would know that if the bloodstain was at a different place than the bullet hole, it meant that Betsy was not lying down when she was shot. I could see Klein knitting his brow, working out the physics. I refused to abandon the topic.

"Now, sir," I went on, "looking at this photograph here. This bloodstain is approximately six inches from where the bullet went into the mattress?"

"Yes sir."

"Can you deduce from this photo that Betsy was not lying against the mattress at the time she was shot?"

"Objection."

"Sustained."

Testing Carney's resolve, I persisted. "If the person was lying against the mattress right here, and the bullet exited from the skin right into the mattress, you expect blood in the bullet hole, wouldn't you?"

"Objection."

"Sustained."

Never surrender: "There was *no* blood in the bullet hole?"

"Doesn't appear to be, no."

"I notice there is not really a lot of blood on the mattress either, is there?"

"No sir."

"And you know the wound in this case would cause a lot of bleeding, don't you?"

Kern was on his feet: "Objection. Calls for a conclusion."

"Sustained."

I pushed on: "Can you deduce from this photograph, sir, that after the shooting the person was removed from the mattress fairly quickly?"

"Objection."

"Sustained."

It didn't matter. Klein, the man with the two master's degrees, was leaning forward in his chair, elbows on knees, chin in his hands. I was sure he understood what I was getting at.

I picked up a photo that showed a hole in the wall. I figured that this might be important later, that Kern could try to argue that Steve's fist had made the hole—a sign of a violent fight shortly before the fatal shot. In fact, Steve had told us that the hole had been made quite a while before the night of the shooting.

"Photographs can be ambiguous, can't they?"

"Possibly, yes."

I pointed out flakes of what appeared to be white powder below the hole in the wall. I then showed him another photo with white dots sprinkled about.

Price thought the first photo showed flecks of plaster, while the second showed "an imperfection in the film."

I stared at him: "The white dots here that one sees on the wall are imperfections in the film. The white dots we see on the rug are plaster?"

"Yes."

"The picture is strewn with white dots, isn't it?"

"Uh-huh."

"Are you sure that is a defect in the film?"

"I can't be positive, no."

"Or is it plaster just falling off the wall because it's old?"

Kern jumped up. "Objection. Asking the witness to speculate."

"Sustained."

The prosecutor was helping me along. "In fact," I said, "all we can do is speculate, isn't that right?"

"Objection!"

Judge Carney overruled him, and I repeated my question: "All we can do is speculate about that?"

"I suppose."

Price acknowledged that, when examining the wall, he had noticed flecks of skin, meaning that someone had suffered an injury while punching the hole in the wall. I had him admit that he had examined Steve's fist and found that there was no skin missing, no signs of any injury that would indicate he had made the hole in the wall.

"And you examined Betsy Turner's hand to find out there's nothing on her hands to show that she in any way punched this wall?"

"Yes."

"In fact, you weren't even sure when this hole was made. It could have been anytime in the past?"

"Yes."

"Now, when you took Mr. Hicks to the police department, did you have his hands swabbed?"

"No sir."

One would think that the police would have wanted to prove Steve's hand had been in close proximity to the gun when it was fired, but they hadn't examined his hands.

I pulled out photos of the corpse taken where it had been found, at the bank. Price acknowledged that there was no indication—from Betsy's clothes, her body or her delicate necklace—that she had been involved in a fight.

I showed Price a photo of Betsy taken during the autopsy. "She still has eye makeup on, doesn't she?"

"It would appear to be, yes."

"Don't young ladies take their makeup off before going to bed?"

"Objection."

"Sustained."

I couldn't let this go. Kern was drawing a picture of Steve luring Betsy to bed, coldly lying next to her until she fell asleep, then pressing the gun to her side and shooting her. It was a loathsome image, but one fact made it unconvincing. Grasping a close-up photo of Betsy's face taken during the autopsy, I drew lines around the faded remnants of foundation and mascara. I made sure the women jurors got a good look at Betsy's face.

I then showed Price a photo of the open nightstand drawer and directed his attention to the empty soft-drink bottles and cans on top of the stand. "Where did they come from?"

"Those are from the reserve officers who sealed off the apartment."

"You mean the soda bottles and cans were placed there by *police* officers?"

"By police officers, yes."

Crime scenes can be contaminated by the weather, souvenir hunters, paramedics or the victim's family, but police officers are supposed to know better. I forced Price to admit that the lead homicide detective supervised the charting and photographing of the blood spatters, weapons and even bits of fallen plaster. If necessary, his job was to keep the crime scene technicians on site for days. He conceded that contamination could render evidence useless.

"You mean contamination like Coke bottles?" I asked.

"Objection," Kern shouted. "Argumentative."

"Sustained."

The Coke bottles were symbolic. The Plantation police thought they had Steve Hicks locked up tight for first-degree murder. They hadn't worried that Liz Hartman was a rookie technician because they didn't really care what she did. They didn't care about getting good photos or making diagrams or preserving the integrity of the crime scene.

"What size mattress was on the bed?"

"It was queen size."

I asked about the sheet found in the closet: "The sheet with a hole in it, exhibit 37, is a twin, right?"

"I don't know."

I held up the photo of the sheet with a square cut out of the center. "Did you measure it?"

"No sir."

"Did it fit the mattress?"

"I don't know."

It was a sheet for a twin, so it couldn't possibly have been put on the queen-sized bed. Later, in my summation, the sheet would become another symbol of police indifference to the evidence, but for now, I just let the question linger in the jurors' minds.

Finally, I questioned Price about the motive: "Were you able to find an insurance policy that upon Betsy's death Steve Hicks would receive any money?"

"No sir."

"Did they jointly hold any stocks or bonds or certificates of deposit?"

"No."

"Any jointly owned property?"

"I myself was not involved in this facet of the investigation, if in fact it was done."

"Do you know whether or not any examination was done to see if there was *any* financial motive *whatsoever* for Steve Hicks to kill Martha Turner?"

"I have no knowledge of that."

As Price left the stand, I thought we had made some inroads, but we still had a long way to go.

Detective Nick Ranieri had driven Hicks back to the police station, where he gave a taped twenty-minute statement at 6:55 p.m. on Saturday. By then, Steve had been awake for thirty-six hours.

With Ranieri on the stand, Kern played the entire tape. Hicks spoke in an exhausted monotone as he described the events of Friday evening, going to a bar by himself, having problems with his car, Betsy coming to meet him, then returning to the apartment, where Betsy insinuated that he might have been seeing another woman, and picked up the gun in the bedroom, and Hicks warned her that it was loaded.

Ranieri asked Hicks, "How many rounds were in the gun?"

"There was one."

"Why was one bullet in there?"

"The round was stuck in there."

He said he lay down opposite her on the bed. "She had the gun in her hand. I don't remember exactly what was said but like I—you know, I just repeated the warning and I went to grab the gun to put it away and that's when I heard the shot."

"Okay. So did you ask her to hand you the gun or did you just go and pull the gun or—"

"Well, I did say, 'Give it to me.' But I don't remember her reply."

"Okay. So then you took the gun from her at which time it discharged?"

"It dis—dis—"

"Was she holding it from giving it to you?"

"We both had our hands on it at the same time, but like I said, she was holding it with the thing on it and when I went to grab it, I said, 'Give it to me, let me put it away.' When I grabbed it, it knocked the little handkerchief off and then it went off."

Hicks said he carried her down to the Mustang and began the search for a hospital. Betsy was groaning. "I told her to hang on, we'll be there real quick." After a while she grew silent. He checked her pulse and realized she was dead. "I was hysterical. I just—I didn't know what to do. . . . I still can't explain my actions."

After abandoning the Mustang at the bank, he went back to the apartment and washed the sheets and his clothes in the laundry room. "See, I didn't wash that stuff for a while. I . . . was really just incoherent. I turned the mattress over and I tried to lay down and I couldn't. . . . My mind was just racing." He told Ranieri that he put the gun in a paper bag in the storage room. "I don't know why this happened to me. I've never done a damn thing wrong in my life. I'm sorry that it happened and I'm sorry that I did not just go ahead and call the police and tell them. . . . I just didn't think about it."

When the tape finished, Kern said, "No further questions."

I asked Ranieri when he had taken responsibility for the investigation. He guessed that Price had handled the case for the first week, and then he had taken over, but he said he really hadn't had to do much.

"Detective Price basically wrapped up the investigation?"

"Pretty much, yes sir."

Ranieri acknowledged that this was the first time he had ever been the lead detective in a homicide case. I decided to take a small gamble with the don't-ask-a-question-you-don't-know-the-answer-to rule. I risked it with Ranieri because he had followed Price to the stand immediately—they had had no opportunity to coordinate their stories. "There was no demonstration as to how the gun was shot there, was there?"

"Not that I remember."

A *major* point for us—and a direct contradiction of what Detective Price had said.

The next day Kern called George Ilaria, who lived in unit 202, just below Steve's apartment. Kern showed him an aerial photo of the apartment complex and the surrounding area. At the prosecutor's request, Ilaria circled with a red marker the Humana Bennett Hospital, a couple of hundred yards from the apartment.

He didn't say that it was difficult to get to the hospital from the apartment complex. You had to leave the complex, turn right, go one block, turn left and then go four blocks and find the hospital entrance, which was tucked behind a Kentucky Fried Chicken restaurant.

Kern asked about the night Betsy died. Ilaria said he was awakened at 2:30 a.m. by a woman's screams He heard a "heavy discussion" for about five minutes. He said he never heard a shot. Kern looked pointedly at the jurors. I was certain that he would argue that the shot—he had already had an officer say that .357s made a huge noise—must have been muffled as part of Steve's murder plan.

Ilaria said that later he was awakened again by a sound that sounded like "shuffling and moving." A door slammed. "That was the end of the noise."

In my cross-examination I brought out that neither Ilaria's wife nor his brother-in-law, who were asleep in the apartment, had heard a thing, and that he had heard no violent confrontation:

"To me, it didn't sound like an argument," he said. "There was no voice raising or threats of any type."

"So it sounded like two people were discussing an important matter?"

"Yes." There was no yelling, no cursing, no threats.

I asked about what he thought of as a door slamming. Perhaps he had heard the gunshot.

"Did you hear something like this?" I asked as I slapped a hand on the witness rail.

"All I can say it sounded like a normal door closing, but, of course, it is magnified at that time of the morning."

"You heard a noise like a door closing, but louder?"

"That's correct."

Kern led Liz Hartman through the work she had done in the bank parking lot, where she had taken photos and collected Betsy's clothes. Then she had gone to the Medical Examiner's Office to photograph the corpse and was given hair combings, nail clippings, swabs and a tube of heart blood. Later, Detectives Price and Ranieri asked Hartman to take photos of blood on the stairs and in the bedroom of the apartment. She also took scrapings of the stains. She found Betsy's purse. It contained $51.03, a brush, a checkbook and credit cards. In the apartment's storage area, she inspected a brown paper bag containing a revolver, a white handkerchief and a box containing forty .357 Magnum cartridges.

Mark Seiden, who was assisting me, started Hartman's cross-examination by digging into her background. He brought out that she had not gone through the local community college's program for crime scene technicians. She had been on the job only three months. It was her first homicide investigation.

Mark summarized what she had *not* done at the bank. She hadn't gone through the glove compartment. She hadn't processed the car for fingerprints, though there were bloody handprints on the car. She didn't check the engine temperature, didn't open the hood to see if the radiator was hot or cold, didn't check the exhaust. Any of those things would have given an experienced investigator an idea of the time the car had been left there. She didn't check the fuel gauge or the odometer reading. She did not bag the corpse's hands. She made no notations about the corpse's body temperature or post-mortem lividity. (Lividity, which is the pooling of blood in the body when circulation stops, can establish the position of the body at death.)

"You took some pictures?"

"Yes sir."

"And they didn't turn out too well, did they?"

"No sir."

"Do you know why?"

"Should have used a different camera lens."

Mark picked up the photos and asked her what they showed. Some were vague blurs. A couple were taken from an apartment window; you could make out the outline of trees, but that was all. One showed a parked car, which was in focus, in out-of-focus surroundings. What was this shot supposed to show? No one knew, not even Ms. Hartman. Another photo was surprisingly sharp, but it showed nothing more than a red car, a yellow fire hydrant and a tree. My favorite was almost entirely black, with just a small strip at the bottom showing some part of the apartment. The unasked question: Why had Kern introduced all these photos into the record?

Concerning the sheet with the square cut out of it, Mark asked: "Did you take that particular sheet and stretch it over the bed to see whether or not that particular hole corresponded to any stains on the bed?"

"No sir."

"As a matter of fact, nobody did that?"

"Not to my knowledge."

Hartman was proving a prime example of our theme: The Plantation police thought they had the case wrapped up.

Kern called James Patrick Ongley, the assistant medical examiner who performed the autopsy. Ongley testified that he had spent at least two hours at the bank parking lot before the corpse was removed. "She had no shoes on. There was no dirt or debris on the bottoms of her feet." He estimated that Betsy died sometime between midnight and 6 a.m.

The doctor told the court that "the muzzle of the barrel was close or next to the skin. You have an imprint of the barrel forming on the skin." The entrance wound was near the waistline. The bullet traveled through the liver and kidneys before exiting on the left side. The trajectory was slightly from front to back, with a small upward slant. Cause of death: Severe bleeding from the wounds to the liver and kidneys. Death would have occurred within fifteen minutes.

I focused the cross-examination on the careless investigation. While most homicide detectives call the Medical Examiner's Office as soon as they find a body, Ongley hadn't been notified until two hours after the corpse was found.

"The police should call you as soon as they find the corpse?"

"That's typically how it's done." Ongley explained how body temperature and lividity can indicate an approximate time of death if they are observed soon enough. The doctor also said he would have wanted to be on hand to make sure that the evidence was handled properly.

I noted that it had been drizzling while investigators were at the bank, and that that had produced condensation on the corpse. "And condensation is one of the things that damage the collection of gunshot residue?"

"Among many, yes." Usually, Ongley admitted, a corpse's hands are swabbed at the scene. Either taking off the T-shirt or the drizzle could have removed the residue. Eventually, the hands were tested, back at the Medical Examiner's Office. No residue was found.

"The absence of gunshot residue means nothing, does it?"

"That's very true."

"It's only the *presence* of gunshot residue that means anything?"

"Yes."

"Somebody can actually fire a revolver in front of a forensic scientist, have their hands swabbed right then and have the swabbings analyzed right then and there, and swabbings may come back negative?"

"That's true."

"Now, no blood on the top of her feet and no blood on her legs would indicate that she probably did not walk or remain erect at any time after she was shot?"

"That would indicate that, yes."

"So it's reasonably certain that she was carried from wherever she was shot?"

"It is consistent with that, yes."

Ongley also stated that there were no marks on her hands, no broken fingernails, no bruises or wounds anywhere on her body to indicate that she had been involved recently in a fight.

"Based upon the bullet track, the deceased would be in more or less a semi-reclining position at the time the shot exited?"

"Yes."

"Semi-reclining lying on the bed?"

"Yeah."

Semi-reclining was different than lying down. We were certain that Kern wanted to have Betsy lying down at the time of the shot, to suggest that she had been sleeping when the trigger was pulled. Ongley also acknowledged that Betsy did not have a "chored exit wound," the kind that occurs when a body is pressed tightly against something, yet another indication that her body wasn't lying on the mattress when the shot was fired.

The doctor said the wound had caused "a fatal injury."

"How many minutes after the bullet struck would death have been absolutely certain?"

"One minute, two minutes, five minutes. If the person was then given the maximal treatment; that is, got to emergency right away, the person wouldn't have lived anyhow." If Steve had found an emergency room right away, Betsy Turner would still have died.

People might expect a .357 Magnum revolver to make an explosive sound, but Ongley confirmed that wasn't necessarily so if the muzzle was right against the body.

"People would describe a contact or near contact gunshot as an unusual noise or thud rather than a sharp crack?"

"Yes."

Finally, we wanted to focus the jury's attention on the most crucial fact of Ongley's testimony: The location of the bullet wound was not where a killer would intentionally shoot someone.

"If I intended a death blow using a .357 Magnum revolver, I would shoot you in the face, or the back of your head."

"Yes."

"And if I placed the muzzle right over your heart and pulled the trigger, that would kill you pretty quickly, too?"

"Yes."

"You almost have to be a physician to know about livers and kidneys and richly vascular organs, wouldn't you?"

"Yes, where they're located."

"There's nothing from your forensic examination that proves this was *not* an accidental shooting, is there?"

"That's correct."

On re-direct Kern shot back: "Doctor, is there anything in our forensic examination to say that this was *not* a deliberate murder?"

"No," said the careful medical examiner, "there's not."

The prosecutor had regained a little ground, but he asked one question too many: "Of course, if someone had not been aware, or asleep, you wouldn't expect to find any defensive mechanisms or indication of defensive mechanisms, would you?"

"Right. That's correct. If you are not aware, you're not going to defend."

Kern was suggesting that Betsy had been asleep when she was shot. Smart move, if the evidence backed him up.

The next day Kern opened with Robert Cerat, a crime scene specialist with the Broward County Sheriff's Office. Cerat was a professional—ten years as a detective, five years on crime scenes. On the Sunday morning following the shooting, he had been asked to look at Hicks's apartment. He had also examined Hicks's .357 Dan Wesson revolver and discovered it had no fingerprints. "It had nothing on it. It was just cleaned, almost like it was brand-new." Kern got him to say that this was "unusual" for a gun that had just been fired. The detective suggested that a towel could have been used to wipe off fingerprints.

In our cross-examination Cerat acknowledged that the lack of fingerprints didn't prove anything. Any kind of accidental rubbing could have removed them.

As the detective was leaving the stand, Judge Carney announced that he had noticed that Juror Klein was taking notes. I took this to be a good sign. Klein was keeping track of the details. Our case rested on those details. The judge, of course, admonished Klein to stop taking notes. I've never understood this rule. Everyone in the courtroom, the judge included, could take notes, except the very people who have to remember the facts. Nevertheless, I was certain that Klein's attentiveness would mean the other jurors would turn to him for answers in deliberations. I decided to concentrate even more on him.

• • •

As the trial progressed, Kern devoted a lot of time to the location of hospitals. Several police officers testified about the location of hospitals; on cross-examination each admitted that police were *trained* to know about hospitals. Then a nurse from Doctor's Concial—the hospital where Steve said the front doors were locked and he couldn't find the emergency room—testified that the emergency room was easy to locate. Kern handed her some nighttime photos that showed a brightly lit emergency sign. It had the candle power of a marquee on the Las Vegas strip. The nurse identified the photos and they were admitted into evidence.

An alarm bell began ringing loudly in my brain. I had visited the hospital at night, to see it exactly the way Steve had seen it, and I didn't recollect that the emergency sign near the entrance was as prominent, as bright, as it appeared in these photos. They had been taken by Detective Cerat, who had just been on the stand, yet Kern had not asked him about the photos. While any witness with knowledge of a location can verify that a photo is accurate, it seemed strange that Kern had waited for Cerat to leave the courtroom before bringing out his photographs.

The photos flashed through my mind the rest of the day. That night I took copies of the photos and drove back to the hospital. The emergency sign was much dimmer than it appeared in the pictures. The next morning before court, we went to a professional photographer, who examined the photos carefully. He was certain the images had been manipulated in a darkroom enlarger to brighten the appearance of the sign.

Kern now focused on the gun—and on Steve's statement to police that there was only one round in the revolver because it had gotten stuck there. The State's main gun witness was Patrick Garland, a firearms specialist with the Broward Sheriff's Office. He testified that he had fired the weapon ten times and not once had a round stuck in a chamber. Garland did observe, however, that the revolver had small white fibers in one chamber and that the handkerchief tested positive for residue from gunfire. That backed up

Steve's statement that the handkerchief had been on the gun when it was fired.

After a break another Broward Sheriff's detective, Randy Goldberg, took the stand. He was the blood spatter expert. Goldberg gave a description of his specialty, calling it a science that "goes back to the days of the Bible." On cross-examination we brought out that nothing in the blood spatters indicated that there had been a fight or that there had been a murder.

When we arrived at court the next morning, Judge Carney announced that Juror Klein had asked to speak to him. This was unsettling news because we had directed so much of our case at Klein. I waited nervously while the bailiff brought Klein to the jury box. He sat there alone, his colleagues remaining out of earshot in the jury room.

"As we were leaving the courtroom yesterday," Klein stated, "a juror I was standing next to spoke to one of the witnesses." The juror was June Habicht, an elderly woman. The witness was Detective Goldberg. "She said to him either 'good job' or 'you did good.' Something to that effect. And she only had one sentence out and I grabbed her arm, and she says, 'Oh, I forgot.' And I said, 'You are not to speak to a witness.' And she says, 'I misunderstood. I thought we could after the witness has testified.' And I said, 'No, I don't believe we are allowed to speak to a witness at any time, plus I believe that we are not supposed to form opinions until the entire trial is over and we are to deliberate.' "

Choosing Klein was paying dividends. We had picked him for his intelligence, and now we found out he was taking a leading role in the jury room. It was obvious he was going to be the foreman.

Judge Carney sent Mr. Klein back to the jury room and ordered Ms. Habicht brought out. The elderly woman was mortified that she had done something wrong. "I said in going by him, 'Good witness,' meaning that some of the other witnesses it was difficult to pay attention and really understand what they were saying and I was impressed by his technicality and his expertise on the subject that he was being interviewed about." She stated Goldberg didn't reply to her comment.

Privately, I thought it was good news that Ms. Habicht was having a hard time understanding the State's witnesses, and a mistrial would be to Kern's advantage because he now knew my theory of defense and could prepare to combat it. But as a matter of law, I had to make an objection for the record, in case we needed to appeal the verdict. I meekly requested a mistrial while silently praying it would be denied. The judge didn't disappoint me.

Kern next put on a series of witnesses who had known Betsy Turner. He was searching for any hint of a motive. Crimes without a motive are rare. At the end of the trial the judge would instruct the jurors that Kern didn't have to prove a motive, but their common sense will require one.

The first witness was Julie Pownall, who had been a co-worker of Betsy's for ten months at East Coast Graphics, a printing company. She stated that Betsy had worked her way up quickly, starting as proofer and then being promoted to head of the proofing department, in charge of five people. Pownall had seen Betsy only twice outside of work. When Kern asked whether Betsy ever told her anything about her personal life, Pownall responded: "She was very quiet about that." On Friday, June 27, her last day at work, she had seemed in good humor.

Kern asked her if she had ever seen Betsy injured. We objected immediately. At a sidebar Kern proffered that Pownall would state that she once saw Betsy bruised. Betsy had told Pownall that she had gotten drunk and fallen down, but Kern suggested that Hicks had hit her. The judge sustained my objection: "The questioning may attach a very sinister meaning to it." The prosecutor asked her an inconsequential question and gave up. We asked Pownall no questions at all: She had said nothing to suggest that Hicks had committed a murder.

Kern continued his search for a motive by calling Betsy's mother, Betty Turner. These are the moments that drive lawyers to drink: a mother's face plainly exhibiting pain and sorrow over her child's death while also flashing hatred at the accused. Mrs. Turner had written a letter to the judge expressing her anger: "She loved him and got death. We loved her and got life (without her). He loved no one but himself. Please don't let him get less. He used her, abused her, killed her and dumped her dead body in a parking lot as if she were nothing to him. He must pay for it." That letter was inadmissible, but her bitterness would seep into her testimony in ways that I couldn't challenge without fear of losing the jury.

In 1984, the mother said, she visited Atlanta and Betsy told her about meeting Hicks: "He was a bartender at a restaurant there and she wanted me to meet him. She was very infatuated with him." Later, after Hicks left Atlanta for South Florida, Mrs. Turner gave her daughter money so she could move down and join him.

After a few months in Plantation, in August 1985, Betsy went back to South Carolina for a vacation. "She was very upset, very unhappy and very emotional and so very much in love." She wanted to go back to Hicks despite the turmoil.

I doodled as Kern traipsed through this testimony. Nothing that Betsy's mother was saying implicated Steve in a murder, and I hoped it was obvious to the jurors that the prosecutor had put her on the stand only to stir their emotions. Several times I objected to Kern's questions, cluing the jury to his manipulation. Despite these frequent protests Kern kept asking irrelevant personal questions. Mrs. Turner tried to help him out, describing her daughter's love for a man obviously unfit for it.

Two months before Betsy's death, Mr. and Mrs. Turner flew down for a three-day weekend, staying at a Holiday Inn near Hicks's and Betsy's apartment. Steve and Betsy took them sightseeing, to Shooters, a bar on the inland waterway, and to a historic house. Mrs. Turner said they seemed happy at the time. Despite the fact that Hicks wasn't working and that he wasn't yet divorced from his wife, Mrs. Turner said, Betsy was delighted to be living with him. When Hicks announced that he was thinking of moving back to Atlanta, Betsy started thinking of moving back, too.

On cross, I had to counter Mrs. Turner's implications without appearing to be harsh. I began by politely scoring a series of small points. When Betsy returned to see her folks in South Carolina, she said she missed Hicks.

"They talked every day?"

"I think every day."

"She was unhappy being separated from him?"

"Yes, she was."

As Kern had elicited sympathy for Betsy, I had to see what Mrs. Turner could say about Steve's better points. She acknowledged that when Steve's mother was dying of cancer in Georgia, Steve went there and stayed by her side for the last two weeks of her life. Then he took in his grandfather, who was elderly and perhaps senile.

"Steve was worried about his grandfather?"

"Evidently," she said between pursed lips. A grudging admission.

"At eighty-six, he's not able to take care of himself?"

"I wouldn't say he could live alone, no."

When she and her husband visited Betsy in South Florida, Mrs. Turner acknowledged that Steve had been a gracious host. "In fact, Steve even cooked the dinner?"

"Yes, he cooked. . . . He was very very congenial, very nice."

"They appeared to be a happy couple to you?"

"They did."

With that, I stopped, figuring that I had countered some of the sympathy Kern had elicited from the jury.

We were deep into the State's case, and Kern had yet to put on a single witness who had suggested *any* reason Steve would want Betsy dead. After the lunch break he called Margie Hightower, one of Betsy's old friends from Atlanta.

Hightower was a secretary with a young son; she was going through a divorce about the time she and Betsy began working together at an Atlanta printing company. One night the two of them went to Penrod's, an Atlanta bar where Hicks was working. Betsy was taken with him, and within a short time they were seeing each other regularly. Hicks was separated from his wife, but saw his young son regularly.

Hightower claimed to be friends with Hicks as well as Betsy, and after they moved to Florida she sometimes had lengthy phone conversations with each of them. "He always thought she was immature. He had told me that he was always debating on whether the relationship would work out, if he should stay or if he should go. He would tell me that he really didn't trust her and you could not marry someone that you didn't trust."

Several times Hicks returned alone to Atlanta to see his son. A few weeks before Betsy's death, Hicks took Margie out to dinner. He told her he was thinking of moving back to Atlanta, to go into business with his wife. "He was trying to convince Betsy that she should stay in Fort Lauderdale, that she had a good job. . . . If they moved back, they could not live together. I had asked him if his wife knew about Betsy and he said no."

"On that night did he talk about his wife?"

"He told me that he had helped her move." She added that Hicks was worried that if his estranged wife knew about Betsy, she might retaliate by not allowing him to see his son.

"Did he ever discuss his wife's financial situation with you?"

"He had just commented that she came from a very wealthy family. You know, that it was a family-owned business and that she would, you know, inherit whatever. You know, once her mother was gone she would inherit that, that would be her business." The business was a bartending school.

"Did he tell you what Betsy's reaction was?"

"She wanted to move back, of course, but he was just trying to convince her that, you know, she had a good job, she should stay there. He told me that he was afraid that if he left she would try to kill herself."

"How did that come up?"

"Just in the conversation over dinner, it just came out. He just said he was afraid if he left that she would try to kill herself."

"Would that be totally out of character for Betsy?"

"Yes, *totally* out of character."

Suddenly, the pieces fell into place. Kern was laying the groundwork that Steve had tried to make the death look like a suicide. My client had supposedly planned the murder and had planted the idea of suicide weeks in advance when he talked to Hightower. Now I understood why Kern had hinted darkly about the stuck bullet in his opening arguments and why he had Garland testify that a bullet had not stuck in the gun when he tested it. Kern was going to claim that Steve had lied about the stuck bullet because he had contemplated fabricating a story that Betsy had loaded only a single bullet for her own suicide.

Kern: "I hesitate to dwell, but how did this statement of his come up?"

"It came up," Hightower said, "after he was telling me that he was trying to convince her to stay. To me the question came out of the blue." She said

Hicks had showed her presents his estranged wife had given him—a gold chain, a watch, a diamond ring.

That evening, Hightower stated, was the last time she saw Hicks until the trial. But Betsy told her by telephone that she intended to follow Hicks to Atlanta. Four days before Betsy's death, Hightower talked to both of them on the telephone. "He said, 'I hear Betsy is coming up to see you in a couple of weeks.' And I said, 'Yes, that's what she tells me.' I made a comment about, 'I guess you guys are taking separate vacations.' And he said, 'I guess so.' "

When Kern was finished, I had a short conversation with Steve. He said Margie had come on to him, but he had told her he wasn't interested. "She's pissed off. It's all bullshit." How could I show she had shaded her testimony to manufacture a motive? I had to keep rigid control of her questioning because I knew she would keep trying to plant insinuations. But I still had to discredit the ones she had already made. I began slowly.

"When you met Steve at Penrod's did he seem like a nice young man?"

She acknowledged that he was well mannered and good-looking, and Betsy was a bit jealous. I pointed out that in her first police statement she hadn't mentioned anything about Steve telling her that his wife would inherit the family business when her mother died. Then I focused on how she had related that Steve was allegedly planning to divorce his wife *and* go into business with her. "He certainly didn't tell you he was going to go back to his wife and have a husband-and-wife relationship?"

"No, he did not."

This was important because one of Kern's theories was that Steve planned to go back to his rich wife and didn't want an angry Betsy ruining his plans.

I took her through the last evening she saw Steve. They met about 7 p.m. at a bar-restaurant, then shifted to an upscale restaurant and then went to another bar. By the time he drove her back to her car, it was about 2 a.m. During these seven hours she claimed to have had less than three drinks.

I asked her if she had told Betsy about the evening. She said she had.

"Did she ask what the two of you were doing out till two in the morning?"

"No," she said, flushing with anger, "absolutely not."

"Did you ever say anything to her that perhaps might indicate there was more than just friendship between you and Steve?"

"Absolutely not." She glared at me.

"During those seven hours through three bars, didn't you show a little interest in Steve?"

"Absolutely not."

"Seven hours is a pretty long time for just a friendly dinner."

"So what?"

"But no thoughts of a liaison behind your friend's back?"

"Never."

Figuring I had done enough to implant a suggestion that she was angry with Steve for rejecting her advances, I quit while I was ahead.

The State's presentation was finished. For our defense, we needed to rebut two basic theories that Kern had floated.

First, I had to deal with Kern's theory that Steve had originally intended to fake a suicide and then come up with the story about the single stuck bullet. Perhaps Kern was going to argue that Steve had planned to make it look as if Betsy had taken her own life, but when she fought back, he had to come up with a new plan. The only way we could rebut was by putting gun experts on the stand.

Secondly, Kern was suggesting that Steve's motive for killing Betsy was that he wanted to get rid of her so that he could go back to the easy life with his wife. His theory would be that Steve was frightened that his wife might find out about Betsy. Maybe the only way we could rebut that argument was by putting Steve on the stand.

We called Robert Domian, the director of engineering for Dan Wesson Arms, the company that made Steve's revolver. Domian described how reamers in the manufacturing process occasionally left slight imperfections in the six chambers. Some customers had complained that the reamer marks sometimes caused bullets to stick in the chambers and sent their revolvers back to the factory. Because of the complaints, Dan Wesson Arms added a secondary reaming operation to smooth the inside of the chambers and thereby improve extraction. Domian's testimony was straightforward—many manufacturers would never admit to defects—and Kern didn't budge him in cross-examination.

Next, we recalled Thomas Coffaro, a police officer who had seen Hicks walking by the side of the road at about 4 a.m. In the State's part of the case, our cross-examination had been limited to asking about Coffaro's having seen Steve, which was all Kern had asked him. We had a different set of questions for him.

Coffaro testified that late at night two days after the shooting, Steve's brother, Mark, had rushed into the Plantation police station and pleaded for an officer to accompany him to Doctor's General Hospital. Mark said there was important evidence there. Coffaro and Debbie Hessler, a crime scene technician, had gone with him. Mark Hicks pointed out that the hospital doors were locked, just as Steve had said they were on the night of the shooting. Coffaro checked. Mark was right. Not only were the doors locked, but if someone didn't know his way around the hospital, he might turn into the main entrance and not see the emergency room entrance farther down the road.

Mark Hicks showed Coffaro tire marks on the pavement. He thought they might have been caused by Steve's squealing his tires as he raced away to find another hospital. Hessler took photos of the tire marks.

On cross-examination Kern helped us out. "Do you know," he asked, "whether or not there is a sign there that says 'Use Emergency Room after hours'?"

"I don't know if there is a sign there or not," Officer Coffaro replied. "I didn't notice one."

Actually, there was a sign pointing to the emergency room. But it was so small and close to the ground that the officer hadn't seen it. Yet again, Kern proved the wisdom of cross-examination rule no. 1: Don't ask a question unless you know the answer or you don't care what the answer is. Kern lost on both fronts since his police officer now corroborated our defense.

Coffaro was followed by several minor witnesses, including a couple of people who testified about how confusing the layout of Doctor's General was. Then we called Debbie Hessler, the technician who had photographed the tire marks. She stated the marks looked as if they had been made by a driver who had gunned his engine. Hessler had also photographed Betsy's Mustang, but she had not tried to match the tire marks with the Mustang's tires.

"I could not match the tire marks," she acknowledged. "I'm not that qualified." She admitted that experts could have compared the tire marks with the car, but Plantation police had never sought out an expert to make a comparison.

The next morning we put on James E. Buchheit, a driver for Ralph's Towing. He testified that late on the Friday night of the shooting, he was awakened by his beeper and told to pick up an '85 Thunderbird. He arrived to find that the gear shift had fallen off and the car couldn't be operated. He said that Steve and Betsy were standing beside the car. The time was about 2 a.m. — an hour before Betsy's death.

"What kind of mood was he in?" I asked.

"Nice guy. I liked him."

"What did you do with the car?"

"Dropped it off at his apartment like he asked."

"Were you paid?"

"Yeah, by check." Betsy wrote it. He said they seemed to be friendly with each other. "It was a happy mood."

I surprised Kern by re-calling Robert Cerat, the sheriff's technician who had taken the night photos of the hospital sign that the State had introduced earlier. Since I had reexamined the hospital scene and shown the photos to an expert, I had a lot of questions.

"Did you enhance the contrast when printing the picture so the sign appeared brighter?"

"Yes sir, I did."

"How did you enhance it?"

"A technique called burning in."

"What is burning in?"

"It is allowing a certain area of the print to develop longer than the rest of the print. Here, it's the sign that would identify Doctor's Hospital and the sign to identify the street. The flash itself bleached it out so it was a white blob and you couldn't see it, so I burned it in."

"So in the darkroom you brightened those two signs?"

"Yes, during the printing process."

On cross-examination Kern tried to explain away Cerat's work: "Do you know of any procedure where you can exactly duplicate by a nighttime photograph exactly what the eye sees?"

"No sir. There is no lens made that can do that."

Kern continued to question the officer, using technical camera terms that revealed he knew a lot about photography. That wasn't too smart on his part: By revealing his expertise, he gave away that he knew the prints had been altered. He had put himself in the position of appearing to manipulate the evidence.

It was time for our star witness, Massad Ayoob, the "quick draw" expert we had used at the Alvarez trial.[3] For this case, we emphasized not his marksmanship, but his knowledge of weapons. Ayoob had been through the Smith & Wesson Academy six times. During four of those seminars he had finished at the top in his class. He was a certified instructor in unarmed combat and had conducted seminars for the Los Angeles and New York City Police Departments, as well as at the Metro-Dade Police Academy in Miami. He was the handgun editor of *Guns* magazine, and he operated the Lethal Force Institute, a private organization in New Hampshire that had trained two thousand citizens. What's more, he was a friend of Dan Wesson, the owner of the company that had made Hicks's revolver, and had written four articles about Wesson and the guns he manufactured.

We proffered Ayoob as an expert in three fields: Dan Wesson revolvers, the dynamics and reconstruction of shooting incidents, and weapon retention and disarming.

Kern objected to the idea of having Ayoob reconstruct the shooting. The judge sent the jury out and Ayoob described his approach to reconstruction. His technique called for tracing a bullet's path, then working backwards to determine what had happened, using evidence such as powder burns to identify the positions of the victim and the shooter. He said he had used this technique

---

3. Ayoob outsmarted the Alvarez prosecutor while re-enacting the shooting in the arcade.

to reconstruct two hundred shooting incidents, including some for the State Attorney's Office in Miami.

With the jury still out of the room, we laid out all the facts pertaining to the shooting of Betsy Turner, including Steve's size, Betsy's size, the kind of gun, the bullet, the trajectory of the bullet, the burn marks on Betsy's clothes and Steve's description of what had happened. Mark then asked Ayoob, "Do you have an opinion, within a reasonable degree of scientific certainty, as to whether such a shot would or would not be accidental?"

"That's ludicrous," Kern objected. "There are simply insufficient facts for him to make that conclusion. He has to assume the integrity of the testimony."

Judge Carney pondered for only a moment. "Based upon the proffer presented, I will sustain the State's objection," he said. This was a major setback for us. He did, however, concede that Ayoob was an expert on Dan Wesson revolvers and on weapon retention and disarming.

After the jury was brought back in, Mark showed Ayoob Steve's weapon. "First," said Ayoob, opening the bullet cylinder and holding it over his head, "let me assure everybody that the gun is not loaded."

"Have you had a chance to look at the chambers of that particular revolver?"

"Yes, I examined them earlier." He verified that the gun had roughly finished bullet chambers, which was typical of Dan Wesson revolvers before the factory changed its production process. "If you had a gun that was completely clean and cartridges were factory produced and within specifics, the round should fall easily in and out. If, however, you have a round that has a little dirt or Styrofoam from the cartridge box and the gun is not cleaned from previous firings, gunpowder residue will build inside the chambers. You will have enough friction there that, in combination with the rough surfaces of the chambers, could cause a round to stick and would be difficult to extract."

"Has that ever happened to you?" Mark asked.

"Very frequently," Ayoob replied.

An alternate juror called out: "I didn't hear that question."

Ayoob repeated the question and answer. The jury was paying close attention. The prosecutor sensed this because he suddenly bounced up: "Objection unless it happened to Dan Wesson revolvers."

Great question. The judge turned to Ayoob: "Has it ever happened to a Dan Wesson?"

"Three of five I own," Ayoob responded quickly. "It happened so often I took it to a gunsmith."

"You had to have the chambers reamed?"

"Yes, the chamber was reamed out to a high polish. If the jury examines this gun, they will see it looks almost like scoring or striations." Ayoob pulled out a small flashlight. He was taking over the courtroom. He stepped down and stood directly in front of the jury box. "Okay, look down inside the firing chambers," he invited the jurors. He said that a well-made gun would have smooth chambers, and these were rough.

The jurors were captivated by the demonstration. "If anyone has any questions . . . ," Ayoob offered, behaving as if he was giving a seminar. Of course, another outdated rule didn't allow jurors to question a witness.

When Ayoob resumed his seat, he testified that Dan Wesson guns had a light, easy trigger pull, and he pulled out a hand dynamometer to show how one measures hand pressure.

"In a weapon-disarming situation, what is the relative dynamic force in terms of hands' strength?" Mark asked.

"You have the combined strength of every hand that's in proximity to the weapon along with the combined body weight of both parties." He worked out the mathematics. With a male who was six feet one, 205 pounds (Steve's size) and a female five feet one, 110 pounds (Betsy's size), there would be a combined body weight of 315 pounds. Add to that hand strength, assuming that each person had both hands on the weapon, he figured there would be about 700 pounds of total pressure being exerted on the revolver.

"In your experience and your training," Mark asked, "if somebody is trying to retain a weapon and someone else is trying to take one away, how much strength or how much force is used?"

"Maximum."

Mark asked Ayoob to show the dynamometer to the jury. Involving the jurors in an experiment is more convincing than a mere explanation. They watched Ayoob hand the dynamometer to the first juror in the first row. "Understand," he remarked, "that in an actual situation, your adrenaline is pumping, and stress increases physical strength, but this will give a rough idea."

The jurors passed the device from one to another, squeezing it and study-ing the gauge. "Could I ask a question, please?" one juror asked.

Kern objected, but the juror went ahead: "Why are we using the entire hand instead of the trigger finger? I don't understand what this is proving."

Good question. Mark started to repeat it to Ayoob, but Kern objected again. Mark demanded to know why: "How can you object to my asking a wit-ness a question?"

"To counsel answering any juror's question. I think it's improper for a juror to ask a question," Kern replied.

Kern had placed himself in a tricky position. He was trying to stop the ju-rors from getting a piece of information they wanted. The judge overruled the objection, and Mark asked: "Mr. Ayoob, in a weapon-disarming situation, is one finger used or is the entire hand used?"

"No, the entire hand is used."

"In such a situation, is there ever a danger of accidental discharge?"

"There is a *great* danger of that, sir."

With Mark holding a cast-aluminum dummy gun, Ayoob showed in slow motion how a person could disarm a person with a gun and how a weapon might go off.

Mark asked him about the handkerchief. Ayoob said it might block the trigger or hammer but wouldn't silence the shot.

"As an expert in Dan Wesson revolvers, if you were intentionally going to shoot someone, would you place a handkerchief over it?"

"Objection," Kern shouted, but Ayoob, a masterful witness, slipped in his answer, "No." A second later Judge Carney sustained the objection.

Ayoob concluded by saying that a piece of cloth was useful only for keep-ing dust off a gun when it was stored. "Also, if you have the gun in a drawer, a friend or a relative might open it for some household object, and a cover keeps them from being alarmed at the sight of a deadly weapon."

As Kern stood up, I saw that he was clutching a legal pad on which he had scribbled a long list of questions. He was obviously planning a lengthy cross-examination, but it was not to be.

Kern: "Now, you said you give courses to officers on weapon retention and disarmament?"

"Yes sir, I teach in those areas."

"Suppose this were the weapon," Kern said, picking up the dummy weapon that Ayoob had used for the demonstration. "How would you take it away from me if I'm the hostile individual? Suppose you were aside—behind me. Can you come and demonstrate how you would take it away from me if I didn't want it taken away?" That was a mistake. You do not physically challenge Massad Ayoob. He doesn't look powerful—he's a slender five feet ten—but his hands and arms are enormous. He had dedicated his life to weapons and self-defense.

Ayoob stepped down from the witness stand and walked up to the prosecutor. I could tell he was enjoying this. So was I.

"Now," Kern said, "I've got a fair grip on the weapon." Kern was gripping the gun so tightly that his knuckles were white. In one swift motion Ayoob grabbed the gun from Kern and jammed the muzzle into Kern's face.

"Very good," Kern gasped, the muzzle pressing against his nose. His face was ashen. "The point being, though," he went on, trying to regain his composure, "I didn't want the weapon taken away. And, of course, you said, as you testified, maximum pressure of both parties would be applied, is that correct?"

Kern was flustered and he wasn't quite making sense, but Ayoob answered the question: "It is my experience when someone snatches away something you want, your reflex is to snatch that back. Anyone who doubts that, take two children and one toy. Perform the experiment."

Kern should have quit, but instead he plunged into more troubled waters by picking up the Dan Wesson revolver and a box of ammunition from the evidence table. "With the indulgence of the court," he said to the judge, "I would ask you to load that weapon with any one of the six rounds in this box."

Ayoob expressed surprise. "Counsel is asking me to load a revolver in the courtroom?" We had anticipated Kern might try to use Ayoob for such a demonstration. In our experiments, as well as those conducted by the police lab, no cartridge had gotten stuck in a chamber. I assumed that numerous police officers, loading and unloading the gun, had smoothed out the chamber. Ayoob decided that he should say it was too dangerous to put live rounds in a gun in the courtroom. That's precisely what he did now, turning to the judge: "Your Honor, I can't do that. It's too dangerous."

Kern insisted: "Yes, I want you to do it."

Ayoob shook his head. "There are people in the courtroom."

Kern pleaded to the judge: "With the indulgence of the court, I ask you to order him to do this."

Judge Carney frowned. "Okay, but make sure the weapon is pointed in a proper fashion."

Ayoob peered quickly into the chambers. As he told me later, he was trying to find the chamber with the most scars, figuring that it would be the one that the bullet had gotten stuck in. Ayoob then slipped in a cartridge. "Here we have a round in the chamber, counsel."

"Just load them, all six," Kern ordered.

"You want *all six* loaded?" Another note of surprise and concern.

"Yes," Kern nodded. "This is an experiment I will not ask the jury to repeat."

"Counsel," Ayoob responded gravely, "let the record reflect I have my finger clear of the trigger. Upon your requirement I have loaded the revolver in the courtroom." Still, he left the cylinder open.

"I want you to close it," Kern said.

"No," Ayoob replied adamantly, "it's too dangerous."

Again, Kern asked the judge to order Ayoob to obey the prosecutor's demand, and again the judge complied. Ayoob pushed the cylinder back into the frame. It locked. I held my breath.

"Okay," the prosecutor said, "how about unloading it now. Do you see any stick?"

Ayoob turned the gun so that the muzzle was pointing toward the ceiling, flicked a latch and pushed the cylinder open. Five bullets fell out. The sixth remained in the cylinder.

A juror jumped up and pointed at the gun. "Look! It stuck!"

"We have one round stuck in the chamber," Ayoob intoned.

Kern stared at Ayoob and the gun. Finally, Judge Carney asked him to continue. "Ah . . . no questions," he said as he walked back to his seat.

Mindful of Napoleon's third law of infantry tactics—When the enemy is destroying himself, don't interfere—I told the judge that we had no further questions.

"Thanks, Tom," I doodled on my notepad.

At the next recess, Ayoob joined us in the corridor and gloated about disarming the prosecutor. "I could have easily broken his finger," he said, "but I figured it wouldn't have been good for your case."

• • •

We still faced the grim problem of explaining Steve's actions following the shooting. I was reminded of a grisly case some years before involving a woman married to a police officer. One day they argued, and she stabbed him in the heart with a paring knife. He staggered out onto the sidewalk. As he lay there dying, she used a mop to clean up the blood in the kitchen. I knew we had to explain to the jury why she had mopped the floor. It seemed so cold, so heartless. But a psychologist examined her, and he testified that when someone is under great stress it's comforting to do something by rote, something where you don't have to think—like doing housework. I told the jury about A *Tale of Two Cities:* Dr. Manette was in the Bastille for twenty years. His only relief was repairing shoes. After he was freed, he went back to repairing shoes whenever he felt overwhelmed by stress. So, in the case of this woman, we had taken the worst thing against us—the apparently callous act of cleaning the floor—and turned it into something that was not only understandable, but entirely human. Her mopping *proved* the brutal stress she was under.

For a while we had thought about calling a psychologist, perhaps Parke Fitzhugh, the stress expert we had put on the stand in the Alvarez case. He had been very effective in explaining Luis's actions. On the other hand, Steve's actions that evening did not fit into an easy psychological explanation. There are many things a person might do after his girlfriend dies that a psychologist could readily explain, but dropping her off at a drive in teller window is not one of them. Even if we found a psychologist who would explain it, no jury in the world would buy it. The only person who could explain Steve Hicks's actions was Steve Hicks.

Because Steve had given so many statements, it meant that he *had* to testify at the trial to explain the lies in his earlier stories. This put us at a disadvantage. From the beginning, the State knew precisely what Steve would say on the witness stand. Steve's testimony *had* to correspond to the last statement that he had given police. If he deviated from it in any way, the prosecutor would smirk, "This is the fifth version of your story, and you want us to believe *this* one?"

Everything in this case was riding on the defendant's testimony. Steve had told so many stories that the jury had to be convinced of his honesty, down to the last detail. If a single fact sounded wrong now, the jurors could easily decide they couldn't trust this liar.

I started him off slowly. "Steve, how old are you?"

"Twenty-nine years old."

"Where did you grow up?"

"In Miami."

Nine years before, when he was twenty, he had married Kathy. Three years later they had a son, Stephen Jr. Shortly after his birth, they moved to Atlanta, where his wife's family ran a vocational school for bartending. Steve taught at the school and helped with job placement.

"Steve," I asked, "are you nervous sitting in that chair testifying?"

"Yes."

"Why are you nervous?"

"My life is on the line." Steve turned to look at the jurors. "I hope these ladies and gentlemen will give me the chance to explain what happened."

With a few questions, I led him through his life: About three and a half years before, he had separated from his wife. A while after that, he met Betsy. They decided to move to Fort Lauderdale. "My brother had offered me a partnership in the business that he had. I was supposed to come down here, train for a year or two, learn it and open a branch in Atlanta."

"What kind of business?"

"Electrical supplies, dealing with lighting fixtures, anything electrical. We'd sell to commercial and industrial."

He talked about his mother's death and assuming responsibility for his grandfather's care. Betsy and Steve moved into a two-bedroom apartment so that there would be room for his grandfather.

"Who cooked Harry's meals?"

"Generally I did."

With this background establishing Steve as a human being, I turned to the evening of Friday, June 27, 1986. "First of all, who cooked the dinner that night?"

"I did, sir."

"Do you like to cook?"

"Yes."

"After dinner, what happened?"

"I told Betsy I felt like getting out of the house. She wasn't feeling well. She had a headache and we had an after-dinner drink with coffee and she said she wanted to take a shower, and I thought maybe that would help her feel better. I went up to the Farm Store [a local convenience store] and when I came back, I asked her if she minded if I went out because I had been in the house all week, and she said she didn't mind." He drove to the bank, withdrew some money, then went to a bar called City Limits.

"How much did you have to drink there?"

"Three, four, maybe five drinks. I am not exactly sure."

"Did you have a date that night?"

"No sir."

"Did you see any other women?"

"No sir." About 1 a.m. he decided to go home.

"Did you have any problem getting your car?"

"Yes, the valet parker, I guess, thought I had too much to drink and he didn't want me to drive. So I went in and called Betsy."

"So what happened?"

"She came there. I saw one of the guys I had been speaking with in the bar, and he asked me what the problem was. And I told him that they would not give me my car. I felt fine. I thought I could drive, and he said he'd get the car for me. I gave him the stub, and I gave him two dollars to tip the valet parker."

Just as Steve was getting his car, Betsy arrived. She was following him back to the apartment when his car's transmission broke. A police officer called a tow truck. When Steve and Betsy finally got back to the apartment, they had a discussion. "She thought I went to see somebody because we had a hang-up phone call. And I told her that was wrong."

"What do you mean you had a hang-up phone call?"

"Somebody had called. She answered the phone and they hung up."

"When did this occur?"

"About eight-thirty. Shortly before I departed."

"What did you tell her?"

"I told her I didn't go to see anybody. That was it. I mean, I had no reason to see anybody else. I live with you, and that was just basically it."

They decided to go to bed because they were planning an early start in the morning, to run some errands and then go to the beach. Betsy went into the bedroom. Steve got a drink of water, then joined her. "I took a pack of cigarettes out of my shirt and I started taking my shirt off. I asked her if she had a light. She said no, but there should be one in the bottom of the nightstand drawer." The room was dark, except for a light in the closet, and he had to grope to find the lighter. "The gun was in the way of me searching through the nightstand, so I took it out and I placed it on the bed."

"How was the gun kept in the drawer?"

"It was folded with a handkerchief, to keep it from getting dirty." He found the lighter and then went to the bathroom. "I have a colitis condition and if you wait too long, it is too late." He was in the bathroom for three or four minutes.

"What happened when you came back?"

"I noticed that the white handkerchief was in her hand. I asked her not to play with it because it was loaded. I don't know if she knew it was loaded. I proceeded to go over to the bed and I asked if she would hand me the gun. I wanted to put it away."

"What happened?"

"I went for the gun, and it went back and forth, and then it just went off."

"What happened then?"

"I said, 'God, no.' Betsy said, 'Take me to the hospital,' and I reached around and underneath her and all I could feel was wet and warm. I went into the bathroom and my hands and my whole arm were covered with blood."

"What did you do?"

"I ran some water on my arms. I went to the closet and took a T-shirt out of the third drawer. I looked on top of the stereo cabinet for some keys. I didn't find them.

"I went into her purse and I got the keys out of there, and I went and picked her up. She was moaning. She wasn't responding to anything I said." He raced down the stairs, carrying her, and put her in the front passenger seat. During the car ride, "the moans were getting lower and lower. I am telling her to please hang on, we are going to get there soon. She never responded. All she was doing was moaning, moaning. I got up to the traffic light and I turned left to the hospital, and I looked straight in front of me. When I pulled in the hospital, it was dark. I was flashing my lights on and off. I didn't see anybody, and I took off. Around the back it was dark. I saw an opening over to the right.

I ran. I parked the car at an angle and I went and I pounded on the door. It is a metal door with a rectangular piece of glass. I could see inside this hallway. All I saw was a metal cart. Nobody answered.

"I couldn't believe the hospital was closed. So I ran back to the car. I said, 'Betsy, the hospital is closed.' She was still moaning, but the moans were getting lower and lower. I am telling her, 'Please hang on, please hang on.' I am just screaming."

Panicked, all he could think of was a hospital he had once seen a few miles away, on Interstate 95 at Oakland Park Boulevard. He raced there. There was no hospital. "I got off on Oakland Park and I came back on and that's when she died. That's when the noise stopped and she just—that was it."

"What did you do then?"

"I didn't know what to think. I was scared. She was dead. I didn't know what to think." Tears were welling in his eyes.

"So what did you do?"

"I went—I just couldn't take it anymore, and I just dropped the car off at the bank. I wanted somebody to find her. I could not deal with it any longer. Every way I turned was wrong, every way I turned." He was blinking back tears.

"When you got out of the car, what did you do?"

"I just ran. I said, 'Betsy, I am sorry.' I didn't know what to do. I ran. I panicked. How else can I explain it? I didn't even feel like it was me. It didn't seem real. I couldn't run far enough. I was so confused I wasn't quite sure which direction to go. I felt sick to my stomach. And then some police were flying up and down the road with their sirens going and the police stopped me, and I told them I was just walking."

"Why did you lie to them?" a ticklish question to have to ask your client in a first-degree murder trial, but there was no coating this pill.

"I was scared. I felt sick. She was dead. I just wanted to hide."

"Where did you go?

"I went home. I went into my bathroom. I got me some tranquilizers and I went to the closet and I grabbed a pillow and blanket. I just sat on the couch, shaking, sick to my stomach."

"Now, after you had been home awhile, did you clean up the apartment?"

"Yes sir."

"Did you call in a missing person's report?"

"Yes sir."

"Why did you do that?"

"I wanted her to be recovered and identified. I don't know. I just felt so bad."

"When the police came to the apartment, you originally lied to them about it?" Another tough question. But to describe what he told the police as "stretching the truth" or "telling a story" would have sounded implausible to the jury. He had lied, and there was no other way to describe it.

"Yes sir."

"Why did you lie to them?"

"I was scared. She was dead. I felt like I had failed."

"That night when you went home from the bar, did you intend to kill Betsy Turner?"

"Absolutely not."

"Did you want her dead?"

"Of course not."

"This was just an accident?"

"Yes sir. I don't understand it either."

"Do you know how the gun went off?"

"No sir. It was going back and forth. I mean, we both had our hands on it. It just went off."

"Thank you, Steve. I have no further questions."

He had been on the witness stand less than thirty minutes—just about right under my theory that the defendant should give the prosecution as little ammunition as possible.

Now, he had to withstand Kern's cross-examination. This was the *entire* case. Steve had already admitted to several lies, and the prosecutor was certain to hammer on the idea that he was lying once again. To the defense attorney, what was about to happen was like letting your toy boat go floating around the lake, completely out of your control.

Kern began with an insinuation: "You have had a lot of time to think about your testimony today?"

"Excuse me?" Steve said, leaning forward.

"You have a lot of time to think about your testimony today?"

"I guess so."

"I can't help but notice the emotion that you displayed a few minutes ago in recounting the events of that night in June. Of course, it brings tears to your eyes even now?"

"Yes."

"Let me guess," Kern said. "The reason it didn't bring tears to your eyes the day you met police officers is because you were on tranquilizers?"

"Sir, I had tears in my eyes then."

"You did? You were equally broken up?"

"I was a little more under control as far as showing tears. I was trembling. I was sick to my stomach."

"And in the course of talking to the police officers, you also broke down several times?"

"I tried to keep myself together, sir. Yes sir. I was under tranquilizers, too."

"Why did you not try to keep yourself together today?"

"I tried."

The prosecutor had struck a small blow for doubts about Steve's display of emotion on the witness stand. Kern asked why two years had passed without Steve's divorcing his wife. Steve shrugged. "My wife and I had discussed divorce." He and Betsy assumed she would eventually mail the divorce papers for him to sign.

"Were you planning to marry Betsy?"

"We had plans."

"You had plans to marry Betsy?"

"Yes sir."

Kern asked whether Steve was still sleeping with his wife during his trips to Atlanta. Steve said no. Kern asked him about the gifts that his wife had given him, implying that there was a close bond between them and that Steve planned to go back to his wife.

"I was *never* going to go back to my wife," Steve said emphatically. "I told that to Margie Hightower and Betsy knew the same."

"Did your wife know about Betsy or not?"

"No sir."

"All these times you visited your son and you never discussed Betsy at all, the woman that you were planning to marry?"

"Sir, my life was my life, and her life was hers."

Kern raised his eyebrows. He said that it was obvious Hicks didn't want Betsy living in Atlanta with him.

"That's not true. It was up to her. I told her that she had a good job down here. She had bills, she was going to have a paid vacation coming up. She was going to get a big Christmas bonus."

"You thought it would be better for her to stay down here with her job in Fort Lauderdale?"

"I was just telling her to look at the practical side."

"Isn't it a fact, Mr. Hicks, that the reason you didn't want Betsy in Atlanta is because you were petrified that your wife might find out about Betsy?"

"No sir. Absolutely not."

"When did you have this great fear that if you left Betsy she would take her own life?"

"I never said that, sir."

"You never told Margie Hightower that if I leave Betsy, she will take her life, or words to that effect?"

"Absolutely not, sir. I didn't say that, sir. Those are *not* my words."

Kern asked about the cleaning Hicks did at the apartment to remove the blood. "Did you use Tide?" he asked sarcastically.

"I believe it was Wisk, sir."

The prosecutor pulled the Dan Wesson revolver and the handkerchief from the evidence table and carried them to the witness stand. "How did you have it wrapped up in the handkerchief?" He extended his hands, offering the items to Hicks.

Steve recoiled. "I would rather not touch that gun. I don't want to touch another gun in my life."

"Well, all right, I will touch it then." Kern put the handkerchief over the gun. "How was she holding it—like this?"

"I don't know exactly how it was because the room was dark and it was wrapped."

"You are not going to give us a demonstration?"

"I would rather not touch the gun, sir." The last thing we wanted was a demonstration.

Kern asked who cut the hole in the sheet found in the closet. Steve said he knew nothing about the sheet. He said he certainly hadn't cut any hole in it after the shooting. The prosecutor continued questioning Hicks about the condition of the apartment without scoring any points. Then he went into agonizing detail about the false statements that Hicks had given to the police. "Were you trying to get them to think that perhaps there had been a robbery?"

"Not at all, sir."

Steve explained how, on Saturday morning, he had started to walk five blocks to the bank to see if her body had been found, but it was raining and he was sick to his stomach, so he turned back. Kern gave that his best shot: "The woman that you lived with for two years, that you were going to marry, that you are in love with—you didn't want to walk five blocks in the rain to see if she had been found?"

"I just walked back, sir, to make another call to the hospital to see if she'd been found."

"When you walked back, you don't know whether she had been found or not?"

"Exactly."

"Let me ask you this: Who is supporting you since you left your job, you say in March of 1986?"

"I was, sir."

In questioning a defendant, I always keep the testimony Spartan. Prosecutors fall into the trap of asking the questions you don't, drawn like a moth to the light. I hadn't asked about how Steve supported himself because I knew Kern would. Criminal defense lawyers live by cross-examination. We understand it's not the time to find out information. On this topic, I had set up a land mine to explode during re-direct.

"You saved so much money from what you made with your brother?" Kern asked.

"Yes, that and some money after my mother's death."

"What were you doing during your unemployment? Just going to bars?"

"No sir. That was only the second time I went out without her. I go to the pool. I take my grandfather out. I would cook his meals."

"You were being a little housewife?" Kern remarked. Not a smart question. An attorney should always know his audience. Several housewives sat on the jury.

"You could basically say that," Steve nodded.

"Did that upset your ego a little bit?"

"I enjoyed it," Steve insisted. "I enjoyed cooking."

On re-direct I finished springing the trap we had set. Kern had suggested strongly that Betsy had been supporting Steve and that Steve resented it. Now, we brought out documents. Steve had received $20,000 from his mother's estate. He used some of it to buy a television and a stereo, then deposited the rest. We had statements showing that Steve had a certificate of deposit worth $17,000 at the time of Betsy's death. He also had a money market account with $4,000 in it and a checking account with $1,000.

"Were you able to support yourself?" I asked.

"Yes sir."

"And did your grandfather have money of his own?"

"Yes sir." He received a Social Security check, Steve said.

Tactics dictated holding back the financial proof until re-direct to give it more punch. I could have presented it during the direct testimony, but Kern then would have never touched it, and the impact would have been negligible. Instead, I had let Kern attack Steve on an issue I could easily disprove. I could tell from the jurors' frowns as they looked at the prosecution table that our counterattack had done its job.

"At this point," I announced, "the defense rests."

Kern began his closing argument by describing this case as a coldly calculated murder worthy of the death penalty, but if the jury disagreed, they could find Hicks guilty of second- or third-degree murder. He suggested that every reasonable man and woman would agree that Hicks was guilty of *some* crime. Florida law allows a conviction on a lesser charge as a compromise. The jurors could feel as if they were making a thoughtful, Solomon-like decision, and a defendant would still get life for second-degree murder.

With years of experience in homicide cases, Kern masterfully discussed the alternatives while continuing to maintain that Betsy Turner's death *had* to be premeditated: "The crux of this case is the defendant's acts in leaving the body of a woman he had been sleeping with, living with, loving with for two years, in a parking lot to make it appear as if she were a robbery victim and then calling in a missing person report. Doing that is totally repugnant to any claim of accident.

"Careless use of a firearm in a bedroom at night could constitute manslaughter, but I submit his acts repudiated even that crime. There is no man, even having killed through manslaughter, who wouldn't rush his girl-friend to a hospital."

Kern found it absurd that Hicks couldn't find an emergency room. "You *can* find it," he said. "It may not be the first door. If you can't find one door, you go to another door. But you can certainly find an emergency room. . . . You wouldn't leave her at a bank parking lot to look like she had been robbed at the automatic teller."

Nothing Steve Hicks had said on the witness stand was to be believed, Kern said. "He began with lies. He continued with lies. This man has zero credibility." He called Hicks's testimony "Class B movie acting." What man would leave the woman he loved in a parking lot? If he was so in love with Betsy, why had two years drifted by without his getting a divorce from his wife? "I say baloney. He has no intention of divorcing that wife. And he has every in-tention of going back to her because the wife has money and security and that's all, I submit, he ever cared about. I submit, he is totally an opportunist without conscience or feeling. . . . he has ice water in his veins."

Kern asserted that the most crucial evidence was missing. "Where is the missing blood? I submit there is a lot of missing bedding material. I submit that she was carried out in bedding material because there is no way under the sun he could have carried her out of that room without leaving a trail of blood. It wouldn't be drops. It would be a big trail all the way down to the car, unless she was well wrapped up in bedding material that wasn't anywhere to be found. And what about the sheet that has a hole in it? That's kind of odd, isn't it?"

Along with the missing bedding material, Kern said, Hicks must have also hidden a pillow—a pillow that he used to muffle the sound of the shot. "Why is there so little noise? A .357 Magnum cartridge spews out fire two inches, sounds like a cannon. Nobody heard a gunshot. . . . It was muffled by the pil-low." Perhaps the fibers in the gun and on the wound had come from the pil-low, he stated.

A missing pillow? I made a note. Like a good blackjack dealer, Kern had kept his hole card facedown until the other hands were played out. A defense attorney's game has to be anticipation: Posit the prosecutor's strategy and undermine it when the evidence is presented. Final argument is the worse place to discover your opponent's plan.

Kern wondered aloud about other things that didn't exist: Why were there no prints and smudges on the gun? Wasn't it obvious that Hicks had wiped it clean? And what about the one bullet that stuck in the chamber? He told the jurors to forget about Ayoob's courtroom theatrics with the gun; a firearms expert from the sheriff's office had tried the same experiment ten times with the revolver, and not once had a bullet stuck.

"Counsel in opening argument asked, 'Where is the motive? There is no motive.' I say baloney. You have got two people living together. You got the emotions from love to hate." Kern proposed that Hicks had to be jealous of Betsy's success. "Resentment—maybe he resented the fact that she was intelligent, articulate. He only has a high school degree. She had been to college. She has a better job than he did. Maybe he resents the fact that a woman is outdoing him. Maybe he blames her. Maybe he's thinking that if it weren't for her, 'I would be in a business now worth a lot of money. I would be back with my wife and child.' He had plenty of reasons. He wanted this relationship to end. He wanted out of it. His self-esteem is suffering. He's not the moneymaker. What does he do for his ego? He brags about the presents that women buy him." He suggested that Hicks kept a gun to make himself feel macho, to compensate for the humiliation he felt about Betsy's success.

There was no testimony about Steve bragging, no testimony about his self-esteem suffering. I could have shouted an objection about the lack of evidence, but if I had done so it would have seemed to the jurors that I was using a nit-picking legal tactic to prevent them from hearing what Kern had to say. I decided it would be better to let him wade as deep as he wanted to into these speculations, then respond in my summation that there was no proof for any of these claims about motive. In chess, this is called a gambit—deliberately sacrificing a piece in order to gain a tactical advantage.

Kern continued: "What I think is really bothering him is his paranoid fear about when he goes back to his wife. What is Betsy going to do? She is going to write that wife a letter and tell her everything. No one is going to fault Betsy for doing that at all. That's his fear: She will get on the phone or write a letter and tell where her precious husband has been for the last two years. That's what he was afraid of."

I was writing furiously. Each of these speculations needed to be rebutted.

Kern insisted there was only one logical conclusion: "It's premeditated murder. That's exactly what he planned all along. It may not have worked out the way he planned. He may have vague thoughts in his mind. 'Well, we will make it look like a suicide.' Then he didn't have the nerve to do it that way and came up with another plan. I submit he was thinking about it when he told Margie Hightower back three weeks before, 'I am afraid if I leave Betsy, she will take her life.' He is thinking maybe that is how he was going to do it."

With that, Kern stopped abruptly.

I picked up my notes and walked slowly to the podium. Twelve faces turned to me. Kern had given a clever closing, and I wanted to quickly undercut his credibility.

"I admire Mr. Kern's skill in fashioning a fictionalized account of this case. It is resourceful and engaging. But just like Detective Cerat's enhanced photograph, it is not fact. In a courtroom, not like on television, the verdict must be based on real evidence, not speculation. Judge Carney will instruct you the burden of proof is beyond a reasonable doubt. This heavy burden is not met by a prosecutor using his overheated imagination to conjure up theories.

"A classic murder investigation revolves around three elements. motive, means and opportunity.

"Motive. What could be more critical in a murder case? We humans don't kill without a powerful motive. Hatred, jealousy, greed. These could lead to murder. Kern and his officers hunted high and low to flush out a motive for Steve to kill Betsy and came up empty-handed. His only recourse is to manufacture one.

"The only benefit to Steve the prosecutor can come up with is that Steve had to kill her to leave her. If he wanted to leave her, it would not be difficult—he would just have to pack his bags and walk out the front door. They weren't married. There is no messy divorce proceedings. No child custody battle. His next variation was that he had to kill Betsy Turner in order to hide her existence from his wife. Can you think of any better way of publicizing their relationship than by killing her?

"Their love affair was hardly a secret. They had lived at his brother's house.

Betsy's parents visited them and they go out to dinner as one big, happy family. My God, they even come to this apartment and Steve Hicks, this guy, this evil man, cooks dinner for everybody. And at the time of the shooting, his grandfather is in the next room. Would you plan to kill somebody with your grandfather in the room next door?

"What does Steve stand to gain by Betsy's death? Is there any life insurance? Did Steve and Betsy own any property together? Does Steve get any money or assets or property because of Betsy's death? Carefully leaf through all these exhibits and you will search in vain to find a motive."

I turned to my second point. "Means. How was this devilishly clever murder accomplished? First, only one shot was fired from Steve's gun." I held up the Dan Wesson revolver. "What does that prove? If Betsy Turner had been shot two, three or four times, Mr. Kern would tell you that was the best evidence of intent to kill—no one is shot accidentally four times. On the other hand, common sense tells us that one shot is consistent with an accident.

"Secondly, can you imagine a person intending to kill somebody by deliberately shooting them once in the hip? If you were shooting to kill, where would you shoot? The overwhelming number of murders occur by a shot to the heart or the head—the two parts of the body where they are going to cause death. But why would you shoot someone in this awkward position, so the bullet goes through the hip, to the kidney, and through the liver? Have you ever heard of anyone *deliberately* shooting someone in the kidney, liver or hip to cause death?

"If Betsy Turner had been shot in the temple, had been shot between the eyes, had been shot in the heart, had been shot in the middle of the chest, it would all be evidence of intent to kill. In fact, you would have heard Mr. Kern argue, what would be better evidence than this that he intended to kill her?

"Let's put these two factors together. Just one shot—to the hip. If you were really intending to kill someone, wouldn't you immediately shoot them again—this time in the head, to be sure they are dead? We know Betsy Turner didn't die for ten to fifteen minutes. Wouldn't a person intending to kill her shoot her again? You couldn't afford to let her live to accuse you of attempted murder.

"And if Steve intended to kill Betsy, why would he wrap the gun in a handkerchief? This skimpy handkerchief"—I held it up for the jury—"would not muffle the noise of the gunshot. Back in the jury room, put this handkerchief over the gun, like this, and see for yourself if it would muffle a shot. It would only interfere with the action of the gun. Use your common sense and your life experiences in deciding whether Steve would set out to deliberately kill Betsy with a gun wrapped in this handkerchief."

Now it was time for point three. "Opportunity. What propitious moment had Steve selected to kill Betsy?" In his questioning of witnesses, Kern had suggested that Betsy had been sleeping at the time she was shot. I had effectively rebutted that theory through cross-examination and Kern had ignored it in his summation. But I did not want the jury to forget that the prosecutor put theories on and off as easily as a person changes clothes. "Let us examine the *location* of the blood on the mattress. Fortunately, we do have one photograph that shows distances and sizes because there is a ruler in it." A good crime scene technician puts a ruler in photographs so that we can accurately determine distances and sizes. "We can see this bloodstain is at least six inches from the bullet hole.

"At one point in the trial, Mr. Kern's theory was that while she was sleeping on the bed, he snuck up and shot her in the hip. But, of course, he had to backtrack from the sleeping theory because there is a little inconsistency. She had her jewelry on. She had eye makeup on. She had her clothes on, and there was no blood in the bullet hole. If she had been asleep, the blood from her exit wound would flow right into the bullet hole where the mattress was flush against her. So Mr. Kern rejects the sleeping theory now."

In a circumstantial case the evidence is a collage of small and disparate facts. The lawyers reason deductively from each fact to a general conclusion. The greater the number of independent facts pointing toward one conclusion the more likely it is true. Summation is the time to recall the important evidence and argue its logical inferences. Now I had to respond to Kern with a point-by-point argument.

"When you are deciding the life-and-death decision in this case, what can you rely on? This massive evidence." I pointed to all the exhibits on the clerk's table. "The evidence, the items, the things gathered by the Plantation Police Department. These are the building blocks that you must analyze, dissect and examine in order to make a decision.

"To put it mildly, the evidence in this case is garbage. That's why the detectives who were in charge of this case are too embarrassed to even admit that they were responsible for the investigation. The evidence collected at the apartment, and in the car, is the lifeblood of this or any criminal investigation. Once it is contaminated, the case is irrevocably poisoned and the truth dies with it. You may wonder, Doesn't the defendant benefit if the police do a slip-shod job? But we are stuck with the evidence that the police detectives collected at the apartment. I cannot be like Mr. Kern and make up the evidence. I was not called to go to the scene of the homicide. We had to rely upon these detectives to do a proper job. Once they ignored or destroyed evidence, it is lost for everyone. Once lost, it is no longer available to Steve to prove his innocence. So it is with this damaged evidence that we must undertake the job of reconstructing the events in Steve's and Betsy's apartment."

The jurors needed to see what I was talking about. I gathered up all the crime scene and autopsy photographs, the bloodstained clothing, the Dan Wesson revolver and all the other exhibits from the clerk's desk, and placed them on a table in front of a cork board. Armed with tacks, Scotch tape, a ruler and a caliper, I intended to storyboard each fact to visually demonstrate Steve's innocence.

"Steve's brother goes to the police and begs them: 'Please go out and look at the tire tracks at the hospital.' This would prove that Steve told the truth. The detectives send Debbie Hessler to take photographs. Mind you, these are photographs that you can barely see." I stopped for a moment, and, one by one, I tacked the blurry photos to the cork board, allowing the jurors to absorb not only the careless incompetence of the photographer, but also, by extension, of the prosecutor who submitted the photos into evidence.

"She *never* takes photographs of the tires from Steve's car. She *never* asks any of the forensic scientists at the Broward County Crime Lab to match up the tires from Steve's car to these tire tracks at the hospital. Is that an unimportant detail? How important has Mr. Kern made Steve's actions at the hospital? He is only able to float this theory because no one made any effort to match the tire marks at the hospital with Steve's tires. A man's life is on the line, yet no effort is made to see if he is innocent. Why? Because they've already made up their minds he was guilty."

Klein was leaning forward in his chair, nodding at many of my arguments. I found myself looking at him during much of my summation, reaching him through eye contact. If anyone could understand the arguments I was making about the botched evidence, it would be a man who had a scientifically trained mind.

"Let's examine the fibers," I went on, speaking directly to Klein. We had always maintained these fibers came from the handkerchief. Kern, searching for any evidence of premeditation, was now claiming the fibers were from a mysterious pillow used to muffle the gunshot. "Why didn't they examine the fibers or the sheets or the pillows? Suppose your child is deathly ill and you take him to the doctor. He draws a vial of blood and holds it up in the air, 'Oh, his blood looks fine; I wouldn't worry about it,' and doesn't send it to the lab to be tested. Would you rely on this diagnosis?

"But Mr. Kern is willing, in a life-or-death case, to say, 'Those white fibers came from a pillow.' Without any proof. Is it fair for a prosecutor to come in at this stage of the trial and claim these fibers came from some nonexistent pillow? Does the need to convict Steve, the need to chalk up another victory, outweigh the requirement that an argument be based on fact?

"Mr. Kern now argues, 'Well, I think that the gun was put in some sort of a pillow to muffle the shot.' Rather than rely on his unsupported speculation, let's look at the evidence." I posted an autopsy photo of the bullet wound on the cork board. "Dr. Ongley, during the autopsy examination, discovered the imprint of the muzzle of the gun on Betsy Turner's skin, just as you see here, and explained that this proved there was nothing between the muzzle of the gun and her clothing at the time of the gunshot. He also found gunshot residue on her clothing. Residue that could not be there if a pillow had been between the muzzle of the gun and her clothing. He also discovered charring, and carbon monoxide inside the wound." I pointed to the area. "He explained that this proved that the muzzle was right against her jeans and her skin. The charring and the carbon monoxide come from the explosive blast of the gun. This could not have occurred if there was a pillow between the gun and the body.

"Mr. Kern conveniently ignores Dr. Ongley's testimony because it is inconsistent with his new guesswork. As the famed scientist T. H. Huxley noted: 'The great tragedy of science—the slaying of a beautiful hypothesis by an ugly fact.' Mr. Kern ignores the ugly facts uncovered by his own expert witness, in a capital case—with a life hanging in the balance."

I went into detail about the problems with the police work: a crime scene technician with virtually no experience; one detective claiming Steve did a demonstration, another denying it. "The first detective obviously enhanced his testimony," I said, "just like Cerat enhanced the photograph." With that I tacked up Cerat's darkroom-enhanced photograph.

I turned to our claim that Betsy was not lying on the mattress at the time she was shot. "She must have been awake and either sitting up or trying to get up."

From my pocket I pulled out the engineer's caliper and placed it against the photographs to show how the relationship between the bloodstain and the bullet hole proved that Betsy couldn't have been lying on the mattress, because if she had been, the blood would be around and in the bullet hole. I added that there were no bruises or marks on either Betsy or Steve to show they had been fighting.

I turned to the issue of the hospital. "I have one question to ask you. If Steve Hicks didn't go to the hospital that night at three or three-thirty, how would he know that the doors to the hospital were locked? How many of *you* know that the doors to that hospital are locked at night? To me, the fact that hospitals lock their doors is a shocking revelation. To be honest with you, I thought hospitals always had their doors open.

"In the quiet of the courtroom, we lose the urgency and confusion of that night. This man is blindly fumbling through his worst nightmare. The night is black. It is three or four o'clock in the morning. He's in a panic. He doesn't have the luxury of two and a half weeks sitting in a comfortable chair thinking over his choices. Is it so absurd, is it so unnatural that he would go to the front lobby entrance of that hospital?" And how had the prosecution portrayed the hospital to the jurors? It had shown them some secretly enhanced photos to make the emergency sign stand out. "I don't see any reason to manipulate evidence just to find somebody guilty of a crime he didn't commit.

"Mr. Kern criticizes what he labels as Mr. Ayoob's demonstration of the cartridge sticking in the gun. That wasn't Mr. Ayoob's demonstration—that was Mr. *Kern's* demonstration. If you will remember, Mr. Ayoob didn't want to put the bullets in the gun because it wasn't safe, and he was ordered by the court to put those cartridges in the gun. He was *ordered* to close the gun. It was only because of Mr. Kern's orders that he did this, and so it is Mr. Kern's demonstration." I reminded the jurors that the gun manufacturer's chief engineer had acknowledged that bullets sometimes stuck.

"And where did the blood go? His latest theory is that Steve is guilty because there is not enough blood. Notice that he waits until the summation to bring this one up. He doesn't ask Dr. Ongley, the expert who examined the body, how much blood there is in the car and on the back seat." I posted a photo showing a pool of blood on the back floor of the car. It was a gruesome picture, but it illustrated my point and it showed the jury I wasn't afraid of the bloody scene. "When he has the expert on the stand who knows about blood flow and the volume of blood in the body, he doesn't ask a single question about what happened to the blood. Instead, he waits until summation when it is too late for anybody to testify about it. Sneaking it in at the last minute, like a sucker punch, leaving us without a defense because the witnesses have left."

Next, I raised the matter of the sheet with the hole in the middle. "If Stephen Hicks had cut this hole in the sheet, why wouldn't he have admitted it? He admitted doing laundry, admitted cleaning the blood off his clothing. If he said he cut a hole in the sheet, that wouldn't add anything. But he didn't do it. I can prove it to you by examining the photographs. Look at this—the bloodstain is larger than this hole. In fact, we can measure the bloodstain." I pulled out my ruler and laid it across the photo. "The bloodstain on the mattress is larger than the hole in the sheet. Therefore, the sheet could not have been cut to remove the bloodstain."

Point made, I moved on: "In another new theory, Mr. Kern theorizes that Betsy Turner died in the apartment, was wrapped in a sheet that doesn't exist, and was carried down to the car. Mr. Kern's theory defies medical fact. When you die your heart stops pumping blood and you no longer bleed. If you are only wounded with your heart still pumping, blood pours out of the wound. That's why you see all this blood in the car." Again I pointed to the photo. "This blood would not have flowed out of her body and on to the back floor of the car unless she was still alive, with her heart beating. Dr. Ongley, the medical examiner, could have explained this. If only he was asked. Ask yourself if this is a search for the truth or a search for a conviction."

I then turned to Kern's argument that because the sleeping neighbor didn't hear the gunshot, Steve must have muffled it with a pillow. "Dr. Ongley testified that with a contact wound, there is not a lot of noise. And, of course, there was nothing between the muzzle of the gun and her skin. There was no pillow, but Mr. Kern had to create one because he needs evidence of premeditation.

"The truth is that Dr. Ongley, the medical examiner, says that the evidence is consistent with an accident. He is not saying, 'I am telling you it was an accident.' He wasn't there. He can't say for certain. But my God, here is a State's main expert telling you the evidence in this case is *consistent* with an accident."

I tacked a photo on the board of blood on the mattress. "Dr. Ongley testified that the liver is like a sponge full of blood, and a tremendous amount of blood would gush out from a gunshot wound. So what can we conclude from this small amount of blood on the mattress? Isn't that consistent with Betsy being picked up off the mattress almost immediately after the gunshot? If Steve had intended to kill her, there would be no purpose in immediately picking her up. He would not need to immediately dispose of the body, but could leave it there while planning his escape. There would be a river of blood on the mattress as she bled for the ten to fifteen minutes of life she had left. There would be no reason I can think of why a killer would have to quickly pick up her body and run outside with it. That could only result in discovery.

"Mr. Kern says that Steve's actions after the shooting proved that it could be nothing but murder. He claimed nobody would panic like that. Nobody would become scared. I am sure Mr. Kern has never been in a panic or scared in his life. But maybe other people have." As I said this, I looked straight at the bar owner who had panicked when robbers pulled their guns. This woman could understand Steve's panic because she herself had panicked. That's why I had picked her, and that's why, at this point in my argument, it was utterly natural for me to look directly at her: "Have you ever heard of a hit-and-run driver? People get in accidents and they panic. Is it so inconsistent with human behavior that at times human beings are overwhelmed by what has happened? They become scared. They hide. They sit in their apartment on a couch curled up in their pillow and sheet. Haven't all of us, to one degree or another, felt at least once that we wanted to hide from the world? Are we so perfect that we can say that we have never had a situation where we are going to panic?

"Who can predict the obstacles that misfortune may place in our path? Life is lived without a chance to practice. We have only one time to live it. We don't always act with courage and judgment and bravery. If it is a crime to be stupid, if it is a crime to be scared, then he is guilty of that crime. But let me tell you something, being scared and panicked doesn't make you guilty of murder. It makes you human."

That concluded my summation. It had been direct and brief—a mere hour and nine minutes. I had responded to all of Kern's points and then stopped. Kern's attempt at a rebuttal was only a repetition of his points. The judge then gave the jury instructions. Shortly after noon the jurors were sent off to deliberate.

Throughout the afternoon we waited—Steve, his wife, Kathy, Kathy's mother and Steve's brother, Mark. Waiting for a jury can be excruciating moments. The afternoon stretched on forever. Finally, the jury adjourned for the night.

The next morning the wait continued. Finally, at three-thirty that afternoon, the jury was brought in. "Have you reached a verdict?" Judge Carney asked.

Gerald Klein stood. As I had suspected (and hoped), he had been named foreman. "Yes," he said, "we have reached a verdict."

"Mr. Foreman," the judge ordered, "please hand the verdict to the clerk."

The clerk inspected the form for a long, awful moment. A look of astonishment spread across her face. She turned and faced the judge. In a stage whisper she said: "Judge, they checked K."

What was K?

The clerk passed the jury form to the judge, who peered at it for a moment, and then passed it back. "Madam Clerk, publish the verdict."

Still with an incredulous look on her face, the clerk announced: "Not guilty."

Gasps filled the courtroom. Steve hugged us and turned to speak to his family. Before he could, a guard walked over and slapped handcuffs on him.

"What are you doing?" I protested. "The verdict was *not* guilty."

The bailiff said it was standard operating procedure in Broward County to take a prisoner back to the jail to see if there were any warrants pending against him.

"You can't arrest him," I shouted, but the bailiff paid no attention. I turned to the judge. "Your Honor, Mr. Hicks has been acquitted, and there are no other charges against him. I can't understand why the bailiffs are handcuffing him."

"Well," said Judge Carney, "this is a normal procedure." He shrugged and walked off the bench.

For the next several hours we were put through a bureaucratic torture. We complained again to Judge Carney, who said he couldn't help. Finally, in early evening, four hours after he was found not guilty, a metal door clanked open and Steve walked out of the jail.

With Steve Wisotsky, a professor at nearby Nova Law School, we launched a class-action suit for all those who were detained in the jail after they were found not guilty. Eventually, the Broward Sheriff's Office settled with Steve for $13,000. Steve didn't get a dime for the eight *months* he spent in jail worrying that he might be sentenced to death. He was compensated only for the four *hours* he had been in jail after his acquittal.

Turning point: We got a big boost when Mr. Klein was put on the jury, because I was confident that he was going to be able to understand all the problems the police caused with the evidence.

But the key was that dramatic moment when the prosecutor insisted that Ayoob try the demonstration. This was not some abstraction about bagging the hands of the corpse. This was something that all the jurors could see right in front of their eyes. When they saw it, the State's case collapsed.

De La Mata

CASH SHOOTS INTO MIAMI WITH THE VELOCITY OF A HIGH-PRESSURE FIRE hose. I'm talking about paper money—not securities, bonds or checks, but the real thing. Green one-hundred-dollar bills adorned with Ben Franklin's portrait. In this international city of many tongues, cash is the universal language.

Many of the bills come coated with white microscopic particles, for if you follow the sinuous river of money back to its source, you find cocaine. Miami's location near the end of the Florida peninsula has made it the perfect spot for the drug trade. To the south, across the Caribbean, is Colombia, where the cocaine is processed and loaded onto twin-engine planes and freighters. The Bahamas and the myriad islands of the Caribbean are convenient way stations for the Cigarette boats and small planes that ferry football-sized kilos to the mainland.

When the smugglers get paid in cash, of course—it's too much of a good thing. One million dollars in hundred-dollar bills weighs twenty-two pounds and stands five feet tall. It's too conspicuous to transport such sums in bulk, so Miami has a huge cash surplus that has fueled an explosion in banks. Brickell Avenue, the city's banking center, has for years been a cacophony of construction—power drills, bulldozers, carpenters, concrete-making construction trucks.

It's the function of banks to take in money and put it to use. That's the way our economy works. At some point, federal prosecutors decided it was a lot easier to go after the bankers, whom they could find with a phone call, than the drug smugglers, who dart in and out of the Caribbean. To launch their offensive against bankers, the feds targeted Fred De La Mata.

On the summer morning in 1988 when he first came to see me, Fred was profoundly dejected. "I can't believe I need a criminal defense attorney," he said with a slight accent. He had closely cropped gray hair, a solid build and the healthy tan of an outdoorsman. Sitting in his finely tailored suit, he looked like what he was—a good, solid banker. But he said that he thought he might be in big trouble. Some "mystery witness" was telling federal prosecutors that Fred had knowingly helped a narco-trafficker launder money to finance his getaway. The whole thing was a lie, Fred said. He had thought he should go straight to the prosecutors, but some friends suggested he consult a lawyer first.

Fred was so agitated that I tried to calm him down by asking him to tell me a little about himself.

He was one of those astonishing Cuban success stories that prove how well capitalism works. After Fidel Castro turned Cuba into a Marxist-Leninist prison, tens of thousands of the country's upper class—the entrepreneurs, the professionals—flocked to Miami. Castro stole not only their nation, but also everything they had. They were forced to start over in a country where they didn't know the language, and in a generation, they took control of the city.

Fred told me he had gone to college in Cuba and was a young employee at Cuba's largest bank when Castro nationalized it. He was fired. He and his wife of a year arrived at the refugee center in Miami with five dollars in their pockets. They moved to New York, where Fred struggled to make ends meet by holding down three jobs. Weekdays, he started at 7:30 a.m., delivering stocks on Wall Street. At 9 a.m. he raced to the bank where he was employed as a clerk. At 5 p.m. he hurried to the U.S. Federal Reserve Bank, where he toiled until 11:15.

In 1965 he found a better bank job in Miami, and in 1967 he went to work for Republic National Bank, a fledgling institution located on the edge of Little Havana. His title was vice president in charge of the international department, which consisted only of himself. Fred lived and breathed the bank. He worked up to sixteen hours a day, even making coffee for the customers. On Saturdays and Sundays he walked the streets of Little Havana, going into the small shops of his fellow immigrants and asking them to open accounts at Republic. His selling point was that if Cuban merchants supported a Cuban bank, it, in turn, would support them. The bank thrived. His international department grew to fifty employees, and Fred swiftly climbed the corporate ladder. In 1985 he was appointed president.

Republic was owned by the Isaías family of Ecuador. Nahín Isaías was Fred's biggest supporter, but a few months after Fred was named president, a band of leftist guerrillas kidnapped Isaías in Quito. They demanded $5 million in cash and the freeing of terrorists from prison. A month after the kidnapping investigators learned where Isaías was being held. Backed by sharpshooters, the police and military commandos rushed a house. The seven kidnappers were killed in the shoot-out. So was Isaías.

The king was dead, and all the princes fought over the throne. Fred had lost his chief backer, and ambitious executives in the bank were jealous of his power. He had built Republic into a thriving enterprise with six hundred employees and $1 billion in assets, but as might be expected, he had made enemies along the way. Now, with federal bank examiners crawling all over the bank, Fred feared he was about to be sacrificed.

He said his problems were caused by a bank customer, Ramón Puentes, whom Fred had known for twenty years as a respectable businessman. Puentes had developed several car dealerships in the Miami area and had invested in commercial properties. He was a good bank customer who always repaid his loans. When the oil crisis hit in the 1970s, other car dealers defaulted on their loans, but Puentes sold off properties, including his house, to repay his commitments to the bank. When Puentes got back on his feet, Republic immediately reopened his lines of credit because of his loyalty and dependability. Puentes was so happy with the bank that he referred other businessmen to Republic, and he even co-signed loans for some of them.

Over the years Fred had gradually built a social relationship with Puentes, as many successful bankers do with their best customers. He had attended the weddings of Puentes's son and daughter, and had gone to Puentes's fiftieth birthday bash. Puentes attended many baseball games of Fred's son, Fred Jr., who was a star player in high school and college. Baseball is a huge sport among Miami Cubans—only in Miami could there be a José Canseco Street—and Fred Jr. developed quite a following. He went on to play minor league baseball in the Baltimore Orioles organization before returning to Miami to start a business career. When Fred Jr. married a local Cuban girl, Puentes paid for their honeymoon trip to the Caribbean. The federal government was now looking at that payment with suspicion because of a loan that Fred had made to Puentes.

One day in the fall of 1987, Puentes ran into Fred in the bank elevator and told him he was seeking a mortgage for a large house in Cocoplum, an upscale neighborhood near Biscayne Bay. He was planning to sell the house for more than a million dollars, but until it sold he was looking for an $800,000 mortgage that would serve as a bridge loan, so he could use the money to invest in other real estate. Puentes said a mortgage company already had approved his request for $800,000, and the deal was scheduled to close the following week, but he thought the company's demand for closing points was too high. He hoped Fred would give him a better deal.

Fred said he would see what he could do. He asked the bank's top real-estate expert to inspect the house. When the man concluded that the house could easily serve as collateral for $800,000, the loan was made. Months after the loan went through, Fred learned there was a problem when agents of the Internal Revenue Service started interviewing officers at the bank. The allegation was that the house was really owned by a major drug dealer named Indalecio "Andy" Iglesias. At the time the loan was made, the feds were closing in on Iglesias, and he needed money to flee the country. He had used Puentes, an alleged co-conspirator in the drug business, to get $800,000 out of Republic National Bank—money that Iglesias had quickly shipped overseas to a Swiss bank.

Iglesias and Puentes, it turned out, had indeed vanished, and arrest warrants were out for both of them. The federal government seized the Cocoplum house, saying it was built with illegal drug profits, and then sold it for $1 million. Ordinarily the government repays banks for any outstanding mortgages, but for the first time that anyone in the legal community could recall, prosecutors refused to pay off a loan on a seized property. They were alleging that Republic had knowingly helped Iglesias flee by turning "tainted" money—the drug proceeds used to build the house—into the "clean" money of a bank loan. The government argued that Republic's loan to Puentes amounted to money laundering. Federal agents were now swarming through the bank, seizing records and interviewing its employees. Fred had been questioned for several hours.

This investigation had already become a public scandal. A few days before Fred came to visit me, *The Miami Herald* ran a front-page story about the loan. Fred said he was shocked by the way his reputation imploded. Puentes had been a respected businessman in Miami for two decades, and Fred was astounded by the possibility that the car dealer might have been seduced by quick drug money. Fred told me he didn't know Iglesias at all. He and his wife had a couple of minor accounts at the bank, and Puentes might have introduced him to Fred once for a brief moment in the bank lobby, but that was it. Federal agents tracked down property documents that indicated the Cocoplum house was owned by a Panamanian concern, Thule Holding Corporation, but foreign ownership of local property was commonplace in Miami, and Puentes had signed documents giving his personal guarantee for the whole $800,000. That's the kind of thing a person would do only if he was the owner of the property.

The bank was now in federal court, fighting a civil forfeiture case to get its $800,000 back. The U.S. Attorney's Office was fiercely opposing the bank. One day the bank's lawyers had rushed into Fred's office and told him that the prosecutors had claimed to have uncovered a bribe that Fred had received in connection with the loan: Iglesias had paid for a Caribbean vacation for Fred and a paramour. Fred laughed. He didn't have a paramour, and he hadn't gone to the Caribbean recently. When the lawyers showed him documents, Fred realized that they concerned the honeymoon trip that Puentes had purchased for Fred Jr. and his bride. The bank's lawyers seemed relieved to hear his explanation, but after that they kept their distance from him.

Before he came to see me, Fred had given a deposition in the civil case and then testified at a hearing. The judge had yet to rule on whether Republic was entitled to get its money back, but then there was a new development. The bank's lawyers had learned about a mystery witness who was supposedly telling prosecutors some incriminating things about Fred.

Fred told me the bank's lawyers had never told him that he should seek his own counsel. They never explained that there might be a conflict between the bank's interests and his personal interests. But some friends had warned him that he should find his own attorney.

I told Fred that he needed a lawyer and shouldn't talk to anyone else, particularly government agents. To drive the point home, I told him about Bob Bennett, a Washington lawyer, who mounted a huge brown trout on his office wall with a brass plaque saying: "I wouldn't be here either if I kept my mouth shut."

•   •   •

The Peter Principle posits that we all eventually rise to our level of incompetence. The Black Principle, developed after years of unscientific observation, posits that the guy on top of the pyramid makes the biggest target.

It didn't take much research to convince me that Fred was a target of federal prosecutors. Poring over the pleadings and transcripts, I realized that they had set a devious trap. The feds were exploiting the civil discovery to squeeze information out of Fred before they filed criminal charges against him.

Their strategy became clear a few days later when the U.S. Attorney's Office asked the judge to reopen the forfeiture hearing to take the testimony of the "mystery witness." He turned out to be René Leonard, a professor of engineering and a contractor who used to have accounts at Republic. Fred told me that Leonard was angry at the bank because Fred had refused to disobey a court order to freeze Leonard's bank accounts so that the accounts could be used to pay off a judgment. He had told Fred, "One day I will pay you back for not helping me."

The day before Leonard was scheduled to testify, Fred called me to say that the bank's lawyers planned to put him on the witness stand to rebut Leonard's testimony.

"Fred, the hearing is just a setup," I told him. "Under no circumstances can you testify."

"Roy, you're just being paranoid."

"It's not paranoia," I replied. "Just my heightened sense of self-preservation."

I warned Fred that government agents had had several months to prepare questions for him, and that he would be opening himself up to a withering cross-examination. Without knowing all the details of the case, he could certainly do himself a lot of damage. Fred reluctantly agreed, but over the next several hours there was a flurry of phone calls from the bank's lawyers to Fred and me. The bank was putting severe pressure on him. Its lawyers told Fred that he would lose his job if he didn't take the stand, and Fred desperately wanted to testify. "All I want to do is say this guy's a liar," he told me.

I told Fred the prosecutors couldn't send the bank to jail. They needed a warm body, and he fit the bill neatly.

Reluctantly, Fred agreed. The next day Leonard took the stand and said that he had told Fred two crucial facts: that the Cocoplum house was really owned by Iglesias and that Iglesias needed the money from the mortgage on the house quickly because he was preparing to flee the country. At the end of the hearing, after Fred didn't take the stand, the government attorney asked, "Where is he to say this conversation didn't take place?"

The next day the bank's owners demanded Fred's resignation. After decades of hard work he was devastated by this public humiliation, not to mention the financial loss. One day he was president of the nation's most important Hispanic-owned bank. The next day he was nothing. His once-pristine image was irrevocably soiled. His fellow bankers shunned him. Embarrassed by the news coverage, he began slinking into his house, hoping the neighbors wouldn't see him. I heard regret in his voice when he asked: Couldn't we have prevented this disaster?

Fred continued to be polite and gracious even as he endured terrible stress, but he and I knew that he had been fired because he had heeded my advice. I felt bad, but my premonitions were soon confirmed.

The U.S. attorney issued grand jury subpoenas for the bank's records. The prosecutors were digging for corporate dirt: falsified accounts, misleading financial statements, bribes, hidden profits. Two weeks later prosecutors issued a thirty-three-page indictment that linked Fred with Iglesias, Puentes and thirteen other alleged drug dealers, saying they were part of a huge conspiracy that involved racketeering and dealing with the notorious Medellín drug cartel. This drug ring was alleged to have smuggled more than $14 million worth of cocaine into the United States.

Fred was charged with two counts—money laundering and accepting a bribe (his son's honeymoon trip). This respected community leader was suddenly facing up to twenty-five years in prison. Obviously, the government had held off issuing the indictment to gather more incriminating information if Fred had testified at the forfeiture hearing. The prosecutors could have charged him separately, but I'm sure they figured that trying an upstanding banker alone would make it more difficult to win a conviction. They preferred having the mild-mannered banker sit at a defense table with a bunch of well-dressed drug dealers.

Since the government knew I was Fred's lawyer, the prosecutors could have simply called and informed me of the indictment, and asked me to deliver Fred for booking. But that wouldn't have made for an exciting "photo opportunity." Instead, FBI agents surrounded Fred's home at 6:20 one morning, accompanied by a Channel 10 crew that the government had thoughtfully notified. When Fred's terrified wife had trouble unlocking the door, the agents threatened to break it down. Finally, she managed to open the door, and the agents burst in, followed by a Channel 10 cameraman. Fred was in his pajamas. His wife was in a nightgown. Agents pushed Fred against the wall and slapped handcuffs on him. Two agents grabbed his arms and walked him slowly out of the house so that the camera could get good footage.

The arrest sent shock waves through Miami. When a man like Fred De La Mata, the respected president of the most prestigious Cuban bank, is arrested, was anyone safe? The banking community was terrified that its mainstay, international trade, particularly with Latin America, was now suspect in the eyes of prosecutors. Was dealing with any offshore entity safe? Was any foreign corporation a possible criminal front in the eyes of prosecutors? How could any banker be completely assured that a company wasn't a front for drug dealers?

Meanwhile, many in the immigrant community were outraged. People like Fred had risen in Miami in good measure because they could speak Spanish and English, making them the ideal facilitators for doing business with Latin America. Of course, many of the drug dealers were Hispanics, and that meant they gravitated to men like Fred. Were all bilingual businessmen now at risk?

Fred's bail was set at $600,000. We got him released after he surrendered his passport. He was out of his jail cell, but he felt trapped in a nightmare. Over the next four months he lost thirty-five pounds. His wife, who had been a homemaker for years, was forced to get a job in the bookkeeping department at a department store. Old colleagues and the bank he had helped build treated him like a pariah. Everything that Fred had spent his life working for was in ruins.

In Florida, the State's prosecutions are conducted on the principle of law in the sunshine. Defense attorneys are entitled to names of witnesses and police reports, and are allowed to question all important witnesses before the trial.

The federal system, by contrast, operates on a moonless night.[1] The defense is kept in the dark. We were not told in advance what witnesses the government would call at Fred's trial, and we had no formal power to require witnesses to talk to us. The unofficial motto of the U.S. Attorney's Office is "Your ignorance is our bliss." In a civil case involving your money, you get full disclosure before trial. In a federal criminal case with your life on the line, you get nothing.

The secrecy in which federal prosecutions are conducted has become so widespread that some judges convene secret (called *ex parte*) conferences with prosecutors to avoid scrutiny by the public and defense attorneys. As one prosecutor boasted: "There is no party like an *ex parte*." I know of instances in which prosecutors have told judges, "We can't have a hearing about this because it would disclose this or that," and the judge then denies the defense's request for a hearing, without the defense even being told about the clandestine conference. Most Americans don't seem to care about these infringements on the constitutional rights of the accused because they think that is the way to put drug dealers and other criminals behind bars, but secrecy has a way of leading to corruption. As the famous jurist Learned Hand once said, "The power of secret inquisition is the greatest threat to democracy."

The secrecy surrounding federal prosecutions in Miami became even more impenetrable after Dexter Lehtinen, a former Republican state senator, was named acting U.S. attorney for the Southern District of Florida in 1988. He turned the U.S. Attorney's Office into a political battleground. A Vietnam vet, Lehtinen liked to tell his assistants that they were at war. He once urged prosecutors on to victory by waving an AK-47 at a staff meeting, and his office walls were covered with platoon flags and posters of people like General Patton. Sometimes he passed out printed placards that said No Guts No Glory. T. D. Allman wrote in *Vanity Fair* that with Lehtinen at the helm, the U.S. Attorney's Office in Miami was "secretive, paranoid, barricaded, gripped by caprices."[2]

Fred's case was the first that Lehtinen took on. Drawing on his experience

---

1. Supreme Court Justice William O. Douglas compared a trial without discovery to a game of blindman's buff.

2. Published in its February 1991 issue.

with the media in political campaigns, Lehtinen used the occasion of Fred's indictment to hold a mammoth press conference. He lectured reporters that the charges against Fred were a clear warning that "in the narcotics world, drug money will continue to haunt you until you go to your grave." The fed's message was clear: Cooperate with the Drug Enforcement Administration and disclose client confidences or end up like Fred De La Mata.

Lehtinen's press conference served as a battle cry for confiscating as much property as possible under the new federal seizure laws. In Miami and elsewhere, federal prosecutors have become pseudo-entrepreneurs, seizing just about anything—bank accounts, cars, boats, planes, houses, businesses. No longer do prosecutors brag about mere trial victories; now they boast about the size of their real estate portfolio. When the U.S. Attorney's Office looked at Fred De La Mata, it saw a billion-dollar bank.

The feds got a hefty chunk of Republic's money even as we were preparing for trial. U.S. District Judge Thomas Scott ruled that Republic Bank had "actual knowledge, if not complicity" that it was helping launder drug money and he said the government could keep the $800,000 the bank had loaned Puentes for the Cocoplum house.[3] Ben Turnbull, president of the Bankers Association for Foreign Trade, called the ruling "a major, precedent-making decision." Bankers throughout the country became afraid that the government's tentacles could reach into their coffers if they made a bad loan.

I worried that potential jurors had read the news stories about the judge's decision. Might these stories lead them to assume Fred was guilty? I knew that Miami Cubans tended to blend their business and their personal relationships, and that the giving of grand gifts was part of their culture. Would a jury understand that? In retrospect, it was easy to see that Fred had gotten too close to Puentes, and that their relationship had clouded his judgment. He should have returned the plane tickets that Puentes bought for Fred Jr. This ethical lapse was causing him a lot of problems, but I didn't think it should send him to jail.

• • •

---

3. Years later, in July 1997, Scott became the U.S. attorney in Miami, replacing Kendall Coffey, who resigned after biting a topless dancer.

Because the prosecution reveals so little information in a federal case, the defense has the burden of finding out what evidence is likely to be presented at the trial. That puts a premium on working closely with your client to learn as many facts about the case as you can. In the months leading up to the trial, Fred remained ever the gracious gentleman, despite the pressure he was under. We collected thousands of pages of bank records, which he tirelessly analyzed for us.

Who would the witnesses against Fred be? I knew where I could find many of them. Dante reserves the ninth circle of hell for the betrayer; the feds reserved the Metropolitan Correctional Center.

From the outside, MCC looks like most prisons. It is surrounded by twelve-foot-high, chain-linked perimeter fences topped with coils of razor wire and by strategically placed gun towers. The inferno is inside: a demonic mass of confidence men, embezzlers, scammers, extortionists, crooked lawyers, dirty cops, junkies, pimps, counterfeiters, racketeers, narcotics dealers and murderers, each looking for a way out. The easiest way is by "jumping on the bus." In prison argot, that means making a deal. There are plenty of other names for it: rat, stool pigeon, informer, *chivato*, snitch. Inmates literally jump on the marshal's bus to testify at the courthouse in exchange for reduced sentences or instant freedom. The MCC is a city of informers, all seeking a "Get Out of Jail Free" card.[4]

When a big indictment comes down, the word quickly spreads through the MCC's underground telegraph. Inmates line up to become witnesses. Girlfriends, lawyers and private detectives are sent to dig through court files for useful information. Sometimes, discovery documents are stolen from defendant inmates to obtain the raw material for constructing a persuasive story. Some enterprising inmates have even been known to conduct seminars on the bigger cases, selling to others information that might be of interest to prosecutors. Usually, information doesn't have to be bought. Many inmates are willing to testify about their own drug deals and add just one name. They refashion events slightly, shading some facts while omitting others.

Iglesias and Puentes remained fugitives, but there were plenty of other drug traffickers eager to make deals. When they agreed to plead guilty and cooper-

---

4. Don't take my word for it. No less of an authority than the chief federal judge in South Florida, Norman Roettger, described the institution as an "anthill of snitches" all conniving a way out (*United States* v. *Sepe*, 1 F. Supp. 2d 1372 [S.D. Fla. 1998]).

ate with the government, we were not informed, so I had to do legal detective
work to find out what was happening. If I saw a sealed document in the court
file, that was a sure sign that a deal had been made. Every week I checked the
clerk's docket sheets to see if they included anything that I didn't know about.

After a couple of weeks the docket sheets disclosed sealed documents had
been filed for John Smith[5] and Duane Munera. Smith, a lawyer, could credi-
bly accuse a banker because he ran Iglesias's money-laundering operation. I
put out feelers to all the lawyers who knew Smith and I scored with one who
had just left the U.S. Attorney's Office. We met at a sidewalk counter on Calle
Ocho. Sipping *café cubano* from a small paper cup, he told me: "Smith is fifty
pounds of shit packed into a ten-pound bag. One swift kick and it's all over
you. The feds don't want to get their pretty suits dirty so they're not using
him." I crossed him off the witness list.

Munera, the subject of the other sealed document, had been Iglesias's
chief enforcer. His indictment listed a large number of automatic guns found
in his possession and it outlined his strong-arm tactics. He had escaped from
the Atlanta penitentiary and been rearrested. Uncomfortable with the Spartan
accommodations in MCC's solitary confinement cells, he struck a sweetheart
deal. As soon as Munera signed on, the prosecutor had him released, even
though he had been caught in a new escape attempt.

By the time Fred's case went to trial in September 1990, the docket sheets
were crammed with sealed documents. Every one of Fred's alleged co-con-
spirators who had been caught pled guilty and agreed to help the prosecution.
The only defendant to face the jury was Frederick De La Mata.

Miami's Old Federal Courthouse has large elegant rooms decorated with
sculptures, columns and murals. At the heart of this Renaissance palace is a

---

5. John Smith is a pseudonym for the real lawyer. This is necessary since the sealed document was another hidden sweetheart deal by the United States attorney. Smith served
only a year and was re-admitted to the bar after his release. Today, he practices real estate
and banking law in Miami.

sunlit, arcaded loggia with a splashing fountain. Our courtroom, in an annex, was far less ornate.

My opponent was Stephen Schlessinger, a veteran prosecutor who had worked in the U.S. Attorney's Office in New York before transferring to Miami. An intense combatant who liked wearing a Los Angeles Lakers T-shirt under his white shirt, Schlessinger was the leading warrior in Lehtinen's prosecutorial army.

Our judge was José A. González Jr., appointed by President Carter in 1978. A fanatical fan of University of Florida football, González had decorated his chambers with Gator memorabilia. He had a reputation as a thoughtful, impartial man who wouldn't be steamrolled by prosecutors.

Jury selection did not take long. Unlike in state cases, where lawyers sometimes question prospective jurors for days, even weeks, before selecting a jury, a federal judge has the power to handle the entire jury selection process. He usually asks the jurors only basic questions, to see if they understand the concept of reasonable doubt and to learn if they have any knowledge about the case that would prevent them from being impartial. I watched with frustration while the judge questioned the men and women who would decide Fred's fate. We ended up with a twelve-member jury that included three black women, two older Hispanic women and a smattering of Anglo males and females, ranging from twenty-somethings to senior citizens.

Schlessinger framed his opening remarks in biblical terms: "This is a case about the wages of sin," he announced. A powerful banker manipulated the bank's rules to clean up drug money and enrich himself through bribery. Schlessinger claimed that the government would prove that the house at 6960 Miraflores Avenue in Cocoplum was controlled by a convicted drug smuggler, Indalecio "Andy" Iglesias. "The question is: What did Mr. De La Mata know and when did he know it?" Schlessinger told the jurors, employing the vocabulary of Watergate.

Schlessinger's theory was that Puentes masqueraded as a legitimate car dealer but was a front man for Iglesias, a major drug trafficker. Iglesias built the house with drug cash, but had to "cash" the house in when the authorities were hot on his trail. Fred was the insider, a corrupt banker. He was guilty of money laundering, Schlessinger said, because he knew the drug-smuggling origins of the funds used to build the Cocoplum house and concealed this information from his colleagues at the bank. He claimed that testimony would show that Fred had rushed the $800,000 loan for Puentes through the bank so that other bank officers wouldn't have time to check on the background of the property. Fred was guilty of bribery because Puentes paid for his money laundering by financing a $3,000 honeymoon trip for Fred's son.

In my opening remarks I walked the jury through the loan process at the bank. I highlighted the documents that showed the loan was issued in the normal course of business. The mortgage was approved by a committee of loan officers and senior bank officials, just as any other loan to a preferred customer such as Puentes. "Iglesias was a highly secretive drug trafficker who worked hard to keep his drug business hidden. It took the DEA years to uncover Iglesias. Yet they expect Fred, without a horde of federal agents at his beck and call, to do it in a couple of days." I said that Fred knew nothing about Iglesias's background and that the drug dealer had gone to elaborate lengths to disguise his connection to the Cocoplum house. Only years later was it learned that there was a link between Iglesias and the house. "In this day and age in Dade County, it's not difficult to deal with people who are involved in drugs," I said.

The U.S. Attorney's Office chose the first day of the trial to announce that Republic National Bank and its employees were targets of a criminal investigation. This was no coincidence. The move accomplished two goals. It treated jurors to lurid press accounts, and it simultaneously torpedoed my defense. We had planned on calling many bank employees—directors, lawyers, officers—to the witness stand, to talk about Fred's reputation and how the Cocoplum loan had been handled. But after being warned they were targets, the employees were told by their lawyers not to testify, just as I had told Fred earlier. No sane lawyer allows the target of a federal probe to testify without the comfort of immunity. I could subpoena them, of course, but they would either be uncooperative witnesses or invoke their Fifth Amendment right against self-incrimination. Once the prosecutor declared all the bankers targets, they would not testify without immunity, which only the prosecutor could ask for. The defense has no power to confer immunity.

Thus, by dashing off one letter, the prosecutor controlled all the important witnesses.

Ironically, Schlessinger found himself in a bind. He needed a grant of immunity for one of his first witnesses. Only the judge could grant immunity, and then only with proper authorization from high officials in the Department of Justice. At a sidebar conference Schlessinger asked Judge González for the grant, even though the formal paperwork from Washington hadn't arrived yet. Judge González, wise in the ways in which the feds often try to manipulate cases, leaned over the bench and stared at him. "Mr. Schlessinger," he said, shaking his head, "I have no problem accepting what you tell me. But I am embarrassed to admit after ten years as a federal judge, I no longer believe all the government's representations."

With that, it was time for the witnesses. In Kafka's *The Trial*, Joseph K. wanders around the courthouse, going in and out of rooms filled with people, trying to find out what's happening to him. I know how he feels. In a federal case, when a witness strides through the rear door of the courtroom, both my client and I turn around to see who it is. Oftentimes, I whisper, "Do you know who that is?" and the client dumbly shakes his head.

When Schlessinger's first witness walked in, neither Fred nor I recognized him. He turned out to be David Ryder, one of Andy Iglesias's henchmen. His swarthy complexion and pumped-up biceps fit the tough-guy role. I was astonished to see that Ryder was wearing a Special Forces T-shirt with the emblem of the United States on it. Prosecutors generally dress up their lowlife witnesses to impress the jury, but this was far beyond the pale.

Schlessinger began by trying to make Ryder seem like an upstanding citizen. Under questioning, Ryder said that he had been a captain in Special Forces and an intelligence officer. After leaving the military he had decided that smuggling cocaine could replace the thrill of commando actions. For four years he had specialized in obtaining speed boats and ferrying drugs from freighters to the sheltered coves and inlets that dot the Florida Keys. He had pled guilty to charges of racketeering and income tax evasion, and had been sentenced to seven years. I made a note: He must be a super–stool pigeon to get only seven years.

Schlessinger tried to preempt one line of attack by drawing out the terms of his witness's plea agreement: Ryder had promised to help the government, and in return the prosecutors had promised not to ask for the maximum sentence for racketeering, which is twenty years. By testifying at Fred's trial, Ryder was maneuvering for a further reduction in his sentence.

Ostensibly, Ryder was put on the stand to establish that Iglesias was indeed a well-known drug dealer. But Schlessinger had a broader, unstated goal: By calling Ryder and other drug dealers to testify, the prosecutor hoped to make Fred look guilty by association—even though Fred had never met Ryder.

Methodically, the prosecutor led Ryder through his drug-smuggling activities. Ryder spoke in the calm tone of a man who might have been buying and selling peanut butter. In one job Ryder rented a waterfront house in Fort Lauderdale to dock a fishing boat used to import a half ton of cocaine. For that trip Ryder was paid $200,000 in cash, which he managed to lose quickly: "I left it one day in a motel parking lot in Key West. I was in a hurry, set it down in a briefcase, got in my car and drove away to eat breakfast. When I got back, somebody had picked it up and gave it to the police. I went to the police and told them it was my money. Through a long legal maneuver, I wound up getting the money back eight or nine months later." He portrayed Iglesias as a brazen smuggler who was far too crude to pass as a legitimate businessman. Iglesias, according to Ryder, had all the Miami cocaine-dealer accoutrements: a solid-gold Rolex watch, diamond pinkie rings, Brioni suits and blood red Ferraris.

By the time Schlessinger was finished with Ryder, it was 5:30 p.m., and we adjourned till the next morning. I knew that Ryder was likely to be the first in a string of sleazy witnesses, and I wanted the jury to see him as an example of the type of criminal who would "jump on the bus" to strike a deal with the prosecutor.

"Good morning, Mr. Ryder," I began. "You and I have never talked before, have we?"

"No."

But hadn't he talked frequently to the U.S. Attorney's Office? Yes, he had. He had been "debriefed" twenty or thirty times. Had he said anything to the prosecutors about Fred? No, not a word.

"That's because you don't know Mr. De La Mata, do you?"

"No, I don't."

"The man sitting down here," I pointed to Fred, "you don't really know him, do you?"

"No, I don't."

Under my questioning he acknowledged that for four years he had no legitimate employment, but he had plenty of bank accounts, including one at Barnett Bank and another at American Bank of Brevard County.

"Did you tell anybody at Barnett Bank that you were a drug smuggler?"

"No, I didn't."

"Did you tell anybody at American Bank that you were a drug smuggler?"

"No, I didn't."

"You kept it hidden as best you could, didn't you?"

"Yes sir."

The same way Puentes and Iglesias would have hidden their drug smuggling from Republic National Bank.

I then drew from him that he had earned a total of $400,000 from his drug smuggling, but he had claimed he had none of it left and therefore didn't have to pay a fine at the time of his sentencing. I asked him about his $275,000 house. He admitted the prosecutor let him keep it.

"What was the name of your mortgage company?"

"It was Sound Mortgage."

"Did they know that you were a drug dealer?"

"Not to my knowledge."

"Did they hire investigators to verify you were a good citizen?"

"Not to my knowledge."

"You just submitted the papers and they looked at them and okayed the loan?"

"Normal bank check."

"And normal credit checks don't show that you're a drug smuggler, do they?"

"I don't think so." His tone suggested that I had asked a stupid question. In a way I had: A banker isn't supposed to be an investigator, but that's what the government said Fred should have been. I glanced at the jurors, who were staring at Ryder with folded arms—a gesture of disapproval.

"You took an oath yesterday, but oaths don't mean much to you, do they?"

Schlessinger leaped up: "Objection!"

"Judge, I need a little latitude here," I pleaded.

"Overruled," said González.

Ryder said he took oaths seriously.

I picked up a copy of his signed affidavit concerning the $200,000 he had left in the parking lot: He swore the money had come from his mother, and he was planning to use it to make a movie. "You signed a false affidavit?"

"I believe that's what I did, sir, yes."

"Because you wanted something, you were willing to lie under oath about it, is that right?"

"Yes sir."

"Nothing as important as getting out of jail—it was just money?"

"At the time, I felt very strongly that the money was mine."

"I assume that you feel just as strongly today about getting out of prison?"

"Not as strongly as that. I'm trying to get my life back the way it was."

"You had no hesitation at all using your mother as a false alibi to get the money back?"

"No sir, I didn't."

He had also claimed that the actor Chuck Norris was going to be the lead in the movie, which would be a documentary about diving for treasure in the Florida Keys. "That was creative scripting?"

"Yes sir," he said uneasily.

"Let me sum up here. Instead of being indicted for perjury, you made a deal to become a witness. You will end up not with additional time in prison, but less?"

"Yes sir."

After Ryder, Schlessinger called Eduardo Cancela. A cocaine importer who had been sentenced to twenty years, Cancela described a 350-kilo deal he did with Iglesias. He claimed that Iglesias boasted about a "personal banker."

In my questioning, I brought out that Schlessinger had promised to appear at Cancela's parole hearing in return for his testimony. I learned this from a subpoena served on the parole commission. I knew there was more, but federal agents are slick enough to fly the perks below the radar—little things like transferring the prisoner to a Club Fed with palatable food and decent tennis, or manipulating a motion to reduce sentence. I asked whether his recollection of precise details of a conversation with Iglesias held several years before had been prompted by Schlessinger's promises to help him get out of jail. "No. It was just a coincidence," he said.

Then came Herbert Kithcart. A West Point graduate and former army captain, he, too, had worked for Iglesias. Once he had helped smuggle 500 kilos of cocaine. He was now in prison for drug trafficking and tax evasion. A motion to reduce his long sentence was pending.

Each of these witnesses, and those who followed, admitted in my cross that they had neither forfeited any drug money nor paid the substantial fines imposed at their sentencing. Each claimed to have lost money dealing in drugs. Their answers drew laughter from the jury.

Schlessinger moved closer to Fred with his next witness, Margarita Iglesias, the former wife of the fugitive drug dealer. She was a dark blonde in her midthirties whose voluptuous beauty was diminished by her many months in prison, where she had languished until her plea bargain with the U.S. Attorney's Office sprang her. Schlessinger tried to elicit sympathy for Margarita by having her talk about her three children. But there wasn't much he could do to clean up her image: She had been charged with money laundering and four counts of tax evasion. She had pled guilty and was awaiting sentencing, which would occur after the trial. She could get three years and a $100,000 fine for each count, but I was certain she would never serve another day in jail.[6]

Under Schlessinger's questioning, Margarita said she met Iglesias in 1976, when he was getting a divorce. He became involved in drugs "to make it rich, to be able to lead the good life." At first, Iglesias imported marijuana from Bimini by boat. He was arrested on Key Biscayne, but the charges were dropped. He was arrested again in Nassau, in the Bahamas, and was fined and released. After earning these merit badges, he hit the smuggling big time, linking up with members of the Medellín cartel and moving cocaine from Colombia to the United States. Margarita knew all about her husband's drug dealing, including the names of the boats he used and how much they carried. Twice, she testified, she carried $100,000 to the Cayman Islands.

After several trips to Colombia, she said, "my husband felt that we were wealthy enough that we could afford the house of his dreams." Andy's version

---

6. I was right. After Fred's trial she received probation.

of the American dream was a $275,000 canal-front lot at 6960 Miraflores. He liked the Cocoplum neighborhood, she said, because it was "very exclusive" and had "big houses."

In preparing for the trial, I had visited Cocoplum. The lush mangroves had been displaced by concrete palaces, reminiscent of Holiday Inns, shoe-horned into small lots. Many were built by the government's star witness, René Leonard, who was an engineer by training, not an architect. Iglesias's dream house proved that money was no substitute for taste. You'd think that with the $2 million that Iglesias had spent on this house, he would have wanted something more than mere square footage, but his five-bedroom house had no elegance. It was all concrete, glass and sharp angles, with a jut-ting roof line and all the grace of the Pentagon.

Margarita said that because Andy wasn't declaring his drug profits to the Internal Revenue Service, they had disguised the ownership of the house by having their attorney, John Smith, put the property in the name of a Pana-manian shell company, Thule Holding Corporation. The nominal president of the company was Antonio Muñoz.

Schlessinger told the jury that it was obvious that the Iglesiases were the real owners of the house: He produced a letter from the Cocoplum Home-owners Association to the Miraflores address with Margarita's name on it, and she stated that she paid her homeowners' fees from a checking account in her name at Republic National Bank. The account listed her address as being 6960 Miraflores.

About the time the house was built, Margarita testified, Andy entered into a smuggling partnership with Ramón Puentes. A boatload of cocaine earned Iglesias and Puentes each a profit of $1 million, but then a relative of Puentes was arrested by the DEA. The two smugglers decided to chill out in Spain for a while, and her husband ordered her to move all their bank accounts to Re-public because "Ramón Puentes had very good contacts at the bank. He felt that if we had our checking account at that bank, because of Ramón's associa-tions there, a few things would be in our favor. One, that we would get speedy clearance of these checks; and two, that if anything were ever to come about, any problems, that we would find out immediately." She said that Puentes's son took her to the bank, where she filled out forms to open the accounts.

In another example of how the drug dealers worked closely with the bank, she said Puentes and Iglesias purchased a large warehouse that Republic National Bank had foreclosed on. "Andy mentioned that it was a very, very good deal." They purchased it for $2 million, though they felt it was worth much more. Puentes and Iglesias made a down payment, and Republic gave them a mortgage for the rest.

I made a note. The warehouse deal had been with Thule Holding Corp. and Puentes. Iglesias's name did not appear in the documents. I didn't see how this could hurt Fred.

Up to this point, Margarita hadn't mentioned Fred or the loan on the Cocoplum house. Finally, Schlessinger asked her about the loan. She said that in the summer of 1987, two contractors who had worked on the house told Andy that they had been served with subpoenas to appear before a grand jury. Fearing that he would soon have to flee, Iglesias decided to sell the house. He asked Puentes to handle the sale. Iglesias's sister, Elena Festa, was the broker. She found a buyer, Margarita said, but that deal fell through. Iglesias and Puentes worked out a deal with a mortgage company to get an $800,000 bridge loan, but Iglesias didn't like having to pay $100,000 in points to close the deal.

"My husband, Andy, he was kind of losing control. He felt he was losing everything." So Margarita spoke with Puentes, who then went to see Fred about getting a bridge mortgage, $800,000 for one year, with four payments that would be for interest only, before the principal was repaid at the end of the year. When the loan was consummated, Margarita said, her husband and Puentes arranged for two large checks to be sent to Swiss bank accounts.

Schlessinger asked her if she or her husband knew Fred. She said that after the closing of the mortgage on the house, she went to the wedding of Puentes's daughter at a church in the Gables, followed by a reception at the Puentes' home. "Mr. Puentes said to me, 'I want you to meet Fred,' and he called Fred, and he said, 'Fred, this is Andy's wife, Margie.'"

"What did Mr. De La Mata say at that time?" Schlessinger asked.

"Nothing. Just said nice to meet you, shook my hand, and that was it."

She said that when Andy decided he couldn't afford to make the $24,000 quarterly interest payment, Puentes said "he was going to talk to Fred and see if there was any way the bank would accept a voluntary foreclosure." Later Puentes "told us we had to make the payment, that the bank would not accept the voluntary foreclosure."

For six months after the loan was made, Andy Iglesias traveled back and forth between Spain and the United States. In June 1988, when he realized he was about to be arrested, he left the United States for the last time. The following month, the bank went to court, demanding its money or the house.

When Schlessinger was finished, I established what kind of person Margarita Iglesias was. "As I understood your testimony today, after years of drug dealing and many millions of dollars, you were unable to make a single interest payment?"

"Well, sir, my husband did spend money very freely."

"I take it that it's all gone and you probably don't have any money left in your wallet?"

"I'm sure I have some money left in my wallet," she said defiantly.

"But, of course, not enough to pay your back taxes or fines?" I asked.

Her only response was a haughty stare.

As with David Ryder, I brought out that she had refused to talk to me, but had had many conversations with Schlessinger. She had begun talking to him while she was in jail, where she was being held without bond. As soon as she started cooperating, she was freed.

"So while you were presumed innocent for eight months, you were in jail, but as soon as you pled guilty, with a plea bargain, the prosecutor had you released from jail?"

"Well, sir—"

"Is that correct?"

"Yes."

"I take it that you were pretty deeply involved in your husband's drug dealings?"

"I was involved."

She had pled guilty only to tax evasion, not to a drug crime, but she clearly had been a major player in her husband's smuggling operations. She said she had watched as a large boatload of cocaine was brought into Miami while the Miami Dolphins were playing in the Super Bowl—a time when virtually everyone's attention, including that of the police, was focused on the game.

"How many drug crimes have you committed?"

"Well, actually, sir. . . ." She evaded the question with a meandering statement before she finally acknowledged, "I would say I am just as guilty because I accepted his deals and his intimate money."

Intimate money. A curious phrase. She said Andy gave her cash—up to $20,000 at a time.

"Where did you spend it?"

"Anywhere I could." She laughed.

"Perhaps you could give me a list."

She mentioned a house on Southwest 115th Terrace, a car, toys, clothes, furniture. "Anything that came to my fancy," she said.

"I take it you enjoyed spending the money?"

"Doesn't everybody?"

"Well, not everybody enjoys spending *drug* money."

"*I* did."

"I take it you didn't have any morals or ethics that prevented you from spending the money?"

"No sir."

She said all her expenditures were in cash, which she and Andy kept stashed around the house—in a floor safe, in a shoebox in a closet, in a compartment hidden in their platform bed. But in the Iglesias household it was easy come, easy go. Andy managed to lose considerable sums in dubious schemes. In one, he gave $725,000 to a guy who had a plan to smuggle gold and Rolex watches into the country, but "it was a con and we lost the money." In another, he invested $250,000 in a car dealership, but the Argentine owners ran off with the cash. Another time he loaned his attorney, John Smith, $250,000 in cash to purchase a house. The lawyer never returned the money, she said.

"Mr. Smith turned out to be a thief?"

"Basically."

I got her to acknowledge that the drug cash used to build the Cocoplum house had never been deposited at Republic. She doled out bags of cash to the subcontractors building the house. This may have seemed like a small point, but it was important legally. Schlessinger claimed it was all a shell game. The drug money went into the house, so the house became the drug money. If you accept that theory, the next step, financing the house, became a way of getting the drug money back out of the house. The truth was that the drug money had gone to workmen and contractors whom the government had never pursued, and not a dollar of it passed through the bank.

Margarita acknowledged that she and Andy went to great lengths to conceal their ownership of the house. Their application to the Cocoplum Home-owners Association said that the owner was Thule Holding Corporation.

"Did it say Andy and Margarita Iglesias?"

"No sir."

"Because you hid the ownership of the home?"

"Sir, we were trying to conceal from everybody possible we owned the home."

I glanced at the jurors, hoping they saw the implication: If a dope smuggler would conceal his ownership from a homeowners association, he was certainly going to conceal it from a bank president.

I showed her other documents, all of which listed Thule as the owner: a city building permit, correspondence with the homeowners association concerning a controversy over their driveway gate, two certificates of occupancy, two leases that showed that the Iglesiases rented the house from Thule.

Schlessinger had portrayed Margarita as almost a victim of her husband. She had worked hard to be a responsible mother and loving wife. I abruptly changed gears: "Several times in this courtroom you have mentioned your children. What ages are they again, ma'am?"

"At the moment, sir, they are five, eight and eleven."

"Did you keep your children isolated from all these drug activities?"

"Yes sir, I did."

"Would you ever allow people to use cocaine in their presence?"

"No sir."

"A good mother wouldn't allow that."

"No sir."

"Do you know Mario Tabraue?" He was a notorious drug dealer who had operated out of a jewelry store in Little Havana.

"Yes sir."

"He was a large importer of drugs."

"Yes sir."

"He's a friend of yours?"

"I knew him."

The network led by Mario Tabraue and his father, a former CIA operative, had spread its tentacles widely, and after their arrest, accusations were made that the Tabraues had corrupted police officers. They were even alleged to have killed and barbecued a colleague whom they caught wearing a wire. The victim was hacked up with a chain saw and then burned with fifty bags of charcoal. I had searched through the files of Mario Tabraue's case and found that thousands of conversations in his warehouse office had been tape-recorded by agents of the Drug Enforcement Administration. One conversation was with Margarita.

"Do you recall taking your children into his office while he was snorting cocaine?"

"While he was snorting cocaine?"

"Yes, Mrs. Iglesias, you know what snorting cocaine is, don't you?"

"Yes sir, I do."

"Do you know there was a room bug taping the conversation between you and Mr. Tabraue?"

"I did afterwards, yes."

"Your children were with you?"

"At one point, yes."

"In fact, your children were captured on the tape saying things?"

"I don't recall."

I was holding the eighteen-page transcript of her conversation with Tabraue. "The transcript shows, Mrs. Iglesias, that Tabraue was snorting cocaine while your children were present. Not acceptable conduct for mother of the year."

She denied he snorted in front of her children. "Mario was a constant user, and he had a nasal problem." He had only been sniffling.

I handed her the transcript with the words "snorting sounds" highlighted in bright yellow. "Was that his post-nasal drip, Mrs. Iglesias?"

"Yes. How can you say snorting sounds to mean that the gentleman was doing cocaine at the moment?"

"Because I took the time to listen to the tape and its unmistakable sounds of snorting lines of cocaine, Mrs. Iglesias." Pressing further on her concept of family values, I got her to admit that she had been so eager to help the government that she even tried to entrap her husband. With the approval of federal agents, she talked to him by phone while he was in hiding overseas, trying to lure him back to the United States so he could be arrested. That didn't work, but it proved how far she would go to get out of jail.

Under my questioning, she admitted numerous other lies. In 1982, when she and Andy had earned $800,000 in drug money, she signed, under penalty of perjury, an income tax statement declaring only $57,186. She had done the same in other years. Like most people in the drug trade, she was a persistent liar, and it didn't matter whether she was under oath or not.

To show that Fred and the Cocoplum house had been singled out by the government for special treatment, I asked about the $500,000 house on Southwest 115th Terrace that Margarita had purchased after separating from Iglesias.

"Was that house bought with drug proceeds?"

"Yes, it was."

When she applied for a mortgage with Savings of America, she said she was earning $450 a week as a secretary at a power boat company.

"Did bank officials say they didn't quite know how a secretary earning $450 a week could buy a house for half a million dollars?"

"No sir." She said she put $170,000 down and claimed she was receiving large sums in alimony and child support. The mortgage payment was $2,400 a month.

When I started inquiring about the lies she told mortgage people, she said she wasn't feeling well. I didn't want to turn her into a sympathetic figure. I suggested a recess.

"No sir," she said tearfully. "I'd like to finish as soon as possible."

"Your Honor," I said, "Mrs. Iglesias is not feeling well, and perhaps we should recess." Cross-examining a crying woman is a dangerous enterprise.

The judge turned to her, and she repeated: "No sir, I can continue."

I pressed on. "Did you tell the bank where you obtained the $170,000 for the down payment?"

"No, I did not say it was coming from drug money."

"Did anybody from Savings of America ask you where the money came from?"

"No sir."

She admitted that she lied many times on the loan application.

"Do you know that it's a federal crime to submit a false statement to a federally insured lending institution in order to get a loan?"

"That's why I pled guilty."

She retreated when I pointed out that the plea to tax evasion had nothing to do with lying on this loan.

"When you sold this house for $525,000, you had already signed your plea agreement with the government?"

"Yes sir."

"Did they ask you to forfeit the proceeds of that house because it was drug money?"

"Originally, the agreement was that I would forfeit the house, but my attorney was able to make some type of arrangement. . . . The bottom line was that I could keep the house."

After that, Schlessinger took care of odd bits of prosecutorial housekeeping. He called a witness who identified travel agency documents showing that Ramón Puentes had paid $3,000 for the Caribbean honeymoon of Fred Jr. and his bride. This was a minor matter, but crucial to prove the alleged bribe. I noted that Schlessinger had omitted one important step in his presentation of the evidence, but I didn't want to alert him to it so he could eliminate the problem.

The next witness was Fernando J. Martínez, Republic's senior vice president in charge of real estate lending. Unlike the previous witnesses, I had interviewed Martínez before the trial, and I knew he was going to be careful and accurate, not shading his testimony toward either the prosecution or the defense.

Schlessinger asked how the typical real estate loan was made.

"For a new customer or an existing customer?"

"Well, all right," Schlessinger said, "let's start with a new customer." The distinction was important, and I jotted a note to myself.

Martínez said that a bank officer gets details about a person's background—financial statements, Social Security number, and so on

"What if it's a Panamanian corporation?" Schlessinger asked.

"Again, are you talking about a new relationship or an existing relationship?"

"Well, let's talk about a new relationship," he said quickly, avoiding the alternative.

"On a new relationship," the vice president said, "the bank usually asks for something about who the principals of that company are. The problem with Panamanian or Netherlands Antilles corporations is that it's impossible to know who the owners actually are, because their stocks are made out to bearer, and anybody can own those stocks." He said that back in 1987, when the Cocoplum loan was arranged, "a lot of real estate deals here were made through foreign corporations because of tax purposes."

"Isn't it fair to say they do it because they don't wish to be identified as the owner of the property?"

"The main reason was tax purposes," Martínez persisted neutrally. "A foreign corporation didn't have to pay the same taxes that a U.S. corporation did."

"Would it be fair to say that you, as an experienced bank officer, were aware that when dealing with Panamanian corporations, the person listed as president of the corporation was not likely to be the real party in interest?"

"Could have been," he acknowledged.

Schlessinger kept pressing the secrecy issue, trying to get Martínez to agree with his theory that there was something automatically suspect about any foreign corporation, but the banker refused to go along. Finally, I interceded: "Objection: He's arguing with the witness."

"Sustained," Judge González said quickly.

Schlessinger asked about Martínez's visit to the Cocoplum house. Fred had requested that Martínez and another bank officer, Félix García, accompany him to see if the house was sufficient collateral for an $800,000 loan.

"Driving to the house, Mr. De La Mata handed me an appraisal report and a real estate listing." The owner was asking $1.8 million. "We arrived at the house. Mr. Ramón Puentes was there. Also a lady. I assume she was a broker handling the sale." They walked through the vacant house and looked at the swimming pool and the dock. "We spent maybe forty-five minutes in the house. We left, and Mr. De La Mata asked me how much did I think the house was worth. I think I said conservatively between a million two and a million five. Mr. De La Mata asked, 'Do you think $800,000 is okay on this house?' I said, 'There is no way we can lose money loaning $800,000 on this house.'"

"And what was Mr. Puentes's connection to this deal, as far as you knew?"

"I understood that he owned the house."

"Who told you that?"

"In the conversation, I don't know with Mr. De La Mata or with him, but my impression was that he owned the house."

"What was it that led you to believe that Mr. Puentes owned the house?"

"The conversation I had, I think I had, with De La Mata. Not exactly sure when the conversation took place, whether in the house, driving to the house, but my impression was that Puentes was the owner of the house."

"Did you inquire as to who lived there?"

"No."

"Is it sometimes important for the bank to know who the owner or the occupant was in terms of assessing the value of the property?"

"I went there basically to see if there was collateral sufficient to support the loan."

"But sometimes it's important, in order to assess the value of the house, to determine who the owner is?"

"I don't see why," Martínez said.

Trying to show that the loan was handled in an unusual way, Schlessinger asked about the bank's senior loan committee, which met weekly, on Thursday afternoons. Martínez said that for the Cocoplum loan, Fred called an informal committee meeting while bank officers were attending a seminar at the Sofitel Hotel. During a coffee break Fred gathered the committee together and said that both Martínez and Félix García had inspected the house. "He explained, I believe, that Ramón Puentes was principal in the transaction. And everybody knew about Ramón Puentes."

"When you say 'principal in the transaction,' does that mean he said that Ramón Puentes was the owner of the property?"

"You know, I don't recall exactly what his words were, but he said he was a guarantor on the loan. . . . My understanding was if Ramón Puentes came to the bank and made a request for a real estate loan, if he's a guarantor of the loan that means he owns the property." At the informal committee meeting, Martinez went on, Fred presented Puentes's personal financial statement and the corporate statement of Thule Holding Corporation, which was also a guarantor.

Schlessinger: "The bank was concerned in 1987 about persons laundering money?"

"Yes."

"And you testified that people frequently use or occasionally use Panamanian corporations to conceal their ownership?"

"Sometimes."

"Why, then, didn't any member of this senior loan committee think to ask who is the real owner of the property?"

Good question. Martínez didn't hesitate: "I think the reason is very simple. The reason is that we had a guarantor that came and asked for the loan. That guarantor's name is Ramón Puentes. Ramón Puentes had been a customer of Republic National Bank for fifteen, twenty years. Republic National Bank had extended loans to Ramón Puentes in the millions of dollars, and always Ramón Puentes had paid his obligations."

A powerful statement—a direct stab at the prosecution's theory that the bank had handled the loan in an unusual manner—and it came from the prosecution's own witness.

Trying to recover, Schlessinger turned to the closing of the loan. "Was there present the same lady that had been present when you inspected the house?"

"I didn't see her."

"And where was Mr. De La Mata at this time?"

"In his office."

"And where is his office located?"

"Seventh floor." Four floors above the third-floor conference room where the closing was held.

At the time I didn't understand the relevance of this exchange and made no note of it. It was only later in the trial that I realized its importance. Schlessinger had hoped to spring a nasty surprise on us, but in Martínez's answer he didn't find what he was looking for, so he had moved on, asking the banker about the manner in which the loan was handled.

"It *was* handled in an irregular manner," Martínez admitted. "However, I think there were reasons behind it, if you want me to enumerate the reasons."

Schlessinger quickly announced that he had no further questions. He wasn't interested in hearing his witness's explanation. That was the end of testimony for the day.

When the trial resumed, I turned Martínez into my witness by emphasizing his experience. He had spent two decades making commercial loans with real estate as collateral. After I had him explain the vagaries of real estate investing in Miami, he said that Republic, as the nation's largest Hispanic bank with roots in South America, made many real estate loans with offshore corporations, particularly ones from Panama. Corporations such as Thule Holding Corporation frequently owned property in South Florida.

After that, I used Martínez to undo each of Schlessinger's insinuations. I began by focusing on the prosecutor's misleading questions about how a loan for a new bank customer was handled. "Why is there a difference between someone coming into the bank for the first time versus somebody who has a history with the bank?"

"Well, with somebody new, you have to check everything—collateral, banking references, character references, credit bureau checks. With somebody that you have a long relationship with, you don't necessarily do that because you already have your own records and experience."

"When you received the loan approval form for the Miraflores house, didn't it have an attachment listing all of Mr. Puentes's existing loans and existing accounts?"

"Yes sir."

"So the bank had sufficient information to make a determination based on its own records?"

"That is correct."

Schlessinger had emphasized that the loan request hadn't been formally examined by the credit department. I pointed out that Félix García, who had gone with Fred and Martínez to examine the house, was the executive vice president in charge of the credit department.

"So when Mr. De La Mata went to this house, he asked you, as the head of the real estate department, and Félix García, as head of credit for the entire bank, to go with him?"

"That is correct."

"Isn't it considered a good idea to bring along senior people on the loan committee to get their ideas about a loan like this?"

"We always do that."

"That was *normal* procedure?"

"Right."

"And if you or Mr. García thought anything was wrong with the loan, you would have said something to Mr. De La Mata?"

"Yes sir."

In fact, because García and Martínez each thought that the house was well worth the loan, and because Puentes was a good bank customer, the loan went through much faster than it would have for a new customer.

I asked Martínez about the loan committee. It had given its approval for the loan at the informal meeting at the hotel, but that was only the first step. "Isn't the loan normally ratified at the next formal meeting?"

"Yes." The Cocoplum loan was ratified at a formal meeting.

"So the informal meeting just gave someone a quick answer?"

"Yes."

He acknowledged that he knew Puentes already had qualified for a loan with Westfield Financial, and that Puentes needed a fast response from Republic or he would go through with the closing with Westfield. Martínez said paper ownership by the Panamanian corporation was irrelevant because Puentes was personally backing the loan, and it was that personal guarantee that really counted.

"In this case, Mr. Puentes signed an *unlimited* guarantee for the $800,000?"

"Right."

At last, Schlessinger called René Leonard, the "mystery witness." He was fifty-one, a heavyset fellow with a large face and thinning, dark hair. He took the stand wearing an intricately stitched and pleated guayabera, a white linen shirt with four pockets favored by Latins in the tropics. Because he had testified in the forfeiture case, I had a good idea what he was going to say, and I was prepared. Leonard could make or break our case.

Schlessinger led him through an impressive list of credentials: He was a professor of mechanical engineering at Florida International University in Miami, and he had built more than 125 houses in Coral Gables, including twelve in Cocoplum. He claimed that 80 percent of his banking business was with Republic, and that a Mr. Del Río served as his personal banker there. He frequently saw Fred at the bank, he said, or at the Big Five Club, which was the leading Cuban social club in Miami.

Leonard was an all-purpose witness. He claimed that he often dropped by the used-car lot of Ramón Puentes, and had his car washed at a place next to Puentes's lot, so he knew a great deal about what Puentes was doing. He also claimed that he had run into Andy Iglesias several times. The first was at a Mercedes-Benz dealership, where both men were looking at cars. A salesman introduced Leonard, the largest builder in Cocoplum, to Iglesias, who had just bought a lot in the neighborhood. From this casual conversation with a se-cretive, high-level drug trafficker, according to Leonard, he learned that Igle-sias was the real owner of the Cocoplum lot: "I would say that he had full control of the property."

In early 1986, Leonard said, he ran into Puentes in a coffee shop and learned that Puentes was now involved in some business with Iglesias in the Canary Islands. In September 1987, Leonard said, he saw Puentes at a late breakfast. The car dealer confided in him: "I need to sell Andy Iglesias's house. I'm his agent."

What else had Puentes told him? Schlessinger asked.

"He mentioned that Mr. Iglesias had some problems and he couldn't come to the United States."

I was watching the jury closely. René Leonard was one of those guys whom everyone has met: a braggart puffed up with self-importance who seemed to know everyone and everything. The jurors were leaning forward and staring at Leonard. I worried that they were taking him seriously.

Under Schlessinger's questioning, Leonard continued his account of coin-cidental encounters: On September 18, 1987, he went to Republic because he was trying to sell a finance company he owned, Safeco Capital, which was licensed by the Small Business Administration to make loans to what Leonard described as "disadvantaged citizens." Under this government program, he ex-plained, "for every dollar I put out of my pocket, the government gives me four" to be loaned out.

He claimed that someone had offered to buy Safeco, which was losing money, but the proposed offer included a letter of credit, and he went to Re-public to find out the implications of the letter. Once again, Leonard, almost like Forrest Gump, fortuitously ran into Fred De La Mata.

"Mr. De La Mata asked me if I knew about a house at 6960 Miraflores Av-enue. I had built a house near there, so I said yes, I know. There are only two houses available there—a doctor's house and Andy Iglesias's house. He told me it was Mr. Iglesias's house."

Leonard said he advised Fred to contact Ramón Puentes "because Ramón told me he needed to sell the house badly. Then I mentioned to him that the reason I had heard [was] that Andy Iglesias was on the run. I remember the sentence I told him: 'He was red hot because the *federales* were after him.' "

Schlessinger: "And how did Mr. De La Mata respond when you told him that?"

Leonard: "Fine. He accepted what I said, and said good-bye." He said he was in Fred's office less than twenty minutes.

All the earlier witnesses had just set the stage for this alleged exchange. Leonard was the first witness to testify that Fred knew that Iglesias was a drug dealer about to flee.

Before Schlessinger finished, he tried to defuse a line of questioning that he knew I would pursue: Leonard had first approached the U.S. Attorney's Office after reading a story in *The Miami Herald* about the government's seizure of Iglesias's house and the scandal over the Republic loan. He claimed he had once been an expert witness for Dexter Lehtinen, and when it was announced that Lehtinen was being named U.S. attorney, Leonard dropped by to congratulate him. While chatting with Lehtinen, Leonard said he mentioned that he knew some things about the Iglesias loan. "I made the mistake of contributing too much information," Leonard told the court, "because I never thought I was going to be called back as a witness. A big mistake."

I was certain that Leonard had been bragging to impress Lehtinen. When Lehtinen's staff asked Leonard to give a formal statement, he panicked. He never expected that his boasts would be taken seriously.

Schlessinger had Leonard describe how he tried to avoid testifying against his "good friend" Fred. "I moved from one house . . . changed phone number to somebody else's name, and I disappeared." The government compelled him to testify by subpoena, and that's how he had ended up in court. This was a clever touch. He made the story more damning by giving the impression it was dragged out of him.

I could see that Leonard took pleasure in telling this story to the jury. Witnesses such as Leonard, who skillfully weave a seamless tale out of half-truths, present a formidable challenge. They chew up unprepared cross-examiners with their improvisations. To pierce the witnesses' veneer takes preparation—examining every relevant record, lawsuit and deposition, and interviewing neighbors, ex-wives, co-workers and bosses, in search of the unexpurgated truth.

Leonard was vulnerable on a myriad of fronts, and I began my questioning, as I had with the other witnesses, by focusing on his character. I asked him if he had ever accepted cash payments from customers when he was building houses in Cocoplum.

He said he had received cash payments no more than twelve times. The largest such payment in cash was $8,000.

"*Eighty* thousand?" I asked.

"No, *eight* thousand."

"So you never received $80,000 in cash?"

"Never," he said emphatically.

I showed him the closing papers from another house on Miraflores Avenue.

He flushed. "Now that you refresh my memory. It was a house I sold. The man gave me $80,000 in cash."

"You mean you had forgotten $80,000 in cash?"

"If you give me three more seconds," Leonard said, "I have a powerful memory. Give me time and you get the truth, nothing but the truth." He rattled off several smaller cash payments.

"So you remember the $1,800, $2,000, but the $80,000 slipped your mind for a while?"

He shrugged.

I asked him about all the banks he had dealt with over the years.

He said he couldn't remember them all. "I know with you," he snapped, "I have to be very careful what I say. Most often you're trying to trick me."

I ignored his attempt at sarcasm and asked about his business with Republic. He said that on September 18, 1987 the day of his alleged contribution with Fred, he said he had only a few hundred dollars in a Republic account and hadn't done any major business with the bank for more than a year before seeking help with a letter of credit to sell his company, Safeco Capital. Though the letter of credit was for more than a half-million dollars, Leonard wasn't certain why he hadn't sought out Del Río, his longtime contact at Republic, but instead had wandered over and chatted with Fred. He claimed that he left several documents involving Safeco for Fred to examine, along with a form for the letter of credit.

"By the way," I asked casually, "do you have that letter of credit form with you?"

"Here with me?" Leonard acted surprised at the question.

"Anywhere."

"I don't have it with me. Whatever I had in my records, I turned over to the government."

Of course the government didn't have it either. I asked whether he had *any* documents to prove that the letter-of-credit deal was real or that he had given any materials to Fred. He said he had nothing.

"Did you submit *anything* in writing?"

"No, because two days later, when I was about ready to sit down and do the application, the purchaser decided not to invest in Safeco."

"Do you have any correspondence, copies of any letters, copies of any documents, showing any contact with Republic National Bank about this September 18 transaction you're testifying about here?"

"No, I don't, sir."

On direct examination he had said he had given one year's financial statements from Safeco to Fred, but in his deposition from the forfeiture case he had claimed they had covered five years. How could he explain the discrepancy?

"Sir, you're trying to trick me. Since I didn't read the deposition, I don't remember exactly—can't remember whether it was three, five, two. I say it was at least one."

"Do you remember the maxim that a liar has to have a good memory?"

Schlessinger was on his feet: "Objection."

"Sustained," the judge said quickly.

Leonard was leaning forward, as if he were about to lunge at me: "Are you trying to call me a name?"

I hesitated a moment. Dealing with a man who was ostensibly a dignified university professor, I had to watch my step. A brilliant cross is thoroughly undermined if it generates sympathy for the witness. Jurors usually side with the witness rather than the attacking lawyer, so I had to retreat. I shouldn't be calling the witness a liar. Better that the jurors reach that conclusion on their own.

"I withdraw that comment," I said, bowing my head slightly. "And I apologize."

"Apology accepted." Leonard smiled smugly.

Letting him have his moment, I moved on, asking him whom else he had talked to when he visited the bank that day. He mentioned George De Cárdenas, a well-known public relations consultant.

"Where was this conversation?"

"He was waiting for an elevator in the lobby." De Cárdenas's son was a friend of Leonard's son, and Leonard knew him well. "George De Cárdenas was going through a divorce. He was complaining to me all the time how much alimony he will pay. And he was very bitter about that. And I mentioned to him how beautiful his wife looked. He says, 'Well, it's going to cost me a lot of alimony more or less I give you 10 percent finding fee if you find a husband for her.' "

"In fact, Mr. De Cárdenas was your very, *very* good friend, isn't that correct?"

He looked away. "That was the biggest mistake of my life."

"Because he said you lied about this, didn't he?" It was all right for me to say De Cárdenas had called him a liar, just as long as I didn't say it.

"Objection," Schlessinger shouted.

"Overruled," Judge González announced, giving me wide latitude with this witness. Leonard knew where I was going. When De Cárdenas heard that Leonard had given this testimony during the bank's forfeiture case, he said Leonard had lied.

"You say it's a mistake now because Mr. De Cárdenas said you lied about it."

"No sir."

"And he also testified that you went to his house to try to get him to commit perjury—to support your perjury."

"Objection."

"Sustained."

"When you testified that you were discussing his ex-wife in September of 1987, I assume you're now saying that was just a mistake?"

"No sir."

"Well, Mr. De Cárdenas was not divorced until April of 1988. Are you aware of that, sir?"

That was at least six months after Leonard's conversation with De Cárdenas at the bank. I was setting Leonard up because I planned to call De Cárdenas, who would state that Leonard had fabricated the conversation at the bank. This was crucial because Leonard had no documents to prove he was at the bank that day in September 1987 when he supposedly had his incriminating exchange with Fred, and he desperately needed De Cárdenas's confirmation of meeting Leonard at that time.

"I was aware before, aware today and always aware of that, sir." He claimed that when he visited the bank, De Cárdenas and his wife were separated. He just made a mistake using the expression "ex-wife."

"Isn't it a fact that the conversation you were talking about with Mr. De Cárdenas really happened in August of 1988, eleven months after you claim it happened?"

"No sir."

"Do you remember that on August 13, 1988, that Mr. De Cárdenas had come home from a vacation in the Virgin Islands with your son and his son?"

"Definitely, sir."

"Do you remember that you met them at the airport?"

"Well, I met my son."

"And isn't it true, sir, it was at this airport meeting that this conversation occurred with Mr. De Cárdenas about his then ex-wife and her high alimony payments?"

"No sir."

"Did you go to his house at midnight one night and tell him, 'I'm in a big problem, and can you help me?' "

"Yes and no. I went to his house, but didn't discuss that, sir."

"Did you tell him at his house at midnight on August 16, 1988, that you had this conversation with Dexter Lehtinen and that you had said some things about Mr. De La Mata?"

"No sir."

"Did you tell him that Mr. Lehtinen asked you to come to his office and that you went there and you had lied and exaggerated about things you knew about Fred De La Mata? Yes or no?"

"No sir."

"Did you tell Mr. De Cárdenas that it was very important for you to look like an important person in the Cuban community to Dexter Lehtinen and you didn't want to go back and admit that you lied about Fred De La Mata? Did you say that?"

"No sir, not my way of looking important, believe me."

I moved on to Leonard's sworn statement to the prosecutors. During the first ten minutes in the U.S. Attorney's Office he had been evasive, saying he couldn't remember much. The taking of the statement was stopped, and Sharon Kegerris, an assistant U.S. attorney, had taken him into the hallway.

"Did she say she was worried that you were going to commit perjury?"

"No, she said specifically, I remember, that I was not getting exactly to the point as I had in my meeting with Dexter, and please, say nothing but the truth. She told me by all means the only thing you cannot do is commit perjury."

"So she mentioned the word 'perjury'?"

He wasn't certain. I read again from his deposition, in which he admitted that the prosecutor had warned him, "René, don't commit perjury."

He acknowledged that he had been evasive: "I was mad at the government, I didn't want to be a witness and I hated it."

"Did you testify on page 39 of your deposition that you were an agent of the CIA?"

"Yes."

"Did you claim that you were working double agents for them in New York City?"

"Yes sir."

"*And* you also worked doubling Mexican agents out of Mexico City?"

"Yes sir."

"And that you also went to Indonesia on behalf of the CIA, to double Cuban agents in China."

"That's correct, sir."

Several jurors were smiling, as I was. The image of this overweight engineer in a guayabera playing 007 in the exotic Far East was indeed funny. What a busy guy Leonard was. It was hard to believe that he had found time, too, to run into Puentes, Iglesias and Fred with all this going on. In the 1960s, Miami had been the headquarters for the largest CIA contingent outside Langley, Virginia, and it still is full of CIA wannabes and conspiracy theorists. Occasionally, some of the outrageous stories you hear turn out to be true, but many more are fabrications told by people trading on false reputations. Did the jury sense that Leonard was one of those fabricators?

I questioned Leonard to expose a motive to lie. Because of a lawsuit, his account at Republic had once been frozen, and he was angry about that. He had demanded that Republic unfreeze the account, and Fred had refused. He had also lied several times during his own bankruptcy proceeding. One lie concerned the $80,000 cash payment he had forgotten.

"Did you deny under oath, on May 12, 1986, receiving the $80,000 in cash?" The payment had been part of a complicated real estate deal. I didn't care about the deal and didn't seek an explanation for it. All I wanted was to emphasize that Leonard had previously lied under oath. The unstated implication was if he had been willing to lie under oath then, he would be willing to lie now.

"I don't remember, sir."

I showed him the transcript. "I've highlighted it here in yellow."

"Now that you show it to me, yes, I remember it perfectly."

"And today you admitted you did get $80,000 in cash?"

"Yes sir."

"In fact, the money was handed over to you and one of your associates in the amount of $5 bills, $10 bills, $20 bills, $50 bills and $100 bills?"

"No sir. It was handed to my creditor."

"Was it in fives, tens, twenties, fifties and hundreds?"

"Yes."

"Sir, you took the $80,000 in cash under the table so you could hide it from the bank who had a lien on your receipts."

"Objection."

"Overruled."

"No sir."

I asked him if he had testified that the selling price of this house was about $350,000, and then later acknowledged that the real price was about $430,000.

"I don't remember."

I read from the deposition in which he admitted that he had given a false price for the house because the other party asked him to. "Do you remember giving that answer?"

Leonard leaned back in the witness chair. "Yes sir," he said, giving up.

"Isn't it a fact, sir, that you doubled the price of the value of the house in order to get the loan?"

"I didn't double it. I assumed the house was worth that money. I didn't ask for an appraisal. Maybe my accountant did it."

"Maybe somebody else did it?"

"Ninety-nine percent of the time, it's the accountant doing this." The modern-day version of saying the butler did it.

"Your excuse for filing these false financial statements was that you just were not too careful preparing them?"

"I deny I said that. There's a difference between inflated and false, you know."

Quickly, I touched on his other problems. He had once made a $1,000 campaign contribution to a judge who was hearing his case—an action that forced the judge to recuse himself. Another time his lending company, which was supposed to be for disadvantaged minorities, had made several large loans to his friends and to residents of plush Cocoplum.

"Do you remember testifying that you did not intentionally lie on any of these documents because you were under medication?"

"I was on a real strict diet, potassium, and almost fainted. I went to a doctor and he gave me some bananas and the next day I was fine."

"According to your testimony, you said you were going to a psychiatrist. You didn't say anything about bananas."

"But I remember one day in the deposition I almost fainted."

The hours I had labored over the thousands of documents from Leonard's tangled legal past were paying off.

Once I had undermined his credibility, I moved to specific questions about his alleged conversation with Fred. I had him describe in detail how he entered the bank and found Fred's office in the Republic building. As soon as he mentioned it was on the fifth floor I knew I had him trapped in a lie. In September 1987, Fred's office was on the seventh floor.

I asked Leonard about his visit to Lehtinen's office to congratulate him on his new job. He admitted that the *Herald* story, containing details about Iglesias's drug dealing, Thule Holding Corporation and the Cocoplum house had just been published. Although I couldn't say it yet to the jury, I was certain that Leonard had culled facts from the *Herald* story and embellished them in his own story to Lehtinen. Leonard didn't acknowledge that, but he did admit that "I never thought because of the stupid comment I made I was going to be here under all of this."

That was as good an ending to my cross-examination as I could expect, but

I was about to get some assistance from Schlessinger. On re-direct he tried to repair the damage to Leonard's credibility by asking him about his alleged CIA background.

"Well, definitely, I was trained by the CIA," Leonard insisted.[7] In the summer of 1960, he said, he met at the Miami airport an old neighbor from Havana "who happened to be the most important man of the CIA in Havana, Cuba," and the man recruited him for the CIA. The poor fellow was later executed by a Communist firing squad in Cuba, where he had been using a false name. The only man who could confirm Leonard's story was dead, if he had existed, and if he were dead.

Leonard described his CIA activities in the 1960s. He had been given one week of training in New York City and was then sent out to double Castro agents in New York. He claimed he worked on this project for five or six months. Then he was sent to Indonesia to serve as an embassy translator for an international sports competition. Thanks to him, he claimed, twelve Cubans had defected in Indonesia.

Doubling agents is tricky business. It seemed absurd that the CIA would have given an amateur agent only a week of instruction. And why New York? Why Indonesia? Leonard offered no explanation, but when I glanced at the jury box I realized I didn't have to worry.

The government turned to the reams of documents it had subpoenaed from the bank. A parade of record custodians and minor bank officials took up days of court time. Araceli Cardet, an assistant cashier, described the loan closing for the Cocoplum house. Diana Acosta, a vice president in charge of special loans, described the bank's numerous deals with Ramón Puentes and Andy Iglesias. She thought they were partners in buying a warehouse and arranging for mortgages on several small investment properties. She said Iglesias also

---

7. The CIA has a policy of refusing to confirm or deny whether a person is really an agent. While this makes good sense as a method of protecting the identity of real undercover agents, it allows unscrupulous con artists to masquerade as government agents. I called Langley and asked about Leonard but got the standard runaround.

had personal accounts at the bank: several checking accounts, three certificates of deposit, two IRAs and a safe deposit box.

Although there was nothing unusual about any of Iglesias's dealings with the bank, Schlessinger had Acosta tell the jury that Fred's name appeared on all the Iglesias papers as the account officer. The implication was that Fred had personally handled all of Iglesias's business and knew him very well. Under my cross-examination, however, she explained that after a bank officer brought in a new client, his name was put on all the client's papers, whether or not the officer personally handled the transactions. Because Fred was Puentes's officer and Puentes had referred Iglesias to the bank, Fred's name was automatically placed on all of Iglesias's accounts. She said she never saw Fred and Iglesias together and had no idea if they knew each other.

I had guessed that Leonard was the government's last major witness, but after the bank employees had testified Schlessinger announced that he was calling Elena Festa. I kept my somber trial face, but this was a shock. I couldn't imagine what Andy Iglesias's sister would say. I had sought to interview her, but her lawyer had declined my request. He said she feared that talking to me would hurt her chances for a favorable sentence recommendation from Schlessinger in a money-laundering case. This was another example of why the feds delay sentencing until after the informer testifies. Her lawyer assured me, however, that Festa's only contact with Fred was during the house tour and that she had no damaging testimony to offer.

So why was she here? I looked at her intensely. She was a rather heavy woman, her black hair peppered with gray, her clothes a bit disheveled.

As usual, Schlessinger tried to make his witness with the sleazy connections look respectable. For fifteen years, she testified, she had been a research associate at the University of Miami, working in the department of microbiology. Her husband was a retired policeman. In 1982 she became a real estate broker.

Now to the bad stuff: She was Iglesias's sister and had been charged with racketeering, conspiracy and money laundering. Four days before the trial she had pled guilty to the money-laundering count concerning the Cocoplum house. The not-too-subtle implication was that the refinancing of the house must have been illegal since Festa had pled to it.

The other charges against her had been thrown out, thereby avoiding a mandatory minimum ten years in prison. Her sentencing was scheduled for two months hence, in front of Judge González. "I have an agreement that if I say everything truthful and to the best of my knowledge," she said, "the U.S. Attorney's Office will make some recommendation at the time of my sentencing." She spoke her lines well.

Festa said that she had tried to sell the Cocoplum house in the summer of 1987 because "my brother had some financial problems, and he needed cash, and the house was free and clear." She said that she knew that the house had been built with the proceeds from drug trafficking. She had arranged for an appraisal of the house so that her brother could get a loan. One day Puentes called and told her to unlock the house so that some Republic officials could inspect it. Puentes, Fred De La Mata and two other men came to the house.

That wasn't the first time she had met Fred, she claimed. Two years before she had been at one of Puentes's car dealerships when her brother, Andy, introduced her: "This is my sister, Elena. This is Frederick De La Mata."

Now Festa had to deliver. To garner a reduction in her sentence, she had to provide "substantial assistance"[8] to the prosecution. Our government only pays COD. No reduction until the government is satisfied. It would be hard to imagine a more blatant invitation to perjury.

Festa said that at the Cocoplum house, Puentes introduced her casually to Fred: "He said, 'By the way, Fred, you remember Elena. This is Andy's sister.' And that's all that was said. 'Hi. How are you doing?' That was it."

Then she said: "I went to the closing with Ramón Puentes and Antonio Muñoz." Muñoz was the president of Thule Holding Corporation. I had talked to several people at the bank who had been at the closing, and none had mentioned that she was present. I wondered what was coming up.

---

8. Sentencing guideline 5K1.1 provides that a prosecutor can seek a lower sentence for a witness who "provided substantial assistance in the investigation or prosecution of another person." Government prosecutors call pointing the finger "cooperating," which sounds more palatable than "ratting," "informing," or "snitching." George Orwell, in 1984, called manipulating words like this to hide their true meaning Newspeak, like calling a dictator "Big Brother." Paying a witness for testimony, whether in cash or something more valuable like a reduced sentence, is bribery. Bribery is a crime because it is a powerful inducement to lie.

She claimed that at the closing there was a big argument because Mark Kimmel, the lawyer for Puentes and Muñoz, presented them with a large bill for legal services. Puentes was angry. "Muñoz speaks a little bit of English, but Ramón doesn't. Muñoz tried to translate for Ramón, asked me to please ask the lawyer why the fees were so high. Ramón was carrying on, cussing all attorneys as SOBs, pretty loud. Then Frederick De La Mata came in from the hallway. He told Ramón in Spanish to calm down. He said that, you know, he got what he wanted, the mortgage was there, all they had to do is sign the papers."

"What did Mr. Puentes say, if anything?" Schlessinger asked.

"Ramón said, 'Wait till Andy see this bill. He's really going to hate it.' And Frederick De La Mata said, 'Don't worry about it. We got rid of the debt.' " By that, she said he meant "the white elephant of the house."

Here was a direct allegation that Fred knew that the house belonged to Andy Iglesias.

Festa had more. After all the documents were signed, she said, "we all went out [into] the hallway, Ramón still arguing about Mark Kimmel's fees. Mr. De La Mata came out from one of the offices. He hugged Puentes, and Puentes said, 'Hey, Fred, thank you, I really owe you a big one. I'm not going to forget you, man. Why don't you come to the car lot to celebrate with us with a glass of wine?' Mr. De La Mata said he couldn't do it, but he was glad he could help, and that was just about it."

She also said that she went with Puentes from the bank to Puentes's car lot, where Iglesias was waiting. They opened a bottle of wine. Puentes was ecstatic. Festa claimed that the car dealer told Iglesias, "I think you better call Fred and say thank-you."

In the following months, according to Festa, Puentes called her many times, asking how the sale of the house was coming along. "He was worried about not being able to pay the mortgage." Finally, she said she told him, " 'Ramón, why don't you just let the bank have this house?' He said he couldn't do that. Fred personally got this mortgage, and he wanted this loan off the books as soon as possible. He said, 'Fred is going to lose his job if we can't do something about it.' I said, 'I can't believe just because of one mortgage he would lose his job.' He said, 'You just don't understand, Elena. There's lots of pressure on him.' "

Four days before the trial Festa had no incriminating information about

Fred. But with her neck on the line, her "memory" improved as the plea bargain grew sweeter. Festa had salted her testimony with hints that Fred had known that Iglesias was behind the loan. I wasn't prepared for this. The government's shroud of secrecy had screened Festa from us until now. If I had known what she was going to say, I would have asked Araceli Cardet, the assistant cashier who attended the closing, about who was present, whether Fred and Festa were there. In a pre-trial interview, Cardet had told me that the closing had gone smoothly: She didn't mention a dispute about attorney's fees. Only now did I realize how shrewd Schlessinger had been in arranging the order of his witnesses.

I now recalled that when the banker Martínez was on the witness stand, Schlessinger had asked him whether he saw at the closing the same lady whom he had seen at the house. Martínez had said no, and Schlessinger had quietly shifted on to other questions. That woman was Festa.

How could I attack her? I started, as I had with the other witnesses, by making it clear to the jury that she had refused to talk to me before the trial, but had eagerly talked to the prosecutors in return for a deal that had been worked out just before the trial began. As I began questioning her about her deal, Schlessinger rose. "Your Honor," he said, "there's something that I need to divulge to Mr. Black."

We approached the bench, where Schlessinger whispered to the judge that he hadn't expected the trial to go this fast, so he hadn't had time to prepare Brady material, which is any information that could be favorable to the defendant or tends to discredit a government witness. Before the trial began, the judge had ordered the government to give us all Brady material. Of course, there had been nothing about Festa, and I was sure that Schlessinger had given us nothing because he was holding her back as a surprise witness.

At the bench, Schlessinger informed me that other witnesses had told investigators that Elena Festa had transported $200,000 in drug cash to Panama in 1983 and taken another $200,000 in cash to Spain in July or August 1984.

In the midst of my cross-examination, I had no way to check out these new leads, no time to explore what other witnesses might have to say about Festa. Schlessinger had cleverly saved Festa to the end. I certainly didn't want to call back previous government witnesses to challenge Festa's veracity because that would also give these drug dealers another shot at us. Of course, I could make

Schlessinger's deliberately late disclosure a point on appeal, but the appellate courts have ruled that even disclosure at the last minute is acceptable.

All I could do was explore the deal she had made with the government. I got her to admit that in return for her cooperation, prosecutors had thrown out a charge that she had conspired with her brother to distribute cocaine—a charge that could have meant a twenty-year prison sentence. Was she guilty of distributing cocaine? She claimed that she wasn't.

"You say that you're *not* part of your brother's drug enterprise?" I asked with surprise.

"No. My attorney explained to me that I may be guilty, I may not be guilty. By closing my eyes to what was going on around me, that doesn't make me innocent."

She also had been charged with racketeering for participating in at least two of her brother's drug activities.

"Did you take $200,000 in cash from the United States to Panama in 1983?"

"No, I did not."

"Are you aware there are people who claim you did?"

"Yes, I am."

"But you deny that occurred?"

"No, I—I took an envelope to Panama that [John Smith, Iglesias's attorney] gave me. A brown envelope. Also, I took a package he told me was a bar mitzvah present. I took what he told me was two little Tonka trucks."

Festa probably felt safe giving this story because, as a government witness, she had no reason to fear prosecution for perjury unless she hurt its case. As a government agent once told me: "Lies in favor of the government are always the truth."

She also denied taking cash to Spain. "They said I took the money inside a girdle. I cannot put that much money inside a girdle."

"So if a witness claims that you transported $200,000 in cash in your girdle, you say it's a lie?"

Schlessinger objected, but the judge quickly overruled him. He was granting me wide latitude because of Schlessinger's late disclosure.

"That's right," Festa said.

If I had received the Brady material well before the trial, I could have dug deeper into her story. As it was, there was nothing more that I could do except to show how closely she had been connected with drug dealers. She admitted that she had helped Mario Tabraue purchase a house and a warehouse. She had helped create phony documents to disguise the fact that one of her brother's cohorts, David Ryder, had paid $400,000 in cash for a boat used for drug smuggling. And she had helped Ryder rent a house on a Fort Lauderdale canal so that they could off-load one of their drug-running boats there. Still, she denied she had known what was going on: "I assisted in renting the house. I did not know at that time it was going to be for any drug activities."

She also admitted assisting in the sale of another of her brother's houses to an agent of either the DEA or the FBI, she couldn't remember which. This had happened in 1983, at the height of Iglesias's drug smuggling. Had the government seized this house? Had it taken the house away from the federal agent? Had it refused to pay off the loan on that house? No, it hadn't.

With that point made, I let Festa go. I didn't ask her anything about her alleged conversations with Fred because I didn't want to give her the chance to repeat her lies to the jury. I would wait until we presented our case to attack her again.

Festa was the government's last witness. The jury was given a recess.

As I always do at the end of the prosecution's case, I made a motion that the government had failed to prove its accusations. I asked that both charges be thrown out, but I focused on the bribery charge. Although Schlessinger had put on witnesses who testified that Puentes had purchased airline tickets for Fred Jr. and his bride, the prosecutor had never established a quid pro quo between these tickets and the Cocoplum loan. A non-corrupt offering, a gift that carries no obligation, is not a bribe intended to exact a favor. The gift had not been concealed, whereas a bribe is usually concealed. The wedding was a legitimate event. Judge González agreed. The bribery charge was thrown out.

The judge's decision presented us with a dilemma. Testimony about the tickets had been given, but the jurors hadn't heard our explanation. My original plan had been to put on several witnesses who had attended the wedding and play a videotape of the reception highlighting the many lavish gifts. That idea was out the window now.

The judge would not tell the jury that the bribery charge was dismissed. He would only say that it was "no longer available for your consideration." The ambiguity of that phrasing caused me to worry that the jurors would still think the gift pointed to Fred's guilt on the money-laundering charge. I had to hope that the jurors now would just forget the prosecution's testimony about the bribe.

With the bribery charge gone, and because of the prosecution's target letter to Republic bank officers on the first day of the trial, our defense was slimmed down to practically nothing. We had two witnesses who were Fred's closest associates at the bank. They wanted to testify despite their lawyers' advice. I decided to call only a handful of witnesses to dispute the claims made by Schlessinger's witnesses. If I had not wounded them mortally on cross, I was in real trouble.

George De Cárdenas owned a public relations firm called Creative Marketing and Advertising Group. To corroborate his story, René Leonard had told federal agents that right after his meeting with Fred at the bank he had run into De Cárdenas at the bank's elevator. They had talked casually of De Cárdenas's alimony problems. Using a calendar, De Cárdenas explained that because he was divorced in April 1988, the alimony conversation with Leonard couldn't have occurred in September 1987; rather it occurred in August 1988. The conversation happened at the airport on his return from a trip to the Virgin Islands with his own son and Leonard's. Later Leonard had tried to get De Cardenas to lie and back up the story he had told Lehtinen. Leonard begged him: "You know how we Cubans like to talk."

Mirta Núñez, a Republic bank vice president, testified that she, not Fred, dealt with Puentes and Iglesias. She had never seen Iglesias and Fred together at the bank. Iglesias's account records had Fred's name on them because Fred was the officer responsible for bringing Puentes to the bank and, in turn, Puentes had brought Iglesias in as a customer. She also drew a floor plan of the bank. In September 1987, Fred's office was not on the fifth floor, where Leonard claimed the meeting occurred, but on the seventh.

María Elena Reyes, a Republic vice president overseeing commercial loans, had presented the proposal for the loan on the Cocoplum house to the bank's loan committee. She agreed to testify despite the target letter to the bank and an even more personal type of intimidation. Her lawyer, outraged at the government's tactics, told me that Schlessinger had threatened her and that an IRS agent threw a file at her because she wouldn't modify her testimony to say that Fred knew Iglesias was behind the Cocoplum loan.[9] Her loyalty to Fred outweighed her fears. She told the court that the loan was not unusual and, at two points over prime, it was a great deal for the bank. She affirmed that Fred was not at the loan closing.

Next I called my best witness to rebut Elena Festa's version of the closing. I had interviewed Raquel Matas before the trial but hadn't thought of her as an important witness. At the time of the closing, she was a junior lawyer with the bank's outside law firm. Now, she was an assistant dean at the University of Miami Law School. It was hard to beat that for credibility—she was no longer connected with the bank, and she had a prestigious job. Even better, she had a clear memory of the loan closing—and documents to back it up. She said she had never talked to Fred about the loan and that Fred wasn't at the closing. She also testified that no one at the closing objected to legal fees. "Not a single objection was raised about it. Nobody was angry or upset."

I had to decide whether Fred would testify. I was sure he would make a great witness, but he might create new problems for himself. Judges grant prosecutors wide latitude in cross-examining a defendant—wide enough to set Fred up for new charges. I had heard rumors that federal investigators were already planning to obtain new indictments in the event he was acquitted. An IRS agent sat at the end of Schlessinger's table, and the specter of a tax witch-hunt loomed daily in my peripheral vision. With a labyrinthine tax code seven times longer than the Bible, it is easy to find taxpayer violations. So I reluctantly rested without Fred's testimony, but I couldn't help wondering whether I had made a mistake.

Fifty of Fred's friends and relatives filled the courtroom to hear the closing arguments. Sometimes this kind of display of loyalty can work against a defendant if the jurors feel threatened—especially when the friends of the

---

9. I was unable to corroborate this accusation because the witness Reyes didn't want to discuss it, perhaps out of fear of offending the government. Schlessinger always acted like a gentleman with me, and no other witness made a similar claim.

defendant don't appear to be upstanding citizens. But Fred's supporters were decent, well-mannered people, and they were so enthusiastic that I doubt I could have talked them out of coming even if I had wanted to.

Schlessinger posed what he defined as the key questions for the jurors: "I think the issue, ladies and gentlemen, is going to come down to simply this: What did Mr. De La Mata know? Did he know this was Andy Iglesias's house?"

He recounted Iglesias's drug dealing and said it had to have been obvious to Fred that Iglesias was a crook. The fact that the house was supposedly owned by Thule Holding Corp. should have been a red flag because offshore corporations were a "popular device for people to conceal the real ownership of property." No bank would loan $800,000 to a shell corporation without knowing who was the real owner. Fred must have known the Iglesiases owned the house because they had a joint checking account at Republic. Their monthly statements were sent to the Cocoplum house. Another tip-off was that the person who showed Fred and the other bank officers around the Cocoplum house was Elena Festa, Andy Iglesias's sister.

Schlessinger said, "In the course of getting this mortgage through the bank, Mr. De La Mata told three lies—three *substantial* lies.

"First, he told his fellow bank officers that the house belonged to Ramón Puentes," Fred must have known that that was a lie, the prosecutor insisted, because Fred had a close relationship with Puentes, and he knew Puentes lived elsewhere. He had even attended a wedding at Puentes's house.

"The second lie relates to the purpose of this loan," Schlessinger continued. Fred had said Puentes wanted the $800,000 to invest in other real estate. But within twenty-four hours, two checks totaling $700,000 went to Swiss accounts. Fred hadn't complained because he knew the money was flight capital.

The third lie was Fred's insistence that the loan had to be approved quickly. The irregular shortcuts—no formal application, approving the loan during a coffee break—were meant to stop bankers from checking records. The discussions with the other mortgage company were bogus, Schlessinger insisted. "There was no reason to hurry."

Schlessinger claimed his theory was supported by two witnesses. If the jurors thought either of them was telling the truth, then Fred was guilty. He acknowledged that René Leonard "is a colorful character who leads a colorful life. . . . His life is not entirely free of controversy and that's, of course, to be expected of somebody involved in the construction business." Quite an understatement for a South Florida contractor.

But in this case, the contractor had no reason to lie. "Mr. Leonard isn't charged with any kind of a crime. Mr. Leonard hasn't been rewarded in any way for his testimony."

Schlessinger then asked the jurors to assess the credibility of Elena Festa. "You may ask yourself what motive she has to lie. I would suggest to you she has no motive, because although she's hoping to get a reduced sentence as a result of her cooperation, she can't get that if she lies."

In closing, he asked the jurors to use their common sense. "Please consider the evidence as a *whole*. If you do so, you will see we have proved the case beyond a reasonable doubt."

How could I make sense of what seemed like a ton of paper and hundreds of exhibits without boring the jury to tears? During the recess I walked around the outside of the courthouse, talking to myself, rehearsing my speech, attempting to psyche myself up, to get the high-voltage energy that I would need for the hour-and-a-half argument.

When I stepped to the podium, I sought to define the terms of our debate. "We all know money laundering when we see it. The phrase is self-defining. Dirty money goes into one end of the washing machine. It is constantly filtered and recycled in countless transactions to disguise its past. It comes out sparklingly clean at the other end ready to be spent.

"Is this what Fred did? Look at what you must believe to think Fred laundered drug money. Iglesias builds a house, not to live in, but as a front to launder his drug money. He spends years building this house, cleverly using his wife to dole out two million in cash to his workers and contractors. Then, just as it is completed, he dumps it for $800,000. He spent $1.2 million to get $800,000. I wouldn't want him to handle my portfolio, but there is a genius to this clever scheme. No one would ever think it was money laundering. No one, except our prosecutor."

I said that Republic's actions were those of a normal bank. "Banks are the middleman in the flow of commerce. We deposit our paychecks in the bank, and it invests our money by issuing loans. Banks are not the FBI. They don't have special agents to investigate their customers. They must rely on the financial statements and information presented to them."

What happened to the drug money? Republic hadn't accepted boxes of drug cash. The cash had gone to those who built the house. I listed several companies and the workmen who built Iglesias's house. "But the government took no action against them. I'm not suggesting that they're guilty of crimes. But if anyone could have recognized the proceeds of a crime it was them. These cash transactions occurred three to four years before Republic National Bank grants the mortgage. Any drug cash is long gone before Republic issues the loan."

I then explored Schlessinger's theory of money laundering. It could entrap innocent people. "Suppose Andy Iglesias gives cash to Puentes, who goes to the auto auction in Orlando and buys cars. He brings them to Miami and gives them to his salesmen, who turn around and sell them to Joe Customer, who gets a loan from Republic National Bank to buy the car. If the cash for those cars were proceeds of a crime, you can find Mr. Puentes guilty if he knowingly takes this cash from Iglesias. But when Mr. Puentes buys a car at the auction, are the sellers guilty of a crime?" And all the others? Throwing out such a wide net could make us all conspirators in money laundering.

I turned to the loan on the Cocoplum house. "Despite Mr. Schlessinger's claim, a loan was approved by Westfield Financial Corporation. The loan approval papers are in evidence as defense exhibit 35. You may read them at your leisure in the jury room. As you know, this loan did not go to closing because it was declined by the Iglesiases."

And why had Iglesias rejected the Westfield loan? "Mr. Schlessinger argues the Republic loan was a front only to get money to Andy Iglesias. The scheme is to get ready cash in Iglesias's hands so he could flee the country." It was the testimony of Schlessinger's own witness, Margarita Iglesias, who disproved this theory. "She testified they rejected the Westfield loan because the interest rate was too high. If the Iglesiases didn't intend to repay the loan, why should they care how high the interest rate was?

"Now, let's look closely at Mr. Schlessinger's 'three big lies.' Number one: Fernando Martínez testifies that Fred De La Mata tells him that Ramón Puentes owns this house. Well, Mr. Martínez never testified to that. He said I *assumed* Puentes owned this house. I assumed it because he's coming in as the guarantor to the loan. He made that logical assumption because of Puentes's guarantee, not because Fred told him that.

"Second lie: The stated purpose for the loan was false. Fred told the loan committee his client wanted cash for another investment that couldn't wait until the sale. The house was for sale. The bank verified that with the broker. The broker was present and showed the house to the bankers. Mr. Schlessinger says the two checks going to Switzerland should have been a red flag to Fred. However, we heard testimony from the bank employee who issued the checks that Fred was not advised where the money went after the closing. Even if he did know, that would not necessarily mean it was not another investment.

"And what is the third lie? The need for speed as he characterizes it. There was no real competition for the refinancing. In fact, Iglesias was so serious about taking the other loan that a check had already been cut by the mortgage company, and we have offered it into evidence as defense exhibit 36."

I turned from the quality of Schlessinger's arguments to the quality of his witnesses. "Mr. Schlessinger suggests, 'Take my case as a whole.' Well, let's take him up on that."

First, I mentioned one of Iglesias's henchmen, David Ryder, who admitted creating false documents and committing perjury to recover his drug money. "If this man could fearlessly deceive federal investigators out of money, what makes you think he wouldn't lie to escape twenty years in prison? His plea agreement, look at defense exhibit 18, required forfeiture of his Merritt Island mansion bought with drug cash. But what does the prosecutor do? Let's sweeten the deal as a little incentive, and let Ryder keep it."

Then I examined Margarita Iglesias. She bought a half-million dollar house using drug cash as a down payment. "She goes to prison, signs the plea agreement, they let her out, and let her keep the house. She sells it and with their blessing keeps the money—the money from the house she bought with drug cash!"

Elena Festa was even less credible. I asked the jurors to imagine what her story would be if she were on trial. "Her defense would be, 'Mr. Schlessinger, I was just a dupe. Andy's my brother, true, but I never helped him in his drug business. I didn't know there was $200,000 in that package. Someone hid it there. I was just being a Good Samaritan taking Christmas presents to unfortunate orphans in Panama.' Imagine how Mr. Schlessinger would ridicule that testimony."

Instead, at this trial, Schlessinger accepted her yarn and allowed her to keep the townhouse deeded to her by Iglesias. "The drug dealers all keep their houses but the bank loses its loan. Is there something wrong with this picture?

"René Leonard believes in being important. He sought to impress Dexter Lehtinen. He likes to impress people. Didn't he impress you with his service in the CIA? He was caught in lie after lie under oath in his bankruptcy case. Can we believe anything he says? He read a newspaper story, then regurgitates it to Dexter Lehtinen. All to be important. How pathetic."

Now, I used an anecdote that has become one of my favorites for summation in these "jumping on the bus" cases. "One of my college roommates was a Native American who told me many of his tribe's ancient myths. Myths are a striking way of teaching youngsters important lessons about life. One stuck with me: A young Indian lived with his tribe in the northern reaches of Montana. One winter day, when it is freezing, he leaves his tepee to hunt. While walking along the side of a frozen lake, he spies a rattlesnake so cold it has frozen solid. This Indian is naturally afraid of the rattler, and he takes out his axe and prepares to chop off its head. When the Indian's arm is poised above his head ready to plunge the axe into the snake, the snake looks up and says, 'Please don't kill me. Take me back to your tepee, warm me up and save my life.'

"The startled Indian replies: 'I can't do that. You'll bite me and I'll die.' The snake says, 'No, I promise if you save my life, I won't bite you.' So the Indian takes the snake back to his tepee and warms him up. As soon as the snake is revived, it bites the Indian. As the Indian lies there, dying, he asks, 'How could you do that? You promised me you wouldn't bite me.' The snake says, 'Yes, but when I made that promise, you already knew that I was a snake.'

"How many false promises do we have to take from these snakes? How many times do they have to lie? How many times do they have to admit they're criminals, felons, drug traffickers? How many times do they have to commit perjury before we finally say enough is enough? Snakes have their own morality. Never blame a snake for acting in character, it's our fault if we trust them.

"The law in its infinite wisdom allows you to say I don't believe the word of a liar, the word of a drug trafficker, the word of a criminal whose testimony is bought by a promise to get him out of jail and to get his house back. The law doesn't require you to let all the real drug traffickers out of jail so that Fred De La Mata can take their place."

Totally drained, my throat sore, I sat down. I felt I had done all I could.

At 12:30 p.m. the jurors began deliberating. I figured they would start with lunch and then discuss the case. But they must not have had much to talk about because at 2:20 they were back with their verdict. Fred's relatives had waited with him, and they filled the courtroom. When Fred heard the clerk read, "Not guilty," he broke down in tears.

When he recovered his composure, he announced to his friends and a covey of journalists: "Everyone wanted to believe all the bad things about me. Now that I've been acquitted, I can have my good name back."

It was not to be.

Unlike his indictment, which had been reported on the front pages of both Miami newspapers and led local television newscasts, Fred's acquittal was virtually ignored. *The Miami Herald* buried the news back with the obituaries and the weather. Fred angrily wrote letters to the various media. To his credit, *Herald* publisher Dave Lawrence wrote a column in which he quoted Fred extensively about the agonizing ordeal he had been through. "No, I am not bitter," Fred said. "Really, I'm not. I just want people to realize that they did something wrong to me."

Fred's victory was short-lived. Eighteen months after his acquittal, in April 1992, prosecutors struck back with a vengeance. Using an obscure civil bank regulation, they indicted him for bank fraud, then used the bank fraud as a predicate crime to accuse him of racketeering under the anti-Mafia RICO statute. To top it off, by invoking a RICO special weapon, they froze all of Fred's assets.

The principal allegation was that he hadn't disclosed to bank officials that he had a financial interest in two lots that had been sold to the bank in the mid-1980s. Was that really fraud? The bank never lost money on the lots and branches did very well. Yet the government managed to turn these two sales into a fifty-nine-count indictment.

I was willing to defend Fred again, but it soon became obvious that the U.S. Attorney's Office didn't want me in this case. Prosecutors froze all the De La Mata family's assets, including Fred's house, his bank stock, his wife's and children's bank stock, and even an account containing money that came from wedding gifts to his daughter. In court, I told a judge that I needed to be paid if I was going to take Fred's case, but that by freezing his assets, the government was effectively denying him his counsel of choice. The government argued that the assets needed to be frozen because Fred might be assessed fines if he was found guilty. The judge accepted the government's argument.

Fred consulted another lawyer, Oscar Rodríguez, who talked with the prosecutors. Oscar told me that if he, not I, represented Fred, the government would allow Fred to mortgage his house to pay for his defense. "They want to know in advance who his lawyer is going to be," Oscar told me. Not only can federal prosecutors take away your business, home, money and other personal property before you've even been convicted, but it can also take away your right to hire the lawyer of your choice. Of course, it's a lot easier for the prosecution to win a case when they can veto the defendant's lawyer.

I was not allowed to defend Fred at his second trial. On December 30, 1992, after eight and a half days of jury deliberations, he and three co-defendants were found guilty. Fred was sentenced to ten years in jail.

That wasn't the end. Later it came out that while U.S. District Judge K. Michael Moore presided over Fred's second trial, Judge Moore was secretly being investigated by FBI agents working with a grand jury.[10] Moore knew about the investigation. Federal prosecutors knew about it. The defense lawyers didn't. Even though FBI agents were closely working with the prosecutors in court each day, the judge failed to disclose this serious conflict. It

---

10. Judge Moore was not indicted by the grand jury, and today he still sits as a federal judge in the Southern District of Florida. Because of grand jury secrecy it is hard to tell if this was a legitimate investigation or just another example of FBI harassment. It is frightening to think that FBI agents can accost a judge who is sitting on one of their cases and threaten him with prosecution. It is only natural to think that a career-destroying threat like this has the potential to affect a judge's decision-making. I can only imagine the anguish Judge Moore suffered through the investigation and the subsequent hearings held on our motions related to it.

would be only human nature to curry favor with the FBI when it was deciding whether to destroy one's career. What an irony: The judge who was trying Fred for failure to disclose a conflict failed to disclose his own conflict.

I reentered the case and with my partner Howard Srebnick filed a motion for new trial. On September 12, 1994, U.S. District Judge William C. O'Kelley from Atlanta set aside Fred's guilty verdict. The government appealed, but the Eleventh Circuit threw out not only the verdict in Fred's case but in twenty-three other trials as well.

Republic National Bank appealed the government's refusal to return the $800,000. In December 1992, more than four years after the loan and two years after Fred's acquittal in his first trial, the U.S. Supreme Court ruled in the bank's favor. Even the conservative Rehnquist court has recognized that the actions of federal prosecutors who had seized $1 billion in assets of alleged drug dealers had gotten out of hand.

Finally, it seemed, the bank could get its $800,000 back, plus interest. But it was not to be. The power of the U.S. Attorney's Office is such that it can overcome even rulings of the Supreme Court. The prosecutors' weapon was the target letter issued to the bank and its officers on the day that Fred's first trial began. For years, the letter had continued to hang over the bankers' heads. In January 1994, Republic made a deal with the prosecutors: In exchange for a promise that the bank and its officers would not be prosecuted for money laundering, the bank agreed to pay $1.9 million in civil penalties and to withdraw its claim for the $800,000. The bank then turned around and sued Fred for all the money it lost to the government.

The sad truth is that Fred's troubles are far from over. No bank will hire him because all banks have to deal with federal regulators. While he confronts his myriad of continuing legal problems, he tries to eke out a living as a consultant. A longtime friend who hired him was harassed by federal prosecutors who demanded to know why he was helping Fred. For his friend's sake, Fred quit the job.

Fred De La Mata is living proof that the federal government will never let go.

Turning point: The cross-examination of René Leonard smashed the core of
the prosecution's case. Leonard, "the mystery man," was the only witness who
wasn't trying to get out of a jail term when he said damaging things about
Fred. Under my cross-examination, the professor's credibility vanished. With
each of my questions about his fanciful CIA past, I could feel the jurors smirk-
ing. Add that to all the other contradictions he had made in sworn statements,
and Leonard ceased to be a factor. Without him, the government had no
case.

Author's Note

Turning court stenographer transcripts into readable prose presents a formidable challenge. Oral speech, full of ungrammatical sentences and ellipses, differs from written prose. Trial lawyers are usually embarrassed when reading raw transcripts. Some of the awkwardness is their fault, while part of it can be blamed on clumsy reporters. In this book, when quoting from trial transcripts, I have edited out many of the oral tics used in everyday speech but have still tried to keep witness testimony as close as possible to the transcripts.

I was also faced with the problem of quoting from final arguments that were hours in length while still giving an accurate feel for their substance. Some license was taken in cleaning up the language and re-arranging the sequence of each argument so it could be summarized and understood in the context of its case. The Knight oral argument differed from the others because it had to be reconstructed without the aid of a transcript. The Eleventh Circuit Court of Appeals tapes the arguments but prohibits attorneys from obtaining copies, so I had to reconstruct that argument from my old notes and from the notes of others who were present in the courtroom.

Acknowledgments

Recently, a tabloid TV show insinuated that it was somehow inappropriate for me to walk with my wife, Lea, into Marv Albert's trial since she looked so glamorous; I assumed he was suggesting that beauty was incongruous in such a drab setting. I laughed and quipped: "You should see her when she really gets dolled up." The truth is that she comes to every trial, rolls up her sleeves and takes on any task, no matter how menial or dirty, to help get the job done. She is a partner in every sense of the word.

Whatever I learned as a criminal defense lawyer came from watching the masters of the universe: Jay Hogan (the sardonic king of demonstrative evidence), David Rosen (for decades he deprived Meyer Lansky of a prison cell), Bob "It's a pizzeria" Josefsberg, Phillip Hubbart, Albert Krieger (Dr. Doom) and Boston's Marty Weinberg. At the same time, a young lawyer could find no finer training ground than the Dade County Public Defender's Office and its dedicated gang of young lawyers, particularly the original ten, who courageously battled a system determined to treat indigents as second-class citizens.

When I was a college junior I read *My Life in Court* by the great New York trial lawyer Louis Nizer. His brilliant stories inspired me to become a lawyer. Once addicted to Nizer's books, I avidly consumed those of F. Lee Bailey, Gerry Spence and Alan Dershowitz.

Writing is a solitary task, normally ill suited to collaboration. John Dorschner is the exception that proves the rule. His grasp of organization and refinement of ideas allowed us to put these stories in a readable form. Unfortunately, the pedestrian prose is all my own.

There are others to whom I am indebted. Howard Srebnick, Scott Kornspan and all the lawyers and staff of Black, Srebnick and Kornspan gave me the time to write. Several people read the manuscript and offered invaluable help: Sandy Marks, Dr. Geoffrey Alpert, Bobbi Berkman and Gayle Wright. Alice Mayhew and Roger Labrie of Simon & Schuster provided invaluable editorial suggestions.

One final note: No civilized society should declare war on its citizens. America's ill-fated war on drugs has created thousands of victims through its excesses and injustices. To Sal Magluta #26012-037, Willie Falcon #26010-037, Victor Prather #11061-112 and Bill Moran #44851-004, I offer Plato's wisdom: "To do injustice is more disgraceful than to suffer it."

Index